Analytical foundations of Marxian economic theory

Analytical foundations of Marxian economic theory

JOHN E. ROEMER
University of California, Davis

The right of the University of Cambridge to print and sell all manner of books was granted by Henry VIII in 1534. The University has printed and published continuously since 1584.

CAMBRIDGE UNIVERSITY PRESS
Cambridge
New York Port Chester
Melbourne Sydney

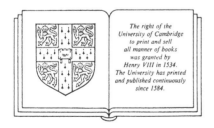

CAMBRIDGE UNIVERSITY PRESS
Cambridge, New York, Melbourne, Madrid, Cape Town, Singapore, São Paulo

Cambridge University Press
The Edinburgh Building, Cambridge CB2 2RU, UK

Published in the United States of America by Cambridge University Press, New York

www.cambridge.org
Information on this title: www.cambridge.org/9780521230476

First published 1981
First paperback edition 1988
Reprinted 1990

A catalogue record for this publication is available from the British Library

Library of Congress Cataloguing in Publication data

Roemer, John E.
Analytical foundations of Marxian economic theory.
1. Marxian economics. I. Title.
HB97.5.R616 335.4 80–22646

ISBN-13 978-0-521-23047-6 hardback
ISBN-10 0-521-23047-0 hardback

ISBN-13 978-0-521-34775-4 paperback
ISBN-10 0-521-34775-0 paperback

Transferred to digital printing 2006

Portions of this publication are adapted from previously published articles by the author. We gratefully acknowledge permission to use these materials:

"A general equilibrium approach to Marxian economics," *Econometrica* 48 (1980): 505–30.

"Technical change and the 'tendency of the rate of profit to fall'," *Journal of Economic Theory* 16(2): 403–24, December 1977.

"Continuing controversy on the falling rate of profit: fixed capital and other issues," *Cambridge Journal of Economics* 3(1979): 379–98.

"The effect of technological change on the real wage and Marx's falling rate of profit," *Australian Economic Papers,* 152–66, June 1978.

"Marxian models of reproduction and accumulation," *Cambridge Journal of Economics* 2(1978): 37–53.

To my parents, Ruth and Milton

Contents

Acknowledgments *page* xii

Introduction **1**

Methodology 1
Summary 10

1 **Equilibrium and reproducibility: the linear model** **15**

1.1 A brief review 15
1.2 A more complete definition of Marxian equilibrium 17
1.3 A model of imperfect competition 23
1.4 Some dynamics in the linear, Leontief model 29

2 **Reproducibility and exploitation: a general model** **35**

2.1 Introduction 35
2.2 Specification of the model 36
2.3 The existence of reproducible solutions 41
2.4 The fundamental Marxian theorem 47
2.5 Exploitation, labor values, joint products, and scarce inputs 51
2.6 The social determination of the value of labor power 52
2.7 The interaction of class consciousness and the choice of technique 55
2.8 Summary 60

Appendix 1: Existence of reproducible solutions with the value of labor power socially determined 61
Appendix 2: Necessary and sufficient conditions for the validity of the fundamental Marxian theorem 64
2.9 Outline of problem 64
2.10 The model 65
2.11 The fundamental Marxian theorem 67
2.12 Conclusion 69

3 The equalization of profit rates in Marxian general equilibrium 71

3.1 Introduction 71
3.2 Marxian equilibrium with finance capital market 73
3.3 Summary: what drives profit-rate equalization in the Marxian model? 81
3.4 Positive profits, positive exploitation, and the theory of profits 83

4 Viable and progressive technical change and the rising rate of profit 87

4.1 Introduction 87
4.2 The value and price rates of profit 90
4.3 The effect of technical change on the rate of profit 97
4.4 Progressive and viable technical change in steady-state growth 105
4.5 Summary 107
Appendix: Frobenius-Perron eigenvalue theorems 110

5 Continuing controversy on the falling rate of profit: fixed capital and other issues 112

5.1 The need for microfoundations: methodology 112
5.2 Miscellaneous arguments against Okishio's theorem 114

5.3 The rising rate of profit with fixed capital: a special case 119
5.4 The general case of fixed capital: the von Neumann model 124
5.5 Conclusion 132

6 Changes in the real wage and the rate of profit 134

6.1 Introduction 134
6.2 Technical change with constant relative shares 134
6.3 A model of relative share constancy within sectors 137
6.4 Technical change and class struggle: efficient versus controlling technical changes 140
6.5 Summary 144

7 The law of value and the transformation problem 146

7.1 Marx's project: where do profits come from? 146
7.2 Marx and the subsistence wage 150
7.3 The law of value 153
7.4 The transformation problem 159
7.5 Summary 160

8 The transformation correspondence 162

8.1 Introduction 162
8.2 The transformation correspondence 162
8.3 Some applications of the transformation correspondence 170
8.4 Summary 175

9 Simple reproduction, extended reproduction, and crisis 177

9.1 Introduction 177
9.2 Simple reproduction 178
9.3 Extended reproduction 182
9.4 Three Marxian crises 192

9.5 A one-sector model 195
9.6 Summary 198

10 Summing up and new directions 199

Notes 211
References 215
Index 219

Acknowledgments

A variety of people have influenced the work that appears in this book. Over the past several years I have had many stimulating discussions with Duncan Foley, although they have not, perhaps, been absorbed according to his design. Leo Hurwicz posed certain questions about the Marxian model in a way that forced me to face them. Roger Howe and Andreu Mas-Colell have been consistent and faithful listeners and critics. Various chapters have been read by Meghnad Desai, Herbert Gintis, Victor Goldberg, and Josep-Maria Vegara, and their comments have affected the final draft. Cheryl Stark typed the manuscript with speed and accuracy and without complaint.

J.E.R.

Acknowledgements

Introduction

Methodology[1]

Although a book in mathematical Marxian economics is no longer a unique phenomenon, its author must still confront the opinion held in many circles, both Marxian and non-Marxian, that such an endeavor is a contradiction in terms. Two lines of defense are available: (1) that Marx himself was not against the use of mathematical methods; (2) that regardless of Marx's position, these methods are appropriate to aid in understanding the social phenomena with which Marx was concerned. Although what Marx believed on this question should not settle the issue, if we consider Marxism to be a science and not a religion, it nevertheless appears that Marx was a supporter of the use of mathematical methods in economics. This is shown by the work of Leon Smolinski (1973), who studied Marx's unpublished as well as published manuscripts for his views on the matter. Smolinski reports there was "not a single injunction against mathematical economics [in] Marx's published or unpublished writings." Moreover, Lafargue attributes to Marx the statement: "A science becomes developed only when it has reached the point where it can make use of mathematics" (Smolinski, p. 1201). Still, the opposing circumstantial evidence remains that Marx made very little use of formal mathematics (beyond arithmetic) in his work. As Marx studied algebra and calculus quite extensively in his later years, why did he not use these tools? Two main reasons are suggested by Smolinski: His economic theories had already been formulated before his mathematical studies became intensive, and his mastery of the application of these tools to economic models was very slight. Indeed, Smolinski provides rather incriminating evidence with regard to the second reason, by showing how inept was Marx's effort to analyze the algebraic relationship between the rate of surplus value and the rate of profit in an unpublished version of *Capital,* Volume III, Chapter III, entitled "The Mathematical Treatment of the Rate of Surplus Value and the Rate of Profit."[2]

Regardless of Marx's position, however, mathematics is a useful tool in Marxian economics. To the extent that abstraction and models are useful, so is mathematics. This would seem self-evident. Several objections nevertheless remain. The most cogent of these seem to be (1) that although mathematics may be useful, it does not accomplish any analytical task that cannot be done without it; (2) that the essential ideas of Marxian social science cannot be mathematized.

Objection 1 does not pass the empirical test of the last century's research in Marxian economics. The use of mathematical techniques can clarify relationships in an unambiguous way; without these techniques, only intuition can be a guide. But the intuitions of two people may contradict each other: When both are forced to state their beliefs in a common (mathematical) language, there is an objective standard for deciding which is correct. This is seen, in Marxian economics, most clearly in the endless discussions of the transformation problem and the theory of the falling rate of profit. Recent theoretical statements of the problems have resolved many (if not all) of the debates. *After* the mathematics has done its job, it is often possible to state the proof verbally – that is, to avoid the "mathematics." Hindsight, however, differs from foresight. If a tool acts as a catalyst, and enables us to see how to perform the task for which it was intended, but without its use, more power to it.

A related point to objection 1 is, as Jacob Schwartz (1961) put it, that "mathematics, in doing its good works, has a way of drawing attention to itself." This is perhaps at the heart of the objection of many Marxists to the use of mathematics. They fear that introduction of the tool distracts attention from the burning social issues of the underlying investigation, and gives the inquiry a gamelike character. This is, no doubt, a danger, but the reciprocal accusation can just as well be made against those Marxists who write pages of "dialectical" reasoning, reveling in the Talmudic play possible in that medium. Any methodology can be abused.

Objection 2 is a more serious point, for certainly mathematics can play only a partial role in Marxian social science, or in any social science, or in any science. Indeed, the essential aspect of a science is confrontation of theory with facts, and mathematics does not produce facts. More specifically, the historical materialist method is central to Marxism, and mathematics does not produce history. The question of the applicability of mathematics, then, must necessarily be limited to its role in Marxian social theory, a theory being a way of interpreting historical fact. Here one must distinguish between a theory and its models. In my terminology a theory is not by its nature mathematical. Theories live in an intuitional domain. One tests the consistency of a theory by making models that are schematic representations of the theory and that may use mathematics. A model allows statements to be made that have an undeniable truth value (within the model): Statements made in a theory do not have this logical status. There may be several models of a single theory, some of which verify the theory, others of which nullify it. For example, now that some have produced models of the falling-rate-of-profit (FRP) theory that nullify the theory (as in Chapters 4 and 5 of this book), others are trying to produce models that verify it. If pro-FRP models are successfully produced, they will clearly differ from the anti-FRP models in their assumptions, and such a confrontation will force a more careful refinement of what the underlying theory is. That is, a theory, living in the domain of intuition, necessarily has a certain vagueness. The vagueness is brought into sharp focus by the articulation of contradicting models of the (same) theory.

It is in this sense that "mathematics," or models, cannot capture all that is contained in a theory. A model is necessarily one schematic image of a theory, and one must not be so myopic as to believe other schematic images cannot exist. Nevertheless, this is not a reason not to use mathematics in trying to understand a theory: for, as has been pointed out above, the production of different and contradicting models of the same theory can be the very process that directs our focus to the gray areas of the theory.

It should be underscored that this discussion applies only to the use of models to test the consistency of a social theory, not the usefulness or accuracy of a theory. The usefulness or accuracy of a theory is tested by confronting it, or its models, with history and data.

Using the distinction that has been stated above between a theory and its models, it is now possible to admit the sense in which objection 2 is viable. Because a social theory, by this definition, is a proposal for ordering and understanding a particular set of historical occurrences and behavior, it does not have the status of a statement in logic. A model, however, contains logical statements. Hence, a model can never replace a theory; that is, a model can never capture every nuance the theory might imply. We might construct models that attempt to capture, schematically, what we conceive of as some of the postulates of the historical–materialist theory, in order to examine whether certain conclusions logically follow from a historical–

materialist perspective. Nevertheless, no model can ever hope to capture fully the theory of historical materialism. It is as if a theory is an object in an infinite-dimensional space, and a model gives us a projection of the object onto a small subspace. Different models produce different projections; with more models, more projections, we get a more accurate feeling for the implications and the limits of the theory, but we can never capture every dimension of the theory from its models. With sufficient modeling, however, we may come to feel that we have exhausted the interesting content of the theory, and so, for all practical purposes, it is understood.

If one adopts this epistemological posture, it becomes clear that although it is true that models can never entirely capture a theory, that is not a reason not to build models of the theory. Quite the opposite: Models provide perhaps the best way of trying to explore the theory. Thus, although objection 2 is valid in the sense described, it does not follow that mathematical modeling should be abandoned.

We have addressed the issue of whether models can necessarily capture everything contained in theories. Another level of objection 2 is that there are specific concepts of Marxian theories – such as class, power, struggle, consciousness, hegemony, and so on – that are not so amenable to mathematical modeling as are the notions of price, quantity, technology, and so on. This, I think, is not the case. The obvious explanation is that we cannot imagine, perhaps, how to mathematize "class struggle" because no one has ever tried – or, more accurately, there is no social science that has tried for 100 years to do so. But even if we *can* mathematize the notion of, say, class, is there a purpose to it? Here the proponents of objection 2 and objection 1 might unite and say: "Class cannot be mathematized. But even if you can do it, what will be gained in the process? The subtle issues concerning class cannot be clarified with mathematical modeling."

However, I would argue, as an example, that the inability of Marxists to understand what has transpired in the socialist economies since 1917 is intimately related to an imprecise and vague notion of class. We have a theory of class, and we have understood many dimensions of the theory. But now a historical experience has occurred that exposes our ignorance of the complete theory. That is, there are dimensions of the notion of class that have only become important to our understanding of reality since 1917, and we have little intuition with regard to what is happening in those dimensions. It is time, therefore, to attempt to produce models of the theory of class that can enlighten us as to those hidden dimensions. To be specific: Soviet society has developed in a way that no Marxist would have predicted in 1885 or 1917. There is no agreement among Marxists on the extremely fundamental, and apparently simple question: What *is* the Soviet Union – capitalist, socialist, or something else? To resolve this question, one must understand how to define *class* when the means of production are not privately owned, investment is centrally planned, and so on. In other words, our accepted theory of what constitutes class is exposed as being vague when we try to apply the theory to a new situation – namely, Soviet society. When the vagueness of a theory becomes critical in our ability to use the theory to interpret reality, it is an appropriate time to tighten our understanding of it by constructing models of the theory. Not only do I think that the Marxian notion of class can be modeled, more important, I think that such modeling can illuminate the gray areas of the theory, and enable us to understand the class nature of modern Sovietlike (or, let us say, socialist) societies.

Perhaps a historical parallel is useful here. The prime example of modeling an ethereal concept, in Marxian economics, is the theory of exploitation. Exploitation is a concept like class, power, struggle, consciousness; it might appear to be a concept that mathematics could only reify, but not clarify. Marx wished to understand how exploitation could exist under capitalism, a mode of production in which exchanges are mediated through competitive markets. Under feudalism and slavery, the existence of exploitation posed no riddle because of the overtly coercive mechanism for the expropriation of labor. If one had lived under feudalism, the theory of exploitation as the expropriation of surplus labor would have seemed utterly clear: It is only with the advent of competitive markets that the vagueness became apparent in this theory. How is surplus labor expropriated when there is no *corvée,* but only a labor market? (If you ask the wage worker how long he must work to reproduce his family, he will reply, "Forty hours a week"; if you ask the serf, he will reply, "Only three days for my family, the rest of the time I slave for that jerk on the hill.") Marx resolved the vagueness in the received theory of exploitation by constructing an essentially mathematical model, and extended the applicability of the exploitation theory to capitalism.

To review this example: Before the advent of capitalism, one might have held that the theory of exploitation necessarily entailed a coercive institution for the exchange of labor. If exploitation means the expropriation of surplus labor, of one class by another, then the historical experience of slave and feudal societies would lead one to believe that a necessary aspect of the theory of exploitation was a coercive institution for labor exchange. Marx observed that this perception of the theory did not work for capitalism: He wished to claim that exploitation was still occurring, despite the absence of a coercive institution for labor exchange. (Indeed, that is the motivation for Marx's effort to explain the existence of exploitation in the presence of "fair" or competitive markets.) One response to capitalist reality was to say that there could not be exploitation, because markets were competitive. This, in fact, is the essence of the neoclassical approach. Marx's approach was, in the terms of this discussion, to say that our previous perception involved false inferences concerning certain hidden dimensions of the theory. As long as society had experience only with coercive institutions for organizing labor exchange, it was not necessary to understand precisely what the theory looked like along that dimension. Now that history has given us a mode of production with, at least in principle, a noncoercive labor exchange mechanism (a competitive labor market), one must attempt to model the theory to see what it predicts in this new situation. Marx's discovery was that the theory of exploitation works through more mysterious channels than one might have thought. Exploitation is a logically consistent idea even in the presence of competitive markets.

An important task for Marxists today is to extend the theory of exploitation so as to be able to evaluate whether exploitation can exist under socialism. To this end, a model-building, mathematical approach should be as useful as it was for Marx. Indeed, we find ourselves today in a theoretical predicament quite analogous to the one in which Marx found himself. We have a fairly good understanding of the dimension of the theory of exploitation that can be labeled "degree of coerciveness of the institution of labor exchange." The dimension of the theory that we have not had cause to examine, until the last sixty years, is the one labeled "public ownership of the means of production." Just as neoclassical economists are incorrect in assuming that the presence of a labor market means exploitation cannot exist, so Marxists, or more generally, historical materialists, would be incorrect in assuming that the absence of private ownership implies the abolition of exploitation. We lack, however, a model of exploitation under these conditions that can help us evaluate if, in fact, the theory is still applicable under socialism. Judgments on the issue of whether exploitation exists in the Soviet Union differ widely among Marxists, because we have no precise understanding of the relevant dimension of the exploitation theory.

This ends the apology for the mathematical model-building method in Marxian economics. Doubtless most of these arguments apply to social science as a whole, and doubtless many have been stated more completely, and with more sophisticated philosophical apparatus, elsewhere. I feel, nevertheless, that it is necessary to include such a statement here.

Two more important methodological issues remain concerning the approach I have taken: the validity of a microfoundations approach in Marxian economics, and the validity of an equilibrium approach.

The *microfoundations* approach consists in deriving the aggregate behavior of an economy as a consequence of the actions of individuals, who are postulated to behave in some specified way. I have taken this approach throughout the book. For example, in the chapters on the falling rate of profit, it is postulated that a technical innovation is introduced only if it increases profits for a capitalist. This micro approach is different from a macro approach, which might say: We postulate that technical change takes the form of an increasing aggregate organic composition of capital. From the micro vantage point, one is not allowed to postulate an increasing organic composition of capital unless one can show what individual entrepreneurial mechanism leads to it. Marxists might question the microfoundations methodology because one of the forceful points of Marx's theory is that the individual is not the relevant unit to examine – it is the class. This might lead one to try and build a model in which classes are the atoms of the system.

I think it should be possible to produce such a model, but I do not believe that model would be contradictory to the ones I have described in this book. The reason is this: That individuals act as members of a class, rather than as individuals, should be a theorem in Marxian economics, not a postulate. Marx's point is that despite the capitalist's incarnation as a human being, he or she is forced by the system to act as an agent for the self-expansion of capital. Workers, similarly, may have their individual yearnings and habits, but conditions of life force them to acquire a class consciousness and to act, at times, as agents of the working class as a whole and not as their own agent. (This might be the situation, for instance, in a strike, where the striker takes great chances for the good of the strike, which are not personally worthwhile.) In each case, Marx has claimed that although people exist organically as individuals, we can *conclude* that they act as members of classes. It is in this sense that class behavior is a theorem and not a postulate of the Marxian theory. [I have discussed this particular theorem of class consciousness elsewhere (Roemer, 1978b and 1979a.)]

Thus, it is not antithetical to Marxian theory to produce models using the microfoundations approach. In particular, I suggest that one theorem of Marxism is a "microfoundations of class" analysis.

Taking the argument a step further, I would say that it is not only admissable, but important, to take a microfoundations approach in Marxian theory. A common error in Marxian discussions is *functionalism:* to assume that a mechanism necessarily exists to perform actions that must be performed to reproduce the system. Put more simply, if the occurrence of *X* will further the reproduction of capitalist relations, then *X* occurs. For example, if racist attitudes exist among the working class, then capital will be strong. Therefore, capitalism foments racism. What is missing here is a description of the mechanism by which this is accomplished. It may be in the interest of capital as a whole to maintain discriminatory wage differentials for black and white workers of equal productivity, but why should the individual, profit-maximizing capitalist respect this differential when he or she can increase profits by unraveling the differential – that is, by hiring only black workers at a slightly higher wage than they are receiving under the racist regime? [For one answer to this question, see Roemer (1979c).] If we postulate capitalism as a system of anarchic, competitive capitals, each bent on its own expansion, we must face this sort of contradiction from functionalist arguments. Another example comes from some Marxist–radical theories of education. Capitalism does not require a highly educated working class, so the theory goes, but it does require a well-socialized and docile working class. Schools, then, will serve the role of socializing and channeling people into capitalist society, but not of educating them. Now, this conclusion may be true, but the functionalist nature of the argument eclipses the mysterious and difficult part of the phenomenon – how does capitalism ensure this role for schools, when teachers try to teach, students try to learn, and so on? A third example is the role of the state. The capitalist state acts in the interests of the capitalist class – that is the theory. But the theory cannot be convincing unless one can demonstrate the mechanism by which this occurs, especially because capitals do not have a habit of cooperating with each other, as the primary aspect of each capital's existence is self-expansion and competition against other capitals.

What one requires, then, are microfoundations for the role of racism, education, and the state under capitalism. Other examples abound. In the cases when capitalism is guided as if by an invisible hand to coordinate its preservation in the ways mentioned, one requires an explanation of how anarchic capitals produce such a result.

A second form of functionalism that exists among Marxists is the converse of the first form: If *X* has occurred, then *X* must be in the interests of capital. We again can take an example from education: Because we observe compulsory education, it must be that capital requires such for its reproduction. But this may not be the case: Compulsory education may exist because the working class fought for it. One can find many examples of this form of functionalism in Marxian work: The general consequence of the error is to attribute an omnipotence to the capitalist class that it does not possess in Marxian theory. The capitalist class is pushed along by historical developments: Not everything that happens under capitalism was planned by it, nor is in its best interests. In fact, according to Marx, the general tide of historical development favors the working class. Again, a defense against this form of functionalism is a microfoundations approach.

There is a third form of functionalism among Marxists that, strangely, seems diametrically opposed to the first two forms: If the occurrence of *X* is necessary for the *demise* of capitalism, then *X* will come to pass. We can see the general rule of which these different functionalist forms are special cases if we phrase the general functionalist position this way. We postulate a certain outcome for the social system; functionalism then takes the form of claiming that only events occur which lead to that outcome. In the first two forms of functionalism discussed, the outcome is the reproduction of capitalist relations; in the third form, the outcome is the transformation of capitalism into socialism. Perhaps the first two forms of functionalism are short-run variants, and the third form is a long-run variant of the general functionalist interpretation of Marxism.

Examples of the third form of functionalism in Marxian economics are prevalent in crisis theory. The system must have crises, because crisis is necessary for capitalist demise. The rate of profit must fall, because only in this way can crisis be brought about. The working class must become impoverished, because otherwise it will never perform its revolutionary task. Bourgeois democracy must transform itself into fascism, because only fascism will heighten the contradictions of capitalism sufficiently to produce revolutionary transformation, which must occur. These arguments are less than convincing; the form of functionalism they involve is similar to that of the utopian socialism of Marx's time, which postulated socialist transformation without a mechanism. Marx's method was to counter utopian thinking by trying to expose the mechanism that would bring the socialist transformation about.[3]

Finally, the *equilibrium* method has been used in the models in this book. While I have defended the approach of mathematical modeling, and the microfoundations approach, I have less confidence about the equilibrium method. Like many economists of my generation, I am strongly influenced by the power of the equilibrium method: of examining a model when it is at rest, so to speak, in the sense that all the rules that describe how its parts work are simultaneously fulfilled. What is disturbing about the equilibrium method is that it pictures the typical position of the system as a position the system rarely or never enjoys. Of course, no sophisticated economic model builder would claim that economies are in equilibrium in the sense of a static equilibrium model. A model is only an ideal type. However, there seems to be a deep contradiction between using models whose main analytical trick is to postulate a position that is precisely at variance with the most interesting and important aspect of capitalist economy as described by Marxian theory – its incessant, contradictory motion. There is, therefore, the danger that if this intuition is correct, the equilibrium method will prevent one from seeing the most important aspects of the Marxian theory of capital. Knowing no other method, I use the equilibrium method, with the vague thought that, when rereading these pages in twenty years, its obsolescence as a modeling tool for Marxian theory may be clear. (I might add that there is plenty of precedent in Marx's modeling of his theory for the equilibrium method: Consider, for example, the notion of equalization of profit rates among capitals, or the models of balanced growth designed to show that capitalism was capable of reproducing itself.)

Summary

From the preceding discussion, it should now be clear what I am attempting. The goal is to convey my perception of aspects of Marxian economic theory by posing specific models. Furthermore, the aspects of the theory that are discussed are classical ones; there is no attempt to extend the theory to deal with new problems, such as the question of exploitation under socialism discussed above.

In Chapters 1 and 2 the concern is with the Marxian notion of equilibrium, and the theory of exploitation. A definition of equilibrium is proposed that includes not only the usual concept of competition of capital and profit maximization or the accumulation of capital (leading to an equalization of profit rates), but also formalizes the Marxian notion of the reproducibility of the economic system. The model is examined in a general equilibrium framework. Within this framework, exploitation is defined, and the equivalence of exploitation and positive profits is shown. In Chapter 1 the model is developed with the usual Leontief–Sraffa–Morishima linear input–output specification of production. In Chapter 2 the model is extended to a more general production environment: It is assumed that production sets are convex sets. The purpose of this general treatment is to show that the Marxian theories of equilibrium and exploitation do not depend on the usual linear specification of production, but are very general – as general, for all practical purposes, as the neoclassical model, which has been developed for convex production sets. In addition to this main theorem, there are various sidelights in these chapters; in Chapter 1 there is a discussion of differential profit rates and imperfect competition in the linear model, and in Chapter 2 there is a modification of the exogenous subsistence bundle assumption which is ubiquitous in Marxian mathematical models, and we allow workers' consumption to be socially determined by technology.

In the first two chapters, one important market is missing, a credit market. In Chapter 3 this omission is rectified by postulating that capitalists can borrow and lend capital among themselves, at an interest rate. This allows a discussion of the foundations of the equalization of profit rates in the Marxian model, and the differences between the Marxian and "neoclassical" positions on the rate of interest as a return to capital.

These three chapters constitute the first part of the book. Chapters 4, 5, and 6 are the next part, and are concerned with the theory of the falling rate of profit. In Chapter 4 the relationship between the value and price rate of profit is studied, and it is shown that competitively induced technical innovations can only cause the equilibrium rate of profit to rise in a linear production model, with only circulating capital. Technical innovations are described along two dimensions: whether they are viable (will competitive capitalists introduce them?); and whether they are progressive (are they socially desirable?). The relationship between viable and progressive innovations is explored. One interesting result is that viable innovations are not necessarily progressive, nor are progressive innovations necessarily viable. At first glance, this appears to contradict a neoclassical theorem, as it implies that the invisible hand does not work very well. The exploration of this anomaly awaits the reader in Chapter 4.

Despite an increasing awareness among Marxists of the rising-rate-of-profit theorem of Chapter 4 (which, it should be pointed out, is not original with this author, but has been discovered by various investigators over the past forty years), models continue to be put forth to resurrect the falling-rate-of-profit theory. Chapter 5 addresses itself to these models. The conclusion of the chapter is that none of the proposals is convincing. Perhaps the most important such models to evaluate are the ones involving fixed capital. It has been claimed by several authors that the rising-rate-of-profit result is an artifact of pure circulating capital models, but in the presence of fixed capital, competitive innovations can lead to a falling rate of profit. This position is rebutted in Chapter 5 by a theorem which states that in a general model with fixed capital, the von Neumann activity analysis model, competitive innovations result in a rising rate of profit. There seems no hope for a theory of the falling rate of profit within the strict confines of the environment that Marx suggested as relevant.

One of these confines is the assumption that the real wage remains fixed before and after technical innovation. Indeed, if the real wage rises, the rate of profit may fall with technical change. In Chapter 6 it is shown that if the real wage increases after technical change, so that workers maintain the same relative share in net product that they had in the old equilibrium, then innovations that were competitively introduced will cause the rate of profit to fall. This focuses attention on the relationship between technical change and induced changes in the real wage, which is a topic addressed in contemporary Marxian discussions of the labor process. The chapter concludes by showing how these modern concerns with the nature of technical change mesh with the classical question of the falling rate of profit.

Chapters 7 and 8 discuss the transformation problem. Already, in Chapters 1–3, it has become clear that the Marxian theory of exploitation can be constructed completely independently of the labor theory of value as a theory of exchange. In Chapter 7 this important point is expanded and specifically confronted. It is maintained that Marx used the labor theory of value as a theory of exchange, at *some* level of abstraction, and his theory of exploitation was then developed as a corollary to the exchange theory. That is, the theory of exchange was the conduit through which the labor theory of value was brought to bear in deriving the theory of exploitation. In Chapter 7 the point is made that the role of the labor theory of value in the theory of exploitation can be developed entirely independently of its role in Marx's exchange theory. It is maintained that the most fruitful interpretation of Marxian value theory entails discarding the labor theory of value in its role as exchange theory, and maintaining it only in its independent role in the exploitation theory. In doing this, we are also led to an interpretation of the logical status of the subsistence wage concept in Marx, and in the reformulation of Marxian value theory, we are able to discard the subsistence notion. This approach enables, also, a new interpretation of the Marxian "law of value," which is presented as a theorem in Chapter 7. This chapter will no doubt be viewed with some controversy; it is maintained that the "transformation problem" is most fruitfully resolved by the model presented.

Chapter 8 is a technical study of what I have called the "transformation correspondence." It is a continuation of the model of Chapter 7, and asks: What is the range of prices that can correspond to a given social rate of exploitation? Answering this question provides some insight into the conventional approach to the transformation problem, and allows comment on various issues, such as the relative importance of "marginal utilities" and "class struggle" in determining relative prices.

In the general equilibrium models of Chapters 1–3, the concern was with the Marxian theory of value and exploitation. As such, the model in those chapters abstracted from questions of unemployment, state expenditures, and the possibilities of a discrepancy between supply and demand. In Chapter 9 we model various classical Marxian theories of crisis, by introducing these aspects into a model. First, simple reproduction is studied, a situation where capitalists consume the entire surplus. Then, extended reproduction is studied. These Marxian notions are modeled: an industrial reserve army in general exists, which puts downward pressure on the real wage; the unemployed are supported at some subsistence level by a state tax on profits; there is, in general, a discrepancy between *ex post* and *ex ante* investment. (Perhaps this last notion in this form is better credited to Keynes than to Marx, although Marx was an ardent opponent of Say's law.) It is shown that the industrial reserve army's effect on wages can lead to a profit-squeeze crisis; the state's role as taxer of profits can lead to a fiscal crisis; and the possible discrepancy between actual savings and desired investment can lead to a realization or underconsumption crisis. The model is schematically represented in a convenient diagram that enables one to see how the various crises occur.

Some advice on how to read this book would perhaps be useful. I have tried to avoid a misleading simplicity, which could be achieved by stating theorems or their proofs imprecisely. For the reader who wishes to follow the argument in detail, such a simplicity would lead only to confusion. The cost of my approach is that the book does not make for casual reading. I have tried to compensate for this by providing ample discussion of the implications and motivations of theorems. I hope the book can be read at two levels: One level skips the proofs of theorems. The reader who follows both the proofs and the surrounding discussion will find that the level of familiarity assumed with results used in mathematical economics jumps abruptly in the proofs. In addition, some chapters are easier than others. Chapters 2, 3, and 8 are more technical than the rest.

The book is not intended as a first exposure to mathematical Marxian economics. In general, I have avoided developing models that are available from other authors, and have concentrated on what I hope are fresh approaches. The reader who has not seen the Leontief-Sraffa-Morishima approach to the labor theory of value and prices of production will probably have a difficult time. Two recent books that provide a clear and elementary presentation of the mathematics and economics of linear models relevant for Marxian analysis are Pasinetti (1977) and Steedman (1977). More advanced treatments can be found in, for instance, Nikaido (1968) and Schwartz (1961). The other kind of mathematics used in this book is the apparatus of fixed-point theorems and continuous correspondences, which is useful for the study of general equilibrium. The most succinct summary of these tools is to be found in Debreu (1973). Another classic source is Arrow and Hahn (1971).

1 Equilibrium and reproducibility: the linear model

1.1 A brief review

We begin with a discussion of what constitutes an equilibrium, in Marxian terms, of a capitalist economy, and for this chapter study a linear, Leontief specification of production.[1] Capitalists all have access to the same Leontief production system $\{A, \mathbf{L}\}$, where

A is an $n \times n$ input matrix of commodities

$\mathbf{L}$ is a $1 \times n$ vector of direct labor inputs

If $\mathbf{p}$ is a $1 \times n$ commodity price vector and the wage is normalized at unity so that prices $\mathbf{p}$ are interpreted as wage prices, then the usual notion of an equilibrium-price vector in a Marxian system is a vector $\mathbf{p}$ for which there exists a nonnegative number π such that

$$\mathbf{p} = (1 + \pi)(\mathbf{p}A + \mathbf{L}) \tag{1.1}$$

The vector $\mathbf{p}A + \mathbf{L}$ is the vector of unit costs of production (assuming that there are no fixed capital costs), and so π may be interpreted as the uniform profit rate for the economy. There may be, of course, many pairs $(\mathbf{p}, \pi)$ satisfying Equation 1.1.

We add more information to the system by requiring that workers each receive a *subsistence vector* of commodities $\mathbf{b}$, an $n \times 1$ vector. By subsistence, we mean simply that the wage must be precisely sufficient for $\mathbf{b}$ to be affordable, thus

$$\mathbf{pb} = 1 \tag{1.2}$$

Here, the unit of time that denominates $\mathbf{L}$, which is the same unit of time for which the wage of unity is paid, is to be thought of as one working day.

Combining (1.1) and (1.2), we see immediately that

$$\mathbf{p} = (1 + \pi)\mathbf{p}(A + \mathbf{bL}) \tag{1.3}$$

Thus, for a vector $\mathbf{p}$ satisfying (1.1) and (1.2) to exist, it is necessary and sufficient that the *augmented input coefficient matrix* $M \equiv A + \mathbf{bL}$ possess an eigenvalue $1/(1 + \pi)$ that does not exceed one, to which can be associated a nonnegative eigenvector $\mathbf{p}$. According to the Frobenius–Perron theorem, if M is an indecomposable matrix, then M has a unique eigenvalue that can qualify; that is, M possesses a unique positive eigenvalue to which can be associated a nonnegative eigenvector. It is, furthermore, the content of Morishima–Okishio's fundamental Marxian theorem (FMT) that if the *rate of exploitation e* is positive, then the Frobenius eigenvalue of M will be less than one, and so the associated profit rate will be strictly positive.

The rate of exploitation is defined in terms of the labor time embodied in the subsistence bundle. The vector of labor values is $\mathbf{\Lambda}$, a $1 \times n$ vector, where

$$\mathbf{\Lambda} = \mathbf{\Lambda} A + \mathbf{L} \tag{1.4}$$

Assuming that A is indecomposable and productive, we can write[2]

$$\mathbf{\Lambda} = \mathbf{L}(I - A)^{-1} > \mathbf{0} \tag{1.5}$$

The labor time embodied in the subsistence bundle is therefore $\mathbf{\Lambda b}$; *surplus* labor time in the working day is $1 - \mathbf{\Lambda b}$, and the rate of exploitation is classically defined as the ratio of surplus to necessary labor time:

$$e(\mathbf{b}) \equiv \frac{1 - \mathbf{\Lambda b}}{\mathbf{\Lambda b}} \tag{1.6}$$

Because the FMT has a prominent place in modern formulation of Marxian economics, it is appropriate to provide a quick proof of it.

THEOREM 1.1: Let $M \equiv A + \mathbf{bL}$ be the augmented input coefficient matrix associated with technology $\{A, \mathbf{L}; \mathbf{b}\}$. Suppose that M is indecomposable. Then the unique rate of profit π associated with M is positive if and only if $e(\mathbf{b}) > 0$.

Proof: Let $(\pi, \mathbf{p})$ be the unique pair satisfying

$$\mathbf{p} = (1 + \pi)\mathbf{p}(A + \mathbf{bL}) \tag{1.7}$$

which exists according to the Frobenius–Perron theorem. ($\mathbf{p}$ is determined only up to a scalar multiple; that scalar is determined by Equation 1.2.) It is also a consequence of Frobenius–Perron that, because M is indecomposable, $\mathbf{p} > 0$. Likewise, there is a strictly positive right eigenvector $\mathbf{x}$:

$$\mathbf{x} = (1 + \pi)(A + \mathbf{bL})\mathbf{x} \tag{1.8}$$

In (1.7) and (1.8), the eigenvalue of M is $1/(1 + \pi)$. π may in general be negative. It is our task to show that $\pi \geq 0$ if and only if $e(\mathbf{b}) \geq 0$.

Pre-multiplying (1.8) by the vector $\mathbf{\Lambda}$ and using the definition of e, we may write

$$\mathbf{\Lambda x} = (1 + \pi)\left(\mathbf{\Lambda}A\mathbf{x} + \frac{1}{1 + e}\mathbf{Lx}\right) \tag{1.9}$$

Because $\mathbf{\Lambda}$ and $\mathbf{x}$ are positive, both sides of (1.9) are positive, and we may write

$$1 + \pi = \frac{\mathbf{\Lambda x}}{[\mathbf{\Lambda}A + 1/(1 + e)\mathbf{L}]\mathbf{x}} \tag{1.10}$$

Glancing at the definition of $\mathbf{\Lambda}$ in (1.4) shows, by consideration of (1.10), that $\pi \gtreqless 0$ according as $e \gtreqless 0$. Q.E.D.

1.2 A more complete definition of Marxian equilibrium

In traditional mathematical models of Marxian systems, such as that of Section 1.1, it is simply asserted that a Marxian equilibrium consists of a price system that equalizes the rate of profit in all sectors. There are, however, some problems with this formulation. First, what behavioral specification of capitalists lies behind this definition of equilibrium? The concept of equilibrium in economics is usually the following: It consists of a state wherein, if all agents follow their specified rules of behavior, the consequent outcome is socially consistent. Speaking of equilibrium makes no sense if one has not specified behavioral rules for the agents, in this case, the capitalists. In the Marxian system (as in others), capitalists seek to maximize profits. One should therefore try and derive the equal-profit-rate (EPR) price vector as a consequence of profit maximization on the parts of capitalists.

One might reply that the story behind the pre-model of Section 1.1 is in fact one of profit maximization: If the rate of profit differed among sectors, then capital would flow to the highest-profit-rate sector(s); prices would fall there (due to competition and increased supply), and the profit rates would become equalized. Note, however, that this is a rather complicated dynamic story, in which many points are quite vague. How precisely do prices adjust? In fact, Nikaido claims that under such a dynamic scenario of capital moving to high-profit-rate sectors, there is no necessary convergence to *any* equilibrium price vector (Nikaido, 1978). At most, what can be said of the EPR price notion of Section 1.1 is this: *If* there is an equilibrium of the

Marxian system, then it should be the price vector of equal profit rates. However, this still leaves unspecified what the precise behavior of capitalists is. For instance, in a (neoclassical) *linear* model, if capitalists are profit maximizing at prices that bring a positive profit rate in all sectors, they will invest infinitely, to make infinite profits. Thus, there could be no equilibrium unless $\pi = 0$, which is to say, unless the real wage $\mathbf{b}$ becomes sufficiently bid up by escalating demands for labor so as to wipe out profits. How, then, can the Marxian behavior be specified in a way that allows a positive profit rate in a constant-returns-to-scale technology?

Capitalists, according to Marx, are endowed with an amount of money M, which they seek to turn into more money, M', through investment and sale of produced commodities. This money M does not appear in the formulation of Section 1.1. It is by appealing to the notion of the expansion of a finite sum of finance capital that we shall overcome the problem outlined above.

A second problem with the model of Section 1.1 is that there is no mention of output levels. For a notion of general equilibrium, we would like to specify not only prices, but what output levels are. To be sure, the fact that Marxian "equilibrium prices" are independent of output levels is usually regarded as a virtue: Prices are determined by technical (A, $\mathbf{L}$) and social ($\mathbf{b}$) conditions, and do not depend on anything else. Yet this is a false benefit, for an equilibrium theory should provide some description of levels of output, even if prices turn out to be independent of those levels.

To resolve these problems, we shall treat the economy slightly differently from the treatment of Section 1.1. There are N capitalists; the νth one is endowed with a vector of produced commodity endowments $\boldsymbol{\omega}^\nu$. Workers have no endowments of produced commodities; they have only labor power. We shall assume the same technology $\{A, \mathbf{L}\}$, but it operates in a different way. Production takes time. One enters inputs today and gets outputs tomorrow. Furthermore, capitalists, facing prices $\mathbf{p}$, are constrained in their choice of activity levels by the value of their capital, which is $\mathbf{p}\boldsymbol{\omega}^\nu$. There is no credit market, and they must pay for inputs today. (In Chapter 3 we shall relax this restriction of no credit market, and show that none of the results change.) Capitalist ν starts with capital $\boldsymbol{\omega}^\nu$, which he seeks to turn into more wealth at the highest rate of return. Thus, the program of capitalist ν is

$$\begin{array}{l}\text{Facing prices } \mathbf{p}, \text{ to} \\ \text{choose } \mathbf{x}^\nu \geq 0 \text{ to} \\ \max\ (\mathbf{p} - (\mathbf{p}A + \mathbf{L}))\mathbf{x}^\nu \\ \text{s.t. } (\mathbf{p}A + \mathbf{L})\mathbf{x}^\nu \leqq \mathbf{p} \cdot \boldsymbol{\omega}^\nu \end{array} \qquad \text{(P)}$$

(The constraint says that input costs can be covered by current capital.) Let us call $\mathbf{A}^{\nu}(\mathbf{p})$ the set of solution vectors to this program.

In this economy, for a given price vector **p**, the plans that different capitalists choose may not be feasible in aggregate. That is, we must guarantee, for **p** to be considered an *equilibrium* price vector, that the production choices capitalists make are globally feasible, given social endowments $\boldsymbol{\omega} \equiv \Sigma\boldsymbol{\omega}^{\nu}$. For each ν, let $\mathbf{x}^{\nu} \in \mathbf{A}^{\nu}(\mathbf{p})$ and $\mathbf{x} \equiv \Sigma\, \mathbf{x}^{\nu}$. Then **x** is globally feasible if

$$A\mathbf{x} + (\mathbf{Lx})\mathbf{b} \leqq \boldsymbol{\omega} \tag{1.11}$$

which says that total intermediate inputs ($A\mathbf{x}$) plus wage goods for employed workers, $(\mathbf{Lx})\mathbf{b}$, must not exceed the total supply of goods. (We assume that wage goods are dispensed at the beginning of the period. Thus stocks must be sufficient to accommodate them as well.)

There is a second attribute that Marxian equilibrium should have. We wish to guarantee that the economy *reproduces* itself. The Marxian notion of reproduction means that the system should create institutions and ideology that enable it to continue existing. We do not try to capture this deep idea, but rather the simple economic prerequisite that the economy should not operate in such a way as to run down some necessary stock to zero, in which case further production would be impossible. There are various complicated ways of specifying conditions to assure that this will not happen. A particularly simple way is to require that the stocks, at the beginning of next period, should exceed, component by component, stocks this period. If aggregate stocks this period are $\boldsymbol{\omega}$, then stocks next period will be

$$\boldsymbol{\omega} - [A\mathbf{x} + (\mathbf{Lx})\mathbf{b}] + \mathbf{x}$$

where **x** is the aggregate vector of activity levels operated, only employed workers eat, capitalists do not eat, and all stocks not used are storable. Hence, our requirement for *reproducibility* is

$$\boldsymbol{\omega} - [A\mathbf{x} + (\mathbf{Lx})\mathbf{b}] + \mathbf{x} \geqq \boldsymbol{\omega}$$

or

$$\mathbf{x} \geqq A\mathbf{x} + (\mathbf{Lx})\mathbf{b} \tag{1.12}$$

We can now state the definition of equilibrium. Facing prices **p**, each capitalist maximizes profits using the technology $\{A, \mathbf{L}\}$, subject to his or her capital constraint. Will there exist a set of individually optimal actions for capitalists that are socially feasible and reproduce the economy?

DEFINITION 1.1: A price vector **p** is a reproducible solution (RS) for the economy $\{A, \mathbf{L}; \mathbf{b}; \boldsymbol{\omega}^1, \ldots, \boldsymbol{\omega}^N\}$ if:

(a) For all ν, $\exists \mathbf{x}^\nu \in \mathbf{A}^\nu(\mathbf{p})$, such that (profit maximization)
(b) $\mathbf{x} = \Sigma\, \mathbf{x}^\nu$ and $\mathbf{x} \geqq A\mathbf{x} + (\mathbf{Lx})\mathbf{b}$ (reproducibility)
(c) $\mathbf{pb} = 1$ (subsistence wage)
(d) $A\mathbf{x} + (\mathbf{Lx})\mathbf{b} \leqq \boldsymbol{\omega} \equiv \Sigma\, \boldsymbol{\omega}^\nu$ (feasibility)
We shall also refer to the entire set $(\mathbf{p}; \mathbf{x}^1, \ldots, \mathbf{x}^N)$ as a reproducible solution.

This definition provides a behaviorally specific concept of equilibrium, as our discussion above required. One might still ask for a more amplified behavioral description of workers. In the present model, they are quite inanimate, demanding always the constant vector **b**. Furthermore, one might ask what capitalists consume, and what happens to workers who are unemployed at equilibrium. These are questions that, to some extent, are treated in later chapters in various ways. For the present, however, the purpose is to derive a consistent model of capitalist behavior, from which can be specified an equilibrium concept. Definition 1.1 attempts to capture the idea that capitalists are agents whose role is to transform their fixed sum of capital into the biggest sum of capital they possibly can during the production period.

We can now prove that, in fact, the only possible equilibrium price vector is the equal-profit-rate (EPR) price vector; and that such an equilibrium exists if social endowments $\boldsymbol{\omega}$ are suitably close to the balanced growth ray of the economy.

THEOREM 1.2: Let the model $\{A, \mathbf{L}, \mathbf{b}\}$ be given with A productive and indecomposable, and the rate of exploitation $e > 0$. Let $(\mathbf{p}, \mathbf{x}^1, \ldots, \mathbf{x}^N)$ be a nontrivial RS (i.e., $\Sigma\, \mathbf{x}^i \equiv \mathbf{x} \neq 0$). Then the vector of prices $\mathbf{p}$ is the EPR vector $\mathbf{p}^*$. Furthermore, a RS exists if and only if $\boldsymbol{\omega} \in \mathbf{C}^*$, where $\mathbf{C}^*$ is a particular convex cone in $\mathbf{R}^n$ containing the balanced growth path of $\{A, \mathbf{L}; \mathbf{b}\}$. ($\mathbf{C}^*$ is specified precisely below.)

Proof: Let $\mathbf{x} \neq \mathbf{0}$ be the aggregate activity vector associated with the RS. By Definition 1.1(b), $\mathbf{x} \geqq M\mathbf{x}$. Recall that $M = A + \mathbf{bL}$ is the augmented input coefficient matrix. Notice that, from Theorem 1.1, we infer that $e > 0$ means M is a productive matrix – that is, the Frobenius eigenvalue of M, $1/(1 + \pi)$, is less than unity. It follows from the Frobenius theorem that $(I - M)^{-1}$ exists and is a *positive* matrix, because M is indecomposable. Notice also that because $\mathbf{x} \neq \mathbf{0}$, we must in fact have $\mathbf{x} \geq M\mathbf{x}$; for if $\mathbf{x} = M\mathbf{x}$, then M's Frobenius eigenvalue would be unity, which it is not. But $\mathbf{x} \geq M\mathbf{x}$ implies that

$(I - M)\mathbf{x} \geq \mathbf{0}$; because $(I - M)^{-1} > \mathbf{0}$, this in turn implies that $\mathbf{x} > \mathbf{0}$. That is, at a (nontrivial) RS, *all activities must be operated.*

Capitalists facing prices $\mathbf{p}$, in maximizing profits, will operate only those processes generating the maximal profit rate, and they will operate those processes in (any) convex combination to the limit of their capital constraints (by linearity). This is seen by recalling the capitalist's program (P). Hence, for all processes to operate, it is necessary that the price vector $\mathbf{p}$ generate the *same* profit rate in all sectors. By the Frobenius–Perron theorem, there is a unique such vector up to scale, and its scale is determined by part (c) of the definition of RS. Thus, there is at most one viable price vector, $\mathbf{p}^*$, where $\mathbf{p}^* = (1 + \pi)\mathbf{p}^*M$.

Let $\mathbf{C}^*$ be the convex cone defined by

$$\mathbf{C}^* = \{\boldsymbol{\omega} \in \mathbf{R}^n_+ | (\exists \mathbf{x} \geqq 0)(M\mathbf{x} = \boldsymbol{\omega}) \quad \text{and} \quad \mathbf{x} \geqq M\mathbf{x}\}$$

$\mathbf{C}^*$ is a convex cone, and it is non-empty because there exists a balanced growth path $\mathbf{x}^*$ such that

$$\mathbf{x}^* = (1 + \pi)M\mathbf{x}^* \qquad \mathbf{x}^* > \mathbf{0}$$

where π is the profit rate associated with $\mathbf{p}^*$. ($e > 0$ guarantees $\pi > 0$, from the FMT, Theorem 1.1.) Hence $M\mathbf{x}^* \in \mathbf{C}^*$, with appropriate scaling of $\mathbf{x}^*$. It follows from previous remarks that $\mathbf{C}^*$ is a closed non-empty convex cone in the nonnegative orthant $\mathbf{R}^n_+$. (Note that the only point of $\mathbf{C}^*$ not in the strictly positive orthant is the origin.)

We proceed to show the existence of a RS if $\boldsymbol{\omega} \in \mathbf{C}^*$. Let $\bar{\mathbf{x}}$ be a vector that exists if $\boldsymbol{\omega} \in \mathbf{C}^*$, such that $M\bar{\mathbf{x}} = \boldsymbol{\omega}$ and $\bar{\mathbf{x}} \geqq M\bar{\mathbf{x}}$. Let $\mathbf{p}^*$ rule, as those are the only possible equilibrium prices. Notice in this case that any activity vector that uses up capitalist ν's capital is in fact a profit-maximizing one, because all processes generate equal profit rates at $\mathbf{p}^*$. It follows that

$$\mathbf{A}(\mathbf{p}^*) = \{\mathbf{x} \geq 0 | \mathbf{p}^* M\mathbf{x} = \mathbf{p}^*\boldsymbol{\omega}\} \qquad \text{where } \mathbf{A}(\mathbf{p}) \equiv \Sigma\, \mathbf{A}^\nu(\mathbf{p})$$

[Notice that any $\mathbf{x}$ in this set can be decomposed as $\mathbf{x} = \Sigma\, \mathbf{x}^\nu$, where $\mathbf{p}\mathbf{x}^\nu = \mathbf{p}\boldsymbol{\omega}^\nu$, and therefore $\mathbf{x}^\nu \in \mathbf{A}^\nu(\mathbf{p}^*)$.] In particular, it follows that $\bar{\mathbf{x}} \in \mathbf{A}(\mathbf{p}^*)$. All conditions of the definition of RS are satisfied.

Conversely, let $\{\mathbf{p}^*, \mathbf{x}^1, \ldots, \mathbf{x}^N\}$ be a RS. By linearity, each capitalist must spend the entire value of his or her endowment if he or she is maximizing profits; thus

$$\mathbf{p}^*M\mathbf{x}^\nu = \mathbf{p}^*\boldsymbol{\omega}^\nu \qquad \forall \nu$$

and so

$$\mathbf{p}^*M\mathbf{x} = \mathbf{p}^*\boldsymbol{\omega}$$

where $\mathbf{x} = \sum \mathbf{x}^\nu$. From part (d) of the definition of RS, $M\mathbf{x} \leqq \boldsymbol{\omega}$; because $\mathbf{p}^* > \mathbf{0}$, from the Frobenius–Perron theorem, it follows that $M\mathbf{x} = \boldsymbol{\omega}$ from the last equation. From part (b) of Definition 1.1, $\mathbf{x} \geqq M\mathbf{x}$, and consequently $\boldsymbol{\omega} \in \mathbf{C}^*$.

Hence $\mathbf{C}^*$ is precisely the cone of initial aggregate endowments for which reproducible solutions exist.[3] Q.E.D.

Notice in the proof what assumptions are necessary to show that the EPR price vector $\mathbf{p}^*$ is the only equilibrium price vector: All capitalists face the same technology, capitalists profit maximize, and the system must reproduce. If a capitalist had only the operation of certain sectors available to him or her, clearly reproducible price vectors could exist with different profit rates. (We shall study this more precisely below.) More important, however, is the observation that if the requirement of Definition 1.1(b) of reproducibility is dropped, then there can be equilibrium price vectors that render differing profit rates across sectors. Only those sectors will be operated that enjoy the maximal profit rate. Hence, the classical notion of the reproducibility of the economy is intimately bound up with the equalization of profit rates in this economy.[4]

The reader can easily verify that, although the indecomposability of M is key in this proof, so that all sectors operate at equilibrium, an analogous theorem holds for decomposable technologies. The modification becomes: The price vector must equalize profit rates among all sectors that operate.

Before continuing, let us reiterate the purpose of Theorem 1.2. It makes precise the sense in which the EPR price vector is a set of *equilibrium* prices. Notice that the equilibrium concept is a static one; as was mentioned previously, conceiving of EPR prices as an equilibrium of dynamic capital flow–price adjustment models is problematical.

Notice also that the sense in which a reproducible solution reproduces the system is quite limited: The only workers who get reproduced are those who are employed. [This is embodied in Definition 1.1(b): The only demand for goods by workers is from employed workers, in amount $(\mathbf{L}\mathbf{x})\mathbf{b}$.] Indeed, the model says nothing about unemployment. By pursuing this question a bit, we can tell a story to motivate the assumption that workers receive only a subsistence wage in this model. The scale of aggregate production is limited by initial aggregate endowments. Even if workers received no wage, the aggregate activity vector $\mathbf{x}$ must satisfy $A\mathbf{x} \leqq \boldsymbol{\omega}$. Hence there is some maximal demand for workers implied by society's finite capital stock. If the supply of workers is greater than this maximum, the wage would be bid down to zero by competitive forces. Before the wage falls to zero, however, workers will cease to offer their labor power for sale; in particular, if the wage is not sufficient to purchase some subsistence bundle **b**, then workers will withdraw from the capitalist economy and engage in handicraft production, or some such alternative. Thus the wage will be driven down to the subsistence wage, but no lower. The excess supply of workers forms the industrial reserve army who are indifferent to joining the capitalist sector at wages **pb**, but who are always available should the wage rise. Thus, one story behind the subsistence wage as an equilibrium concept, which we derive from this model, flows from the limited size of the capital stock with respect to the size of the labor force.

1.3 A model of imperfect competition

We next pursue a slight generalization of the above model. Suppose that all capitalists do not face the same technology. In particular, each capitalist has access to only a subset of the technologies for the n sectors. Of course, there may be some sectors to which several capitalists have access. Let us specify that capitalist ν can operate any sector indexed by an integer in the set S_ν, where S_ν is a subset of $\{1, 2, \ldots, n\}$. As before, there is no credit market, so a capitalist can only sink capital into one of the sectors available to him or her. We may define reproducible solutions as before; the only difference is that the program for capitalist ν to which the vectors $\mathbf{A}^\nu(\mathbf{p})$ are the profit-maximizing solutions is more restricted than before, because capitalist ν has access to only certain columns of the technology $\{A, \mathbf{L}\}$. What does the class of prices that support reproducible solutions look like? Clearly, the EPR prices $\mathbf{p}^*$ will be a RS; but there will in general be others. This might be viewed as a model of imperfect competition, because "entry" into the various sectors is limited. Alternatively, we can view S_ν as the information available to capitalist ν.

The perhaps surprising fact is that there are, in general, an infinity of equilibrium price vectors for this economy. In fact, we can use the Kaleckian notion of degree of monopoly (Kalecki, 1954) and assert roughly the following: For each of infinitely many prior distributions of degrees of monopoly among the n capitalists, there corresponds an equilibrium price vector. Hence, at the level of abstraction adopted thus far, it is "market power" that must determine the equilibrium, although there are other possible stories which will be mentioned later.

To see this, let us start with the simplest case. Suppose that the sets $S_1, \ldots, S_N$ of technologies to which the various capitalists have access are pairwise disjoint: $S_i \cap S_j = \emptyset$, for all $i, j = 1, N$. (In particular, in this case we must have $N \leq n$ if all capitalists are to exist in a nontrivial way.) We maintain, for simplicity, the assumption that the technology is indecomposable. Then, as before, all sectors must operate to achieve a RS. It follows that **p** can be an equilibrium price vector if and only if the profit rates are equalized *within* each set S_ν. Formally, let

$$p_i = (1 + \pi_i)\mathbf{p}\mathbf{M}_i \qquad \mathbf{M}_i = \mathbf{A}_i + (\mathbf{bL})_i$$

define the profit rate in sector i associated with a particular price vector **p**. ($\mathbf{M}_i$ and $\mathbf{A}_i$ are the ith columns of the matrices M and A.) Then **p** is a reproducible price vector if and only if:

$$(\forall\nu)(i, j \in S_\nu \Rightarrow \pi_i = \pi_j) \tag{1.13}$$

For if this did not hold for some ν, then that capitalist would operate only the sector(s) of maximal profit rate in his or her available set S_ν. Because no one else can operate the other sectors, by disjointness of the S_ν, reproducibility is impossible. Conversely, if condition (1.13) holds, it is clear any desired levels of activities that are socially feasible can be achieved as individually profit-maximizing for capitalists.

We next prove that we can specify the profit factors to have any desired ratios among the sets $S_1, \ldots, S_N$, and a price vector achieving those profit factors exists.

LEMMA 1.3: Let $d_1, \ldots, d_n$ be any positive numbers such that:
(*i*) $\min d_i = 1$
(*ii*) $\max d_i < 1 + \pi^*$
where $1/(1 + \pi^*)$ is the Frobenius eigenvalue of the matrix M. Then there exists a unique price vector $\mathbf{p} \geq \mathbf{0}$, which is in fact strictly positive, generating positive profit rates π_i in sectors i such that:

$$\text{for all } i, j \qquad \frac{1 + \pi_i}{1 + \pi_j} = \frac{d_i}{d_j}$$

Proof: Let D be the diagonal matrix (d_i). Clearly MD is indecomposable.

MD is a productive matrix: for let $\mathbf{p}^*$ be the eigenvector of M:

$$\mathbf{p}^* = (1 + \pi^*)\mathbf{p}^*M$$

Because $\max_i d_i < 1 + \pi^*$, it follows that

$$\mathbf{p}^*D^{-1} > \mathbf{p}^*M$$

and so

$$\mathbf{p}^* > \mathbf{p}^*MD,$$

showing the productiveness of MD.

Hence, there is a unique vector $\tilde{\mathbf{p}}$ and positive number $\tilde{r}$ such that

$$\tilde{\mathbf{p}} = (1 + \tilde{r})\tilde{\mathbf{p}}MD$$

and so

$$\tilde{\mathbf{p}}D^{-1} = (1 + \tilde{r})\tilde{\mathbf{p}}M$$

or

$$\tilde{p}_i = d_i(1 + \tilde{r})\tilde{\mathbf{p}}\mathbf{M}_i$$

Thus the profit factor in sector i associated with the vector $\mathbf{p}$ is

$$1 + \pi_i \equiv d_i(1 + \tilde{r})$$

and so

$$\frac{1 + \pi_i}{1 + \pi_j} = \frac{d_i}{d_j}$$

Furthermore, $\pi_i > 0$ for all i, because $d_i \geq 1$ and $\tilde{r} > 0$.

Uniqueness of $\tilde{\mathbf{p}}$ follows easily. If $\tilde{\mathbf{p}}$ were not unique, there would exist a vector $\hat{\hat{\mathbf{p}}}$ such that

$$\hat{\hat{p}}_i = d_i(1 + \hat{\hat{r}})\hat{\hat{\mathbf{p}}}MD$$

where $\hat{\hat{r}}$ is defined by the profit rate in the sector i for which $d_i = 1$. Hence

$$\hat{\hat{\mathbf{p}}} = (1 + \hat{\hat{r}})\hat{\hat{\mathbf{p}}}MD$$

contradicting the uniqueness of the Frobenius eigenvector for the matrix MD. Q.E.D.

Note. It can be observed from the proof that the condition $d_{\max} < 1 + \pi^*$ is only a *sufficient* condition for the result of the lemma to hold. In general, $d_{\max}$ can be greater than $1 + \pi^*$ and the result may still hold. We shall not be concerned with a more complete formulation of the acceptable domain of degrees of monopoly.

A direct application of the Lemma 1.3 to the case in point, where $S_\nu \cap S_\mu = \emptyset$ for all ν, μ, shows that a unique equilibrium price vector exists, for any desired distribution of degrees of monopoly $\{d_1, \ldots, d_N\}$ among the various capitalists. Simply assign the number d_ν to all sectors in S_ν.

Consideration of the general case, where S_μ and S_ν may overlap, can now be carried out. We first must define an *admissable* indexing of capitalists. We wish to index capitalists from 1 to N in such a way that a capitalist with index ν never has access to an activity to which capitalist $(\nu + 1)$ does not have access. That is, capitalists are indexed in order of nondecreasing access to information, so to speak. Formally, this may be accomplished as follows.

DEFINITION 1.2: An indexing $1, \ldots, N$ of capitalists is admissable, if, when the sets T_k are formed:

$$T_1 = S_1$$
$$T_2 = S_2 - S_1$$
$$T_3 = S_3 - (S_1 \cup S_2)$$
$$\vdots$$
$$T_k = S_k - \bigcup_{i<k} S_i$$
$$\vdots$$
$$T_N = S_N - \bigcup_{i<N} S_i$$

they have the following property: For some integer $1 \leq \tau \leqq N$, $T_k \neq \emptyset$ for $k \leqq \tau$ and $T_k = \emptyset$ for $k > \tau$.

This somewhat awkward combinatorial definition states that each of the first τ capitalists has access to some process not accessible to capitalists of lower index, but that no capitalist of index larger than τ has access to a process not already accessible to some capitalist of index $\leqq \tau$.

For *any* partition $S_1, \ldots, S_N$ of the activities, it is easily seen there is at least one admissable indexing of capitalists. In general, there are many admissable indexings. For instance, if every capitalist has access to a sector to which no other capitalist has access, then *any* indexing of the capitalists is admissable. The case of pairwise disjoint S_μ is a special case of *this* special case.

We can now state the general theorem.

THEOREM 1.4: Consider the imperfect competition model where capitalist ν can operate only sectors in a subset S_ν of $\{1, \ldots, n\}$. Let $\theta = \{i_1, \ldots, i_n\}$ be any admissable indexing of capitalists. Let

$$T_{i_j} = S_{i_j} - \bigcup_{k<j} S_{i_k}$$

Let there be τ_θ non-empty sets T_{i_j}. Let $d_1 \leq \cdots \leq d_{\tau_\theta}$ be numbers such that

(*i*) $d_1 = 1$
(*ii*) $d_{\tau_\theta} < 1 + \pi^*$

where $1/(1 + \pi^*)$ is the Frobenius root of M. Then there is a unique price vector $\mathbf{p}$ that achieves degree of monopoly d_j for the capitalist i_j to whom corresponds the non-empty set T_{i_j}. That capitalist, at the RS corresponding to $\mathbf{p}$, operates all sectors in T_{i_j}. Conversely, all reproducible price vectors are of this form for some admissable indexing θ and degrees of monopoly $d_1 \leq \cdot \cdot \cdot \leq d_{\tau_\theta}$.

(As in Theorem 1.2, the existence of a RS corresponding to $\mathbf{p}$ is subject to the requirement that the aggregate endowments ω be suitably close to the balanced growth path. In addition, as was mentioned previously, there is in fact slightly more freedom possible on the *largest* degree of monopoly.)

In the statement of Theorem 1.4, for the sake of clarity, it is not specified what degree of monopoly will be enjoyed by a capitalist ν for $\nu > \tau$. The procedure for deciding is this: Insert capitalist ν's set S_ν into the original chain $T_1, \ldots, T_\tau$ and ascertain at what point he or she ceases to have access to new information. That is, define the sets:

$$T_1(\nu) = S_\nu$$
$$T_2(\nu) = S_\nu - S_1$$
$$\vdots$$
$$T_k(\nu) = S_\nu - \bigcup_{i<k} S_i$$

For some $k \leq \tau$, $T_k(\nu) = \emptyset$. Let k_ν be the largest integer k for which $T_k(\nu) \neq \emptyset$. Then capitalist ν will sustain degree of monopoly d_{k_ν} at the equilibrium.

The statement of the proof of Theorem 1.4 will not be provided; the main work is in the theorem's formulation, not its proof, which is a direct application of Lemma 1.3.

Theorem 1.4 is a little surprising: One might think that the technology $(A, \mathbf{L}; \mathbf{b})$ would impose certain restrictions on the partitions $S_1, \ldots, S_N$ of information available to various capitalists, for which there could correspond price vectors allowing all sectors to operate under individual profit maximization, while giving different capitalists different profit rates. This, however, is not so. Any arbitrary partitioning of "information" can support an equilibrium price vector that provides differential returns to the special information possessed by the various capitalists.

How special the information possessed by a particular capitalist is can be gauged by how high is his or her index in some admissable indexing. Suppose, for clarity, capitalist ν's set S_ν is strictly contained in all other S_μ: then he will always be of lowest index in any admissable indexing, and his degree of monopoly will be minimal. The opposite case is of a capitalist who has access to a sector to which no one else has access; then there *exists* an admissable indexing in which his index is the highest, and hence there is an equilibrium price vector at which he possesses the highest degree of monopoly. (Note, however, that there may also be admissable indexings in which he has a low index.) This last point is starkly summarized as follows.

COROLLARY 1.5: Let a partition $S_1, \ldots, S_N$ be such that each capitalist possesses access to a sector accessible to no other capitalist; that is, $\bigcup_J S_i \neq \{1, \ldots, n\}$, where J is any proper subset of $\{1, \ldots, N\}$. Then there is a reproducible price vector assigning the maximal degree of monopoly to any given capitalist.

The second perhaps surprising conclusion of Theorem 1.4 is that, once an admissable distribution is decided upon, only the *ordinality* of degrees of monopoly is determined. The *cardinalities* can range over a continuum.

Thus, we have a hierarchical determination of the degree of monopoly: First, there are upper and lower bounds placed on a capitalist's ordinal ranking in the degree of monopoly based on the amount of information he possesses – this idea is summarized by his possible positions in admissable indexings. Second, given an admissable indexing, the precise cardinalities of degrees of monopoly are (virtually) arbitrary, in ratio (by Lemma 1.3). Thus, as far as the theory developed to this point is concerned, one would be inclined to say that market power determines the precise oligopolistic solution for the price vector.

What has been endeavored in this section has been to provide a basis for further modeling of oligopolistic behavior in the linear Marxian model. We have seen, first, that any partitioning of entry barriers in a linear Leontief technology can support a reproducible solution; but, furthermore, there is a great range of reproducible solutions possible. Which reproducible solution is arrived at can be discussed only with further stipulations on the model.

Finally, it might be mentioned that there is one way of arriving at a determinate solution to the problem without recourse to bargaining models. One can take the point of view that the degree of monopoly is really a differential rent. Imagine that there are two ways of producing each good i: the observed way $(A_i, \mathbf{L}_i)$, and some inferior way $(\tilde{A}_i, \tilde{\mathbf{L}}_i)$. There is limited entry to operation of the observed technique, but free entry to the technique ($\tilde{A}_t$, $\tilde{\mathbf{L}}_t$). It is then possible to construct a theory where the degrees of monopoly are determined by the differential rents of the superior processes over their inferior counterparts. This model will not be presented here, as the supposition of these (non-observed) inferior processes stretches the imagination. At least as a thought experiment, however, the idea deserves mention, as it shows how what may appear to be a pure bargaining–market-power phenomenon in fact has a competitive structure in the alternative opportunities faced by the agents in the bargain. Basically, the argument is this: The degree of monopoly in the auto industry rises as the relative price of autos rises. How high can this degree of monopoly be pushed? If auto prices rise too high, then the inferior auto process, into which there is free entry, becomes profitable, and capitalists rush into that activity and other sectors do not operate, destroying reproducibility. Hence, there is a limit to the degree of monopoly in a particular sector imposed by the productiveness of the (shadow) inferior activity for producing that sector's output. This is the sense in which the degree of monopoly in a sector with limited entry can be viewed as a differential rent over processes into which there is free entry.

1.4 Some dynamics in the linear, Leontief model

We return now to the competitive model of Section 1.2 where all capitalists have access to the entire technology (A, $\mathbf{L}$). Recall from Theorem 1.2 that a reproducible solution exists if and only if the social endowment $\boldsymbol{\omega}$ lies in a certain cone $\mathbf{C}^*$ containing the balanced growth path. This raises the following dynamic question. Suppose that $\boldsymbol{\omega} \in \mathbf{C}^*$, and a RS prevails. At the beginning of the next period, there will be new social endowments $\boldsymbol{\omega}'$, as a consequence of last period's production. Will $\boldsymbol{\omega}' \in \mathbf{C}^*$? That is, would a dynamic model lead to continued reproducibility? In general, the answer is no: It depends on the technology. We shall investigate this question in this section.

We first define a weaker equilibrium notion than reproducible solution. Individual capitalists are not concerned with whether a given equilibrium is reproducible; they simply maximize profits. This motivates the following definition.

Definition 1.3: A competitive equilibrium (CE) with respect to initial endowments ($\boldsymbol{\omega}^1, \ldots, \boldsymbol{\omega}^N$) is a pair ($\mathbf{p}$, $\mathbf{x}$) such that:

(a) $\mathbf{x} \in \mathbf{A}(\mathbf{p}) \equiv \Sigma\, \mathbf{A}^\nu(\mathbf{p})$
(b) $\mathbf{pb} = 1$
(c) $A\mathbf{x} + (\mathbf{Lx})\mathbf{b} \leqq \boldsymbol{\omega}$ $(M\mathbf{x} \leqq \boldsymbol{\omega})$

That is, a CE that is also reproducible is a RS. Even if $\boldsymbol{\omega} \notin \mathbf{C}^*$, competitive equilibria exist.

THEOREM 1.6: For any $(\boldsymbol{\omega}^1, \ldots, \boldsymbol{\omega}^N)$, a competitive equilibrium exists.

Proof: Let $S = \{\mathbf{p} | \mathbf{pb} = 1\}$, the simplex. (Assume that $\mathbf{b} > \mathbf{0}$ so that S is a simplex.) Construct the correspondence $\mathbf{z}(\mathbf{p}) = \{M\mathbf{x} - \boldsymbol{\omega} | \mathbf{x} = \Sigma\, \mathbf{x}^\nu, \mathbf{x}^\nu \in \mathbf{A}^\nu(\mathbf{p})\}$. It is easily verified that $\mathbf{z}(\mathbf{p})$ satisfies the requirements of the fixed point lemma;[5] hence, a vector $\bar{\mathbf{p}}$ and $\bar{\mathbf{x}}$ exist such that $M\mathbf{x} - \boldsymbol{\omega} \leqq 0$ and $\mathbf{x} \in \mathbf{A}(\mathbf{p})$. Q.E.D.

If $\boldsymbol{\omega} \notin \mathbf{C}^*$, what happens? We shall say that a competitive equilibrium is arrived at, $(\mathbf{p}, \mathbf{x})$. The initial endowments for the *next* period will be

$$\boldsymbol{\omega}(t + 1) = \boldsymbol{\omega}(t) - M\mathbf{x} + \mathbf{x}$$

that is, the old endowment plus net outputs $\mathbf{x} - M\mathbf{x}$.

DEFINITION 1.4: A good is in excess supply at a CE $(\mathbf{p}, \mathbf{x})$ if $\omega_i > (M\mathbf{x})_i$.

LEMMA 1.7: If good i is in excess supply at CE $(\mathbf{p}, \mathbf{x})$, then it is not produced:

$$\omega_i > (M\mathbf{x})_i \Rightarrow x_i = 0$$

Also, a good in excess supply is free:

$$\omega_i > (M\mathbf{x})_i \Rightarrow p_i = 0$$

LEMMA 1.8: Let $(\mathbf{p}, \mathbf{x})$ be a CE for technology $\{A, \mathbf{L}; \mathbf{b}\}$ for which it is assumed that $e > 0$. If $\mathbf{p}\boldsymbol{\omega} > 0$, then $(\mathbf{p}, \mathbf{x})$ generates positive total profits.

Proof of Lemma 1.8: Suppose that there were zero total profits at $(\mathbf{p}, \mathbf{x})$. Then each capitalist makes zero profits. Because $\mathbf{p}\boldsymbol{\omega} > 0$, for at least one capitalist, $\mathbf{p}\boldsymbol{\omega}^\nu > 0$. This capitalist will operate a positive-profit-rate activity if there is one, so all activities must have nonpositive profit rates, hence:

$$\mathbf{p} \leqq \mathbf{p}M$$

Let $\mathbf{x}^*$ be the column eigenvector of M. We know that $M\mathbf{x}^* < \mathbf{x}^*$, by Frobenius–Perron. We know that $\mathbf{p} = \mathbf{p}M$ is impossible by Frobenius, because M has a unique row eigenvector, and it is associated with eigenvalue $1/(1 + \pi) < 1$. Hence

$$\mathbf{p} \leq \mathbf{p}M$$

Post-multiplying by $\mathbf{x}^*$ gives

$$\mathbf{p}\mathbf{x}^* < \mathbf{p}M\mathbf{x}^*$$

But $\mathbf{x}^* = (1 + \pi)M\mathbf{x}^*$, which implies that

$$\mathbf{p}\mathbf{x}^* > \mathbf{p}M\mathbf{x}^*$$

This contradicts the original assumption. Q.E.D.

Proof of Lemma 1.7: Consider capitalist with endowment $\boldsymbol{\omega}^\nu$. Let $(\mathbf{p}, \mathbf{x})$ be a CE. Say $\mathbf{p}\boldsymbol{\omega} > 0$. By Lemma 1.8, there are positive total profits; hence there must be a positive profit-rate process, and so capitalist ν can certainly operate this process and make positive profits. By linearity, capitalist ν will therefore operate to the limit of his capital constraint. That is, he will choose a vector of activity levels $\mathbf{x}^\nu$ such that

$$\mathbf{p}M\mathbf{x}^\nu = \mathbf{p}\boldsymbol{\omega}^\nu \tag{1.14}$$

On the other hand, if $\mathbf{p}\boldsymbol{\omega}^\nu = 0$, then certainly (1.14) holds also. Hence, adding gives

$$\mathbf{p}M\mathbf{x} = \mathbf{p}\boldsymbol{\omega}$$

or

$$\mathbf{p}(M\mathbf{x} - \boldsymbol{\omega}) = 0 \tag{1.15}$$

By (1.15) it follows that any good which is in excess supply at CE $(\mathbf{p}, \mathbf{x})$ has zero price. Consequently, the profit rate for operating the activity that produces that good is nonpositive. However, by Lemma 1.8, we know that there are positive profit-rate processes: hence, the nonpositive profit-rate processes will not be operated. Q.E.D.

Using Lemma 1.7, it is possible to construct a complete taxonomy of the CE for the case of an indecomposable 2×2 matrix M. Let M be 2×2, and let $\boldsymbol{\alpha}_1$ and $\boldsymbol{\alpha}_2$ be the (positive) input requirement vectors for operating the first and second processes, respectively, at unit levels:

$$\boldsymbol{\alpha}_1 = M(1, 0)$$

$$\boldsymbol{\alpha}_2 = M(0, 1)$$

Let us suppose that $\boldsymbol{\alpha}_i$ lie as pictured in Figure 1, which is the positive

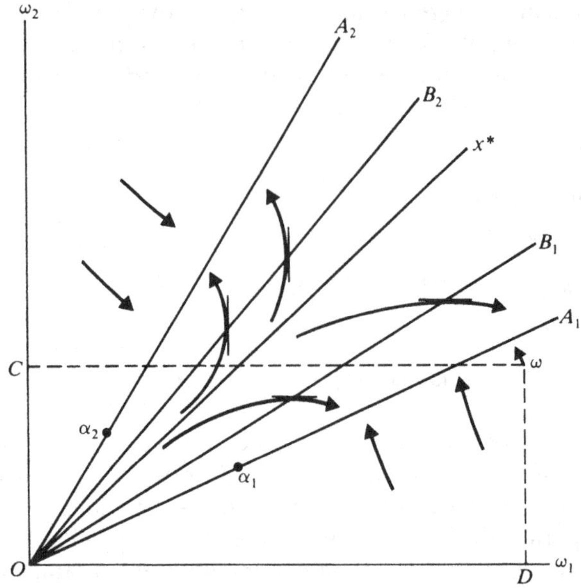

Figure 1

orthant in input-requirements space. Then any vector of outputs $\mathbf{x}$ will generate input requirements lying in the cone A_1OA_2. Suppose that the initial endowment vector lies to the right of the cone, as pictured. Then, by feasibility, any competitive equilibrium ($\mathbf{p}$, $\mathbf{x}$) must have its input requirements $M\mathbf{x}$ lying in the rectangle $C\boldsymbol{\omega}DO$ to the southwest of $\boldsymbol{\omega}$; because $M\mathbf{x} \in A_1OA_2$ also, it follows that good 1 must be in excess supply at competitive equilibrium. It follows by Lemma 1.7 that $p_1 = 0 = x_1$. Thus, only process 2 is operated, and process 2 is operated to the limit of the capital constraint.

To get a dynamic story, we must replace the discrete model here with a continuous model. We shall not do this in all rigorous detail here, but the idea is as follows: We think of $\boldsymbol{\omega}$ not as a stock of inputs to be used up, but as a stock of capital generating capital services over a large number of periods. At each period, the initial endowment of capital, $\boldsymbol{\omega}$, is adjusted by the net product $\mathbf{x} - M\mathbf{x}$, in the sense discussed:

$$\boldsymbol{\omega}(t + 1) = \boldsymbol{\omega}(t) - M[\mathbf{x}(t)] + \mathbf{x}(t)$$

We have observed that if $\boldsymbol{\omega}(t)$ lies to the right of the cone A_1OA_2, then we get a solution $\mathbf{x}(t)$ with the property:

$$x_1(t) = 0$$

$$x_2(t) > 0$$

Furthermore, $M[\mathbf{x}(t)] > 0$, and we therefore have

$$\omega_1(t + 1) < \omega_1(t)$$

$$\omega_2(t + 1) > \omega_2(t)$$

(Observe, also, that $x_2(t) > \{M[\mathbf{x}(t)]\}_2$, by productivity of M.) Hence, the net endowment vector moves toward the cone, as indicated by the arrow in Figure 1.

We can carry out this analysis for other positions of the initial endowment vector, and the phase diagram of Figure 1 is generated.

In Figure 1, $\mathbf{x}^*$ is the balanced growth path. B_1OB_2 is the cone $\mathbf{C}^*$, in which reproducible solutions exist. A_1OA_2 is the cone of feasible input requirements. If $\boldsymbol{\omega}$ lies precisely on the balanced growth path, then there is a competitive equilibrium that keeps it there. However, if $\boldsymbol{\omega}$ lies elsewhere in the cone A_1OA_2, the endowment vector, over time, moves away from the balanced path $\mathbf{x}^*$ toward the boundary of the cone. (On the cone's boundaries, behavior is not continuous.) If $\boldsymbol{\omega}$ lies initially outside the cone, it moves toward the cone. From the figure, it can be seen that the difference between $\boldsymbol{\omega} \in B_1OB_2$ and $\boldsymbol{\omega} \notin B_1OB_2$ is this: If and only if $\boldsymbol{\omega} \in B_1OB_2$, the endowments of both goods increase during that period. Hence, the dynamics are unstable. $\boldsymbol{\omega}$ does not converge to a value inside B_1OB_2.

There is a second case, namely, when the factor intensities are reversed, as in Figure 2. (In the first case, each output was relatively intensive in its own input.) In the factor-reversal case, the phase diagram of Figure 2 holds. Thus, the case of factor intensity reversal does generate stability and a convergence of endowments toward the domain B_1OB_2 where reproducible solutions exist.

This discussion shows that in general there is no convergence toward reproducible solutions. It is possible, though perhaps not fruitful, to interpret the paths that lead away from the cone of reproducible endowments as the paths leading to the "disproportionality crises" of Marx.

More appropriate, however, is to consider a possible alteration of the basic model that should be made if we are to consider it dynamically. Time is of the essence in the model of production constructed in this chapter, and so it is only appropriate to allow capitalists to expect different prices to hold tomorrow than hold today. Instead of assuming that tomorrow's prices will not change, capitalist ν may hold expectations that prices next period will be $\mathbf{p}^{\nu}_{t+1}$, when today's prices are

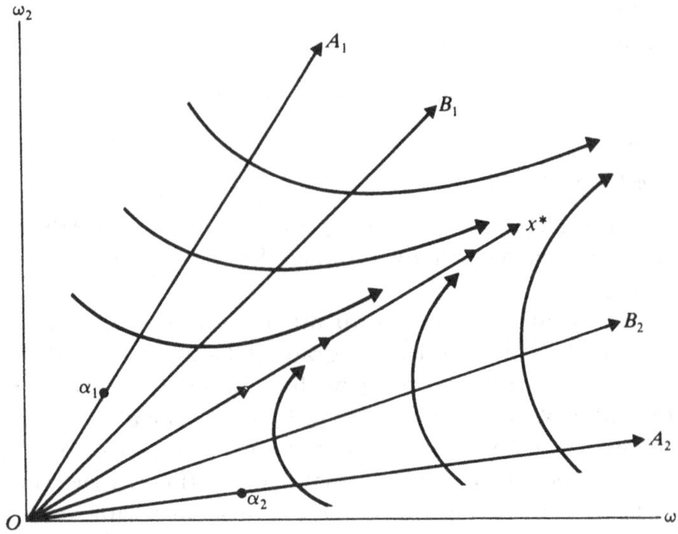

Figure 2

$\mathbf{p}_t$. We would then consider the model of the present chapter as a temporary equilibrium model. In particular, as the economy starts to run out of one good, as happens in the exploding technology of Figure 1, we might expect capitalists to raise their price expectation for the good in short supply, thus making its production more profitable, thus resolving the crisis of exit from the feasible cone **C***. Such complications shall not concern us here.[6] For our purposes, we may consider the model of this chapter to apply to stationary points of capitalists' price expectation functions. If the endowment "converges" as in Figure 2, then in fact stationary expectations are consistent, and the economy eventually converges to aggregate endowments on the balanced growth path.

The main purpose of this chapter has been to define a precise equilibrium concept for a Marxian model, the concept of a reproducible solution. In the next chapter, we investigate the application of this idea to economies with far more general production sets than the Leontief technology $\{A, \mathbf{L}\}$. Our concern shall be to develop the Marxian theory of value in these general economies.

2 Reproducibility and exploitation: a general model

2.1 Introduction

We have shown that the traditional Marxian notion that equilibrium prices must be the vector of equal-profit-rate prices can be imbedded in a general equilibrium framework using the idea of reproducibility, at least in a linear, Leontief model. The task now is to investigate how robust these ideas are if we consider more general technologies. In particular, we shall focus on two important ideas: the existence of reproducible solutions for economies with more general specifications of production, and the validity of the fundamental Marxian theorem – that exploitation is synonymous with positive profits. In Chapter 3 we investigate a third important idea – whether equilibrium prices equalize profit rates among sectors in these more general models.

The answer is that the Marxian concepts, as discussed in Chapter 1, remain tractable, and the important theorems do generalize to a production environment in which capitalists face general, convex production sets. Thus, the ideas developed by Morishima (1973), Wolfstetter (1973), Okishio (1961), von Weizsäcker (1973), Maarek (1975), Brody (1970), and others for linear, Leontief models, and generalized by Morishima (1974) to von Neumann production models, are shown here to depend not at all on the activity analysis specification of production. Convexity suffices to define the concept of exploitation, and to verify the equivalence of profit making and exploitation.

Carrying out the analysis for convex production sets is instructive for another reason: It makes clear precisely which aspects of classical Marxian value theory are *not* robust, but incidental to the main story. In particular, the use of individual labor values of produced commodities falls by the wayside. In Chapter 1, exploitation was defined by using the labor-value vector $\mathbf{\Lambda}$; here, this is no longer possible, nor is it necessary. This enables us to conclude that the Marxian theory of exploitation is independent of the conception of microdenominated, individual labor values. Social surplus value need not be aggregated from individual surplus values!

This position is not new in Marxian debates: It has been argued previously by Morishima (1973, 1974) and, perhaps most forcefully, by Steedman (1977). Those two writers, however, limited their general analysis to the von Neumann model. It becomes, perhaps, even more clear in the convex model studied here that exploitation must be defined independently of microdenominated labor values. Because this issue is of such importance in the Marxian heritage, a special chapter (Chapter 7) is devoted to it.

For most of this chapter, we retain the simplifying assumption that the vector of workers' consumption, **b**, is exogenous. In a full general equilibrium model, one might wish to determine workers' subsistence needs endogenously; and in a final section of the chapter we propose a manner of doing this in a Marxian fashion. That is, we allow **b** to be socially determined, and investigate the consequences for the model.

2.2 Specification of the model

Production

The νth capitalist faces a production possibilities set P^ν. There are n commodities that can be produced, and labor. Vectors $\boldsymbol{\alpha}^\nu \in P^\nu$ will be written as $(2n + 1)$ vectors, as follows:

$$\boldsymbol{\alpha}^\nu = (-\alpha_0^\nu, -\underline{\boldsymbol{\alpha}}^\nu, \bar{\boldsymbol{\alpha}}^\nu)$$

where α_0^ν is the direct labor input, $\underline{\boldsymbol{\alpha}}^\nu$ is the nonnegative n vector of commodity inputs, and $\bar{\boldsymbol{\alpha}}^\nu$ is the nonnegative n vector of commodity outputs. For notational convenience, write $\hat{\boldsymbol{\alpha}}^\nu$ for the n vector of net outputs, $\hat{\boldsymbol{\alpha}}^\nu = \bar{\boldsymbol{\alpha}}^\nu - \underline{\boldsymbol{\alpha}}^\nu$. It is assumed that:

A1. $(\forall \nu)(\mathbf{0} \in P^\nu)$

A2. $(\forall \nu)(P^\nu$ is convex$)$

A3. $(\forall \nu)(P^\nu$ is closed$)$

A4. $(\forall \boldsymbol{\alpha} \in P^\nu)(\boldsymbol{\alpha}_0 \geq 0$ and $\underline{\boldsymbol{\alpha}} \geqq \mathbf{0})$

$(\bar{\boldsymbol{\alpha}} \geq \mathbf{0} \Rightarrow \alpha_0 > 0$, where $\boldsymbol{\alpha} = (-\boldsymbol{\alpha}_0, -\underline{\boldsymbol{\alpha}}, \bar{\boldsymbol{\alpha}}))$

In addition, let $P = \Sigma P^\nu$ be the aggregate production set. It is assumed that

A5. $(\forall$ commodity n vectors $\mathbf{c})$ $(\exists \boldsymbol{\alpha}' \in P)$ $(\hat{\boldsymbol{\alpha}}' \geqq \mathbf{c})$

It follows that A1–A5 are also true for P.

Assumptions A1–A3 need no comment. A4 is a strong form of "no free lunch": Labor is not a producible commodity, and is necessary for any productive activity. A5 says that all (nonlabor) commodities are producible, and that any vector of nonnegative net outputs can be produced.

An explanation is due for why inputs are separated from outputs in the definition of production sets. Time is essential in this sense: Capitalists must pay for inputs prior to production, and must use their capital $\mathbf{p}\boldsymbol{\omega}^{\nu}$ to do this. They cannot borrow against future revenues to finance today's production. Hence, the differentiation between inputs and outputs must be made. For example, in the linear model of the previous chapter, a typical activity vector will be written, under this convention, as

$$\langle -l_i, -a_{1i}, -a_{2i}, \ldots, -a_{ni}, 0, 0, \ldots, 1_i, 0, \ldots, 0\rangle$$

Under the convention that ignores time, this activity vector would be written:

$$\langle -l_i, -a_{1i}, \ldots, -a_{i-1,i}, 1 - a_{ii}, -a_{i+1,i}, \ldots, -a_{ni}\rangle$$

In the latter case it appears as if there is no cost to the capitalist operating this activity from use of input i. This, however, is incorrect. In the model of Chapter 1, recall the capitalist must lay out cost $p_i a_{ii}$, among other costs; this is captured only by viewing production as $(2n + 1)$ vectors.

Exploitation

Exploitation can now be defined.

DEFINITION 2.1: The labor value of commodity bundle **B**, l.v.(**B**), is defined as

$$\min_{\phi(\mathbf{B})} \alpha_0 \qquad \text{where } \phi(\mathbf{B}) = \{\boldsymbol{\alpha} \in P \mid \hat{\boldsymbol{\alpha}} \geqq \mathbf{B}\}$$

DEFINITION 2.2: The rate of exploitation at a point $\boldsymbol{\alpha} \in P$ is

$$e(\boldsymbol{\alpha}) = \frac{\alpha_0}{\text{l.v.}(\alpha_0 \mathbf{b})} - 1$$

For the zero production vector, $e(\mathbf{0}) = \mathbf{0}$.

As defined, $e(\boldsymbol{\alpha})$ captures the notion of the ratio surplus labor time/necessary labor time of classical Marxian value theory. First, consider Definition 2.1. The labor value of a particular bundle of commodities, **B**, is defined as the minimal amount of direct labor needed to produce $\mathbf{B}$ as *net* outputs of social production. (The outputs are net, because it is required that $\hat{\boldsymbol{\alpha}} \equiv \bar{\boldsymbol{\alpha}} - \underline{\boldsymbol{\alpha}} \geqq \mathbf{B}$.) This is the same as calculating the direct and indirect labor time embodied in $\mathbf{B}$, because the indirect labor time is used in producing intermediate inputs needed for $\mathbf{B}$'s production, which is accounted for here by the specification that $\mathbf{B}$ is the *net* output vector.

Some may argue that one should not calculate the labor value of $\mathbf{B}$ using the best available techniques (i.e., minimal labor time) but using "socially average" techniques. This, however, is a mainly semantic matter. By defining l.v.($\mathbf{B}$) as we have done, we are asking for the labor-efficient way of producing $\mathbf{B}$, using the aggregate production set P. If a "socially average" technique is inferior to this, then we would be injecting some sort of inefficiency into our conception of labor values, which is not in the Marxian spirit. One might, alternatively, argue that being on the frontier of the set P means "socially average;" and that socially superior techniques are ones that do not appear in P.

Given the definition of l.v.($\mathbf{B}$), we can define necessary labor time at a point $\boldsymbol{\alpha} \in P$ as l.v.($\alpha_0\mathbf{b}$). This is the labor time socially necessary to produce consumption goods to feed all the workers employed at $\boldsymbol{\alpha}$, of whom there are α_0 in number. Thus, only the needs of employed workers enter into the definition of necessary labor time. Surplus labor time, at $\boldsymbol{\alpha} \in P$, is clearly $\alpha_0 -$ l.v.($\alpha_0\mathbf{b}$). Hence, Definition 2.2 becomes the ratio surplus labor time to necessary labor time.

It is important to note that the rate of exploitation is defined at a point in P. Thus, $e(\boldsymbol{\alpha})$ is no longer a *number,* but a *function, e:* $P \rightarrow \mathbf{R}$. If P is a cone, and so there are constant returns to scale, then $e(\boldsymbol{\alpha})$ becomes a constant function, that is, a number. The functional specification is necessary when P is not a constant-returns-to-scale technology.

It is important to show that $e(\boldsymbol{\alpha})$ is always defined, which is the content of the following.

PROPOSITION 2.1: $e(\boldsymbol{\alpha})$ is well defined $\forall \boldsymbol{\alpha} \in P$.

Proof: It is only necessary to show that l.v.($\mathbf{B}$) is well defined for all commodity vectors $\mathbf{B} \geq \mathbf{0}$. The set $\phi(\mathbf{B})$ is non-empty by A5; g.l.b.α_0 exists because $\{\alpha_0 | (-\alpha_0, -\underline{\boldsymbol{\alpha}}, \bar{\boldsymbol{\alpha}}) \in \phi(\mathbf{B})\}$ is bounded below by 0, by A4. It is then only necessary to show that

$$\alpha_0^* = \min_{\phi(\mathbf{B})} \alpha_0$$

is achieved at a point $\boldsymbol{\alpha}^* = (-\alpha_0^*, -\underline{\boldsymbol{\alpha}}^*, \bar{\boldsymbol{\alpha}}^*) \in P$.

Choose a sequence $\boldsymbol{\alpha}^i = (-\alpha_0^i, -\underline{\boldsymbol{\alpha}}^i, \bar{\boldsymbol{\alpha}}^i)$ in $\phi(\mathbf{B})$ such that $\alpha_0^i \to \alpha_0^*$. It is claimed that $\{\boldsymbol{\alpha}^i\}$ is bounded. For let

$$\boldsymbol{\beta}^i = \frac{1}{\|\boldsymbol{\alpha}^i\|}\boldsymbol{\alpha}^i \qquad \|\boldsymbol{\alpha}^i\| = \max_j |\alpha_j^i|$$

Because $\mathbf{0} \in P$ and P is convex, $\boldsymbol{\beta}^i \in P$. $\{\boldsymbol{\beta}^i\}$ is bounded. Because P is closed, $\boldsymbol{\beta}^i \to \boldsymbol{\beta}^* = (-\beta_0^*, -\underline{\boldsymbol{\beta}}^*, \bar{\boldsymbol{\beta}}^*) \in P$. Suppose that $\{\boldsymbol{\alpha}^i\}$ is unbounded; then $\beta_0^i \to 0$ because $\alpha_0^i \to \alpha_0^*$. Hence $\beta_0^* = 0$. But $\bar{\boldsymbol{\beta}}^* \geq 0$, which contradicts A4 applied to the set P.

Therefore, $\{\boldsymbol{\alpha}^i\}$ is bounded, so by the closedness of P, a convergent subsequence of $\{\boldsymbol{\alpha}^i\}$ can be chosen converging to the required vector $\boldsymbol{\alpha}^*$. Q.E.D.

We shall be interested in points $\boldsymbol{\alpha} \in P$, where $e(\boldsymbol{\alpha}) \geqq 0$. It is possible, of course, that $e(\boldsymbol{\alpha}) < 0$ for some points $\boldsymbol{\alpha}$. It is important to keep in mind that the data used to define $e(\boldsymbol{\alpha})$ are *technology* and *workers' consumption;* that is, $e(\boldsymbol{\alpha})$ is technologically and socially determined. In particular, no price or wealth data are necessary to define $e(\boldsymbol{\alpha})$. The condition $e(\boldsymbol{\alpha}) > 0$ will turn out to be equivalent to a condition of productiveness on the augmented input coefficient matrix, $M = A + \mathbf{bL}$, of the Leontief technology. It can be verified by the reader that if P is the linear technology $\{A, \mathbf{L}\}$ of Chapter 1, then the function $e(\boldsymbol{\alpha})$ reduces to $e(\boldsymbol{\alpha}) = e = 1/\boldsymbol{\Lambda}\mathbf{b} - 1$.

Capitalist behavior

The behavior of capitalists is profit maximizing. Capitalist ν possesses capital $\boldsymbol{\omega}_t^\nu$ at time t. We view the model in a temporary equilibrium framework. Capitalists face prices today, and their objective is to maximize the expected value of tomorrow's endowment $\boldsymbol{\omega}_{t+1}^\nu$. Tomorrow's endowment comes from two sources: the output from production carried on today, and commodities carried over from today to tomorrow; commodity speculation may take place. Formally, if capitalist ν expects prices $\mathbf{p}_{t+1}^\nu$ to rule tomorrow, his program is

$$\text{choose } \boldsymbol{\alpha}^\nu, \boldsymbol{\delta}^\nu \in \mathbf{R}_+^n \text{ to max } (\mathbf{p}_{t+1}^\nu \bar{\boldsymbol{\alpha}}^\nu + \mathbf{p}_{t+1}^\nu \boldsymbol{\delta}^\nu)$$
$$\text{subject to } \alpha_0^\nu + \mathbf{p}_t\underline{\boldsymbol{\alpha}}^\nu \leqq \mathbf{p}_t\boldsymbol{\omega}_t^\nu$$
$$\mathbf{p}_t\boldsymbol{\delta}^\nu = \mathbf{p}_t\boldsymbol{\omega}_t^\nu - (\mathbf{p}_t\underline{\boldsymbol{\alpha}}^\nu + \alpha_0^\nu)$$

That is, capitalists seek to maximize the expected value of tomorrow's endowment $\boldsymbol{\omega}_{t+1}^\nu = \boldsymbol{\delta}^\nu + \bar{\boldsymbol{\alpha}}^\nu$ subject to the budget constraint on production costs and commodity speculation that expenditures cannot exceed present capital $\mathbf{p}_t\boldsymbol{\omega}_t^\nu$. (We take the wage as *numéraire,* and $\mathbf{p}$ is an n vector of wage – prices.)

For the body of the chapter, we shall assume that expectations are stationary: $\mathbf{p}^\nu_{t+1} = \mathbf{p}_t = \mathbf{p}$, for all ν. (Or the analysis can be conceived of as applying in a general expectations framework, at a stationary state, if one exists.) The details of the more general analysis, where price expectations are not stationary, are available in Roemer (1980a).

To this end, we observe that with stationary expectations, the capitalists' objective function takes this simple form:

PROPOSITION 2.2: When $\mathbf{p}_{t+1} = \mathbf{p}_t = \mathbf{p}$, the capitalist's program is

$$\text{choose } \boldsymbol{\alpha}^\nu \in P^\nu \text{ to maximize } \mathbf{p}\bar{\boldsymbol{\alpha}}^\nu - (\mathbf{p}\underline{\boldsymbol{\alpha}}^\nu + \alpha_0)$$
$$\text{s.t. } \alpha^\nu_0 + \mathbf{p}\underline{\boldsymbol{\alpha}}^\nu \leqq \mathbf{p}\boldsymbol{\omega}^\nu$$

Proof: The program is

$$\text{choose } \boldsymbol{\alpha}^\nu, \boldsymbol{\delta}^\nu \text{ to max } \mathbf{p}\bar{\boldsymbol{\alpha}}^\nu + \mathbf{p}\boldsymbol{\delta}^\nu$$
$$\text{s.t. } (i) \quad \alpha^\nu_0 + \mathbf{p}\underline{\boldsymbol{\alpha}}^\nu \leqq \mathbf{p}\omega^\nu$$
$$(ii) \quad \mathbf{p}\boldsymbol{\delta}^\nu = \mathbf{p}\omega^\nu - (\mathbf{p}\boldsymbol{\alpha}^\nu + \alpha^\nu_0)$$

Substituting from (*ii*) into the objective function, and recognizing that $\mathbf{p}\boldsymbol{\omega}^\nu$ is a constant, yields the result. Q.E.D.

This proposition justifies the specification of the capitalist's program of Chapter 1, Section 1.2. Capitalists maximize profits, subject to the capital constraint that they must finance the costs of production inputs from present holdings of capital. In this world, there is no capital market. Such a market will be introduced in Chapter 3.

From now on, all time subscripts on prices are dropped, as it assumed that $\mathbf{p}^\nu_{t+1} = \mathbf{p}_t$ for all ν.

DEFINITION 2.3: The feasible production set for capitalist ν at prices $\mathbf{p}$ is

$$\mathbf{B}^\nu(\mathbf{p}) = \{\boldsymbol{\alpha}^\nu \in P^\nu \mid \alpha^\nu_0 + \mathbf{p}\alpha^\nu \leqq \mathbf{p}\boldsymbol{\omega}^\nu\}$$

(The feasible set consists of those production points at which the capitalist can afford to produce with his capital.)

LEMMA 2.3: $\forall \nu$, $\mathbf{p} \geq 0$, $\mathbf{B}^\nu(\mathbf{p})$ is non-empty, convex, and compact.

Proof: $\mathbf{B}^\nu(\mathbf{p})$ is non-empty because it contains $\mathbf{0}$.

Convexity and closedness are obvious.

Boundedness: Notice that $\{\alpha^\nu_0 \mid \boldsymbol{\alpha}^\nu = (-\alpha^\nu_0, -\alpha^\nu, \bar{\boldsymbol{\alpha}}^\nu) \in \mathbf{B}^\nu(\mathbf{p})\}$ is bounded by $\mathbf{p}\boldsymbol{\omega}^\nu$. By the argument given in the proof of Proposition 2.1, $\mathbf{B}^\nu(\mathbf{p})$ is bounded. Q.E.D.

DEFINITION 2.4: The profit-maximizing set for capitalist ν at prices $\mathbf{p}$ is

$$\mathbf{A}^{\nu}(\mathbf{p}) = \{\boldsymbol{\alpha}^{\nu} \in \mathbf{B}^{\nu}(\mathbf{p}) \mid \mathbf{p}\hat{\boldsymbol{\alpha}}^{\nu} - \alpha_0^{\nu} \text{ is maximized}\}$$

PROPOSITION 2.4: $\mathbf{A}^{\nu}(\mathbf{p})$ is non-empty, compact, and convex for all ν, $\mathbf{p} \geq 0$.

Proof

Non-emptiness. Notice that profits $\mathbf{p}(\bar{\boldsymbol{\alpha}}^{\nu} - \underline{\boldsymbol{\alpha}}^{\nu}) - \alpha_0^{\nu}$ are bounded for $\boldsymbol{\alpha}^{\nu} \in \mathbf{B}^{\nu}(\mathbf{p})$ because $\mathbf{B}^{\nu}(\mathbf{p})$ is bounded (Lemma 2.3). Hence, there is a sequence $\{\boldsymbol{\alpha}^{\nu_i}\} \in \mathbf{B}^{\nu}(\mathbf{p})$ whose profits converge to the maximum value; because $\mathbf{B}^{\nu}(\mathbf{p})$ is compact, there is a limit vector $\boldsymbol{\alpha}^{\nu *} = \lim_{i} \{\boldsymbol{\alpha}^{\nu_i}\}$ that achieves those maximum profits in $\mathbf{B}^{\nu}(\mathbf{p})$. Closedness of $\mathbf{A}^{\nu}(\mathbf{p})$ is obvious; boundedness follows from boundedness of $\mathbf{B}$ and convexity of $\mathbf{A}^{\nu}(\mathbf{p})$ follows directly from convexity of $\mathbf{B}^{\nu}(\mathbf{p})$. Q.E.D.

2.3 The existence of reproducible solutions

The elements of the model are now specified. We can define a *reproducible solution* (*RS*) as a straightforward generalization of the definition of Chapter 1.

DEFINITION 2.5: A reproducible solution for the economy specified is a pair $(\mathbf{p}, \boldsymbol{\alpha})$ $\mathbf{p} \geqq \mathbf{0}$, $\boldsymbol{\alpha} \in \mathbf{P}$ such that:

(a) $\boldsymbol{\alpha} = (-\alpha_0, -\underline{\boldsymbol{\alpha}}, \bar{\boldsymbol{\alpha}})$ and $\hat{\boldsymbol{\alpha}} \geqq \alpha_0 \mathbf{b}$ (reproducibility)
(b) $\boldsymbol{\alpha} \in \mathbf{A}(\mathbf{p}) \equiv \Sigma_{\nu} \mathbf{A}^{\nu}(\mathbf{p})$ (profit maximization)
(c) $\mathbf{pb} = 1$ (subsistence wage)
(d) $\underline{\boldsymbol{\alpha}} + \alpha_0 \mathbf{b} \leqq \boldsymbol{\omega}$ (social feasibility)

Only parts (a) and (d) require comment. Part (a) says that net outputs, at the socially chosen point, should at least replace workers' total consumption – where only employed workers consume. This is equivalent to requiring that the vector of social endowments not decrease in terms of components. Part (d) says that intermediate inputs and workers' consumption must be available from current stocks. Thus, capitalists profit maximize, considering only their capital constraints; prices must be such as to allow input markets to clear.

We shall now prove the existence of reproducible solutions in the economy. The method is somewhat circuitous; we first must introduce the notion of a *quasi-reproducible solution*.

DEFINITION 2.6: Let $W^1, \ldots, W^N$ be positive numbers. (W is to be thought of as the money-wealth of capitalist ν.) Let

$$\bar{\mathbf{B}}^\nu(\mathbf{p}) = \{\boldsymbol{\alpha}^\nu \in P^\nu \mid \alpha_0^\nu + \mathbf{p}\underline{\boldsymbol{\alpha}}^\nu \leq W^\nu\}$$

and

$$\bar{\mathbf{A}}^\nu(\mathbf{p}) = \{\boldsymbol{\alpha}^\nu \in \bar{\mathbf{B}}^\nu(\mathbf{p}) \mid \mathbf{p}\hat{\boldsymbol{\alpha}} - \alpha_0 \text{ is maximized}\}$$

A pair $(\mathbf{p}, \boldsymbol{\alpha})$ is said to be a quasi-reproducible solution (QRS) if
(a) $\boldsymbol{\alpha} = (-\alpha_0, \underline{\boldsymbol{\alpha}}, \bar{\boldsymbol{\alpha}})$ and $\hat{\boldsymbol{\alpha}} \geqq \alpha_0\mathbf{b}$
(b) $\boldsymbol{\alpha} \in \bar{\mathbf{A}}(\mathbf{p}) \equiv \Sigma\, \bar{\mathbf{A}}^\nu(\mathbf{p})$
(c) $\mathbf{pb} = 1$

That is, a QRS takes no account of the vector of physical endowments, and no account of the feasibility of the production plan, in the sense of part (d) of Definition 2.5.

Note. Lemma 2.3 and Proposition 2.4 hold for the sets $\bar{\mathbf{B}}^\nu(\mathbf{p})$ and $\bar{\mathbf{A}}^\nu(\mathbf{p})$.

The method for showing the existence of a RS shall be, first, to demonstrate existence of a QRS.

THEOREM 2.5: Let $\mathbf{b} > \mathbf{0}$. Under A1–A4, and stationary expectations, a quasi-reproducible solution exists, for any nonnegative values $W^1, \ldots, W^N$.

Remark. For technical reasons, a different proof is required if $\mathbf{b}$ has components that are 0. This will be provided subsequently.

The proof will rely on the following lemmas.

LEMMA (fixed point):[1] Let the correspondence $\mathbf{z}(\mathbf{p})$: $S \to T$ be upper hemicontinuous (uhc) from the simplex S to the compact set T. Let $\mathbf{z}(\mathbf{p})$ be closed and convex for all $\mathbf{p}$, and $\mathbf{pz}(\mathbf{p}) \leqq 0$. Then $\exists \bar{\mathbf{p}}$ and $\bar{\mathbf{z}} \in \mathbf{z}(\bar{\mathbf{p}})$ such that $\bar{\mathbf{z}} \leqq 0$.

LEMMA 2.6: $\bar{\mathbf{B}}^\nu(\mathbf{p})$ is lower hemicontinuous.

Proof: Let $\boldsymbol{\alpha}' \in \bar{\mathbf{B}}^\nu(\mathbf{p})$, $\mathbf{p}^\mu \to \mathbf{p}$. We wish to produce a sequence $\boldsymbol{\alpha}'^\mu \in \bar{\mathbf{B}}(\mathbf{p}^\mu)$ such that $\boldsymbol{\alpha}'^\mu \to \boldsymbol{\alpha}'$. Let

$$\boldsymbol{\alpha}'^\mu = \begin{cases} \boldsymbol{\alpha}' \text{ if } \boldsymbol{\alpha}' \in \bar{\mathbf{B}}^\nu(\mathbf{p}^\mu) \\ \lambda^\nu\boldsymbol{\alpha}' \text{ if } \boldsymbol{\alpha}' \notin \bar{\mathbf{B}}^\nu(\mathbf{p}^\mu) \end{cases} \quad \text{where } \lambda^\mu = \max \left\{\lambda \mid \lambda \left(\alpha_0' + \sum_1^n \mathbf{p}_j^\mu \underline{\alpha}_j'\right) \leq W^\nu\right\}$$

λ^μ is well defined. By definition, $\boldsymbol{\alpha}'^\mu \in \bar{\mathbf{B}}^\nu(\mathbf{p}^\mu)$. Furthermore, $\mathbf{p}^\mu \to \mathbf{p}$ and $\boldsymbol{\alpha}' \in \bar{\mathbf{B}}^\nu(\mathbf{p})$ imply that $\lambda^\mu \to 1$. Hence, $\boldsymbol{\alpha}'^\mu \to \boldsymbol{\alpha}'$. Q.E.D.

LEMMA 2.7: $\bar{\mathbf{A}}(\mathbf{p})$ is upper hemicontinuous.

Proof: We show that $\bar{\mathbf{A}}^{\nu}(\mathbf{p})$ is uhc for any ν. It follows that $\bar{\mathbf{A}}(\mathbf{p})$ is uhc.

Let $\mathbf{p}^{\mu} \to \mathbf{p}$, $\boldsymbol{\alpha}^{\mu} \in \bar{\mathbf{A}}^{\nu}(\mathbf{p}^{\nu})$, $\boldsymbol{\alpha}^{\mu} \to \boldsymbol{\alpha}$. To show: $\boldsymbol{\alpha} \in \bar{\mathbf{A}}^{\nu}(\mathbf{p})$. Because $\mathbf{p}^{\mu} \to \mathbf{p}$ and $\boldsymbol{\alpha}^{\mu} \to \boldsymbol{\alpha}$, it is easily seen that $\boldsymbol{\alpha} \in \bar{\mathbf{B}}^{\nu}(\mathbf{p})$. It must be shown $\boldsymbol{\alpha}$ is a profit maximizer in $\bar{\mathbf{B}}^{\nu}(\mathbf{p})$. Suppose not. Then $\exists \boldsymbol{\alpha}' \in \bar{\mathbf{B}}^{\nu}(\mathbf{p})$, such that

$$\mathbf{p}\hat{\boldsymbol{\alpha}}' - \alpha_0' = M' > M = \mathbf{p}\hat{\boldsymbol{\alpha}} - \alpha_0$$

Notice that

$$\mathbf{p}^{\mu}\hat{\boldsymbol{\alpha}}^{\mu} - \alpha_0^{\mu} = M^{\mu} \to M$$

By Lemma 2.6, there is a sequence $\boldsymbol{\alpha}'^{\mu} \in \bar{\mathbf{B}}^{\nu}(\mathbf{p}^{\mu})$ such that $\boldsymbol{\alpha}'^{\mu} \to \boldsymbol{\alpha}'$. Hence $\mathbf{p}^{\mu}\hat{\boldsymbol{\alpha}}' - \alpha_0' \to M'$. Thus for large μ, profits made by capitalist ν at prices $\mathbf{p}$ at point $\boldsymbol{\alpha}'^{\mu}$ are larger than profits made at $\boldsymbol{\alpha}^{\mu}$ at those prices. This contradicts the fact that $\boldsymbol{\alpha}^{\mu} \in \bar{\mathbf{A}}^{\nu}(\mathbf{p}^{\mu})$. It follows that $\boldsymbol{\alpha}$ must have been a profit maximizer at prices $\mathbf{p}$ for ν. Q.E.D.

Proof of Theorem 2.5: Because $\mathbf{b} > \mathbf{0}$, $S = \{\mathbf{p} \geq \mathbf{0} \mid \mathbf{p}\mathbf{b} = 1\}$ is homeomorphic to a simplex. Define for $\mathbf{p} \in S$:

$$\mathbf{z}(\mathbf{p}) = \left\{ \left(\sum_{\nu} \alpha_0^{\nu} \right) \mathbf{b} - \sum_{\nu} \hat{\boldsymbol{\alpha}}^{\nu} \,\middle|\, \forall \nu (-\alpha_0^{\nu}, -\underline{\boldsymbol{\alpha}}^{\nu}, \bar{\boldsymbol{\alpha}}^{\nu}) \in \bar{\mathbf{A}}^{\nu}(\mathbf{p}) \right\}$$

(a) $\mathbf{pz}(\mathbf{p}) \leq 0$.

Notice $-\mathbf{pz}(\mathbf{p}) = \Sigma_{\nu}(\mathbf{p}\hat{\boldsymbol{\alpha}}^{\nu} - \alpha_0^{\nu})$, which is simply the sum of the profits made by the capitalists at the chosen points $\boldsymbol{\alpha}^{\nu}$. Hence $-\mathbf{pz}(\mathbf{p}) \geq 0$, because at worst capitalists operate at zero profits by producing at $\mathbf{0} \in P^{\nu}$.

(b) T, the set of images of $\mathbf{z}$, is compact.

The set $\bar{\mathbf{A}} = \bigcup_{\mathbf{p} \in S} \bar{\mathbf{A}}(\mathbf{p})$ is bounded. For if $\boldsymbol{\alpha} \in \bar{\mathbf{A}}$, then $\alpha_0 \leq W$. It has been shown previously that $\{\boldsymbol{\alpha} \in P \mid \alpha_0 \leqq W\}$ is bounded.

Furthermore the set $\bar{\mathbf{A}}$ is closed: Let $\{\boldsymbol{\alpha}^{\mu}\}$ be a bounded subsequence of $\bar{\mathbf{A}}$. We write $\boldsymbol{\alpha}^{\mu} = \boldsymbol{\alpha}^{\mu}(\mathbf{p}^{\mu})$ to identify the price vector with which $\boldsymbol{\alpha}^{\mu}$ is associated. There must exist a convergent subsequence of the $\{\mathbf{p}^{\mu}\}$, so without loss of generality, assume that $\mathbf{p}^{\mu} \to \mathbf{p}$. That $\boldsymbol{\alpha}^{\mu}$ converges to a vector $\boldsymbol{\alpha} \in \bar{\mathbf{A}}(\mathbf{p})$ is a direct consequence of the upper hemicontinuity of $\bar{\mathbf{A}}(\mathbf{p})$, by the Lemma 2.7.

Hence the set $\bar{\mathbf{A}}$ is compact. Now $T = \bigcup_{\mathbf{p} \in S} \mathbf{z}(\mathbf{p})$ is the image of the compact set $\bar{\mathbf{A}}$ under a continuous function ($\boldsymbol{\alpha} \in \bar{\mathbf{A}}$; $\mathbf{F}(\boldsymbol{\alpha}) = \alpha_0\mathbf{b} - \hat{\boldsymbol{\alpha}}$), and is therefore itself compact.

(c) $\mathbf{z}(\mathbf{p})$ is convex.

Because $\bar{\mathbf{A}}^{\nu}(\mathbf{p})$ is convex, this follows immediately.

(d) $\mathbf{z}(\mathbf{p})$ is closed.

This follows from the closedness of $\bar{\mathbf{A}}^{\nu}(\mathbf{p})$.

(e) $\mathbf{z}(\mathbf{p})$ is uhc.

This follows from the upper hemicontinuity of $\bar{\mathbf{A}}(\mathbf{p})$ (Lemma 2.7). For let $\mathbf{p}^{\mu} \rightarrow \mathbf{p}$, $\mathbf{z}^{\mu} \in \mathbf{z}(\mathbf{p}^{\mu})$, $\mathbf{z}^{\mu} \rightarrow \mathbf{z}$. Write $\mathbf{z}^{\mu} = \alpha_0^{\mu}\mathbf{b} - \hat{\boldsymbol{\alpha}}^{\mu}$, where $\boldsymbol{\alpha}^{\mu} = (-\alpha_0^{\mu}, -\underline{\boldsymbol{\alpha}}, \bar{\boldsymbol{\alpha}}^{\mu}) \in \bar{\mathbf{A}}(\mathbf{p}^{\mu})$. Because $\{\alpha_0^{\mu}\}$ are bounded by W, it follows that $\{\boldsymbol{\alpha}^{\mu}\}$ are bounded and hence possess a convergent subsequence. Let the subsequence converge to $\boldsymbol{\alpha} = (-\alpha_0, -\underline{\boldsymbol{\alpha}}, \bar{\boldsymbol{\alpha}})$. It follows that $\mathbf{z} = \alpha_0\mathbf{b} - \hat{\boldsymbol{\alpha}}$. By the uhc of $\bar{\mathbf{A}}(\mathbf{p})$, $\boldsymbol{\alpha} \in \bar{\mathbf{A}}(\mathbf{p})$ and hence $\mathbf{z} \in \mathbf{z}(\mathbf{p})$.

(f) The conditions of the fixed point lemma are all satisfied.

There exists, therefore, $\bar{\mathbf{p}} \in S$ and $\bar{\mathbf{z}} \in \mathbf{z}(\bar{\mathbf{p}})$, $\bar{\mathbf{z}} = \bar{\alpha}_0\mathbf{b} - \hat{\boldsymbol{\alpha}}$, such that $\bar{\mathbf{z}} \leqq 0$. But this is precisely condition (b) of the definition that $(\bar{\mathbf{p}}, \boldsymbol{\alpha})$ be a quasi-reproducible solution, whereas condition (a) of that definition holds because $\bar{\boldsymbol{\alpha}} \in \bar{\mathbf{A}}(\bar{\mathbf{p}})$. Q.E.D.

COROLLARY 2.8: Let $(W^1, \ldots, W^N)$ be any vector of wealths. Then there exists a set of endowments

$$\boldsymbol{\Omega} = \{\boldsymbol{\omega}^1, \ldots, \boldsymbol{\omega}^N\}$$

such that a reproducible solution $(\mathbf{p}, \boldsymbol{\alpha})$ with respect to $\boldsymbol{\Omega}$ exists under stationary expectations, where $\mathbf{p}\boldsymbol{\omega}^{\nu} = W^{\nu}$ for all ν.

Proof: By Theorem 2.5, a QRS $(\mathbf{p}, \boldsymbol{\alpha})$ exists with respect to wealths $(W^1, \ldots, W^N)$. Say $\boldsymbol{\alpha} = (-\alpha_0, -\underline{\boldsymbol{\alpha}}, \bar{\boldsymbol{\alpha}})$. Let $\boldsymbol{\omega}$ be any vector such that

$$\boldsymbol{\omega} \geqq \alpha_0\mathbf{b} + \underline{\boldsymbol{\alpha}} \quad \text{and} \quad \mathbf{p}\boldsymbol{\omega} = W = \Sigma\, W^{\nu}$$

(Such $\boldsymbol{\omega}$ exists, because by definition of QRS, we have $\mathbf{p}(\alpha_0\mathbf{b} + \underline{\boldsymbol{\alpha}}) \leqq W$.) Because $\mathbf{p}\boldsymbol{\omega} = W$, $\boldsymbol{\omega}$ may be decomposed (in perhaps many ways) as $\boldsymbol{\omega} = \Sigma\, \boldsymbol{\omega}^{\nu}$ such that $\mathbf{p}\boldsymbol{\omega}^{\nu} = W^{\nu}$. It follows by checking the definition that $(\mathbf{p}, \boldsymbol{\alpha})$ is a RS with respect to endowments $\{\boldsymbol{\omega}^1, \ldots, \boldsymbol{\omega}^N\}$. Q.E.D.

The question might arise: Why not adopt the notion of quasi-reproducibility as the equilibrium notion, instead of the stronger concept of reproducibility? There are several reasons. First, although the magnitudes W^{ν} have been called "wealths" to give an intuitive rendition to the proof, it is misleading to think of them as such. In particular, the W^{ν} are given before prices are arrived at. If W^{ν} were money in the bank, therefore, it would not have much meaning with prices undetermined. We cannot assign a valuation to capital before prices are set (shades of the Cambridge controversy). Second, the QRS notion takes no account of feasibility of production, and hence of the notion of time in production. It is true that a QRS replenishes those inputs it uses up [Definition 2.6, part (a)]; but where does it get those inputs from in the first place? There is no market for initial inputs: Somehow each capitalist can automatically cash in his capital W for the necessary physical inputs into production. Clearly this notion is not a substitute for the RS notion; it is, however, a mathematical convenience in proving the existence of the latter.

Let us comment on the domain of possible initial endowments. Notice in this case that we do not have the characterization of the initial endowment domain as a cone, as was true in the linear case. However, Corollary 2.8 shows that endowments held by different capitalists can replicate *ex post* (i.e., after prices are determined) any desired distribution of capital values among capitalists.

We proceed to the existence of reproducible solutions in the general case that $\mathbf{b} \geq \mathbf{0}$. (The reason the proof of Theorem 2.5 does not apply to the case $\mathbf{b} \geq \mathbf{0}$ is that $S = \{\mathbf{p} \mid \mathbf{pb} = 1\}$ is no longer a simplex if $\mathbf{b}$ possesses zero components.) It is assumed that:

A6. (Indecomposability)

$$(\boldsymbol{\alpha} \in P,\ \boldsymbol{\alpha} = \Sigma\, \boldsymbol{\alpha}^\nu,\ \hat{\boldsymbol{\alpha}} \geqq \alpha_0 \mathbf{b})\ (\forall j \text{ s.t. } b_j = 0\ (\exists \nu)\ (\boldsymbol{\alpha}_j^\nu > 0)$$

This is an indecomposability assumption, because it says that if a particular commodity is not a subsistence commodity ($b_j = 0$), then at any reproducible point in the production set, that good must be an input into some capitalist's production process. Put another way, A6 says there are two kinds of goods: workers' consumption goods, and "intermediate" goods, which must enter the production process if the economy is to be capable of reproduction.

Viewed from the Marxian vantage point of evaluating the reproducibility of economies, this assumption is not difficult to justify. If a good is not consumed by workers and is not needed as an intermediate input for reproducible states, then it is an economic appendage in a sense. It may be an intermediate good that *could* be used to reach reproducible states at higher profits than can be achieved without its use. In either case, however, the good in question and all production processes in which it appears *could* be eliminated and a reproducible solution would still exist.

To be more precise, suppose that A6 does not hold. Let $J = \{j \mid b_j = 0 \text{ and } \exists \boldsymbol{\alpha} \in P,\ \hat{\boldsymbol{\alpha}} \geqq \alpha_0 \mathbf{b},\ \boldsymbol{\alpha} = \Sigma\, \boldsymbol{\alpha}^\nu \text{ and } \boldsymbol{\alpha}_j^\nu = 0\ \forall\ \nu\}$. Then define new production sets

$$\bar{P}^\nu = \{\boldsymbol{\alpha} \in P^\nu \mid \forall j \in J,\ \alpha_j^\nu = 0\}$$

It is easily verified that assumptions A1–A6 hold for the restricted production sets $\bar{P}^\nu$ and $\bar{P} = \Sigma\, \bar{P}^\nu$. We may now consider the new economy with production sets $\bar{P}^\nu$ to consist only of the original commodities minus those in the set J. On the new economy specified, A6 therefore holds.

We now prove that quasi-reproducible solutions exist in "indecomposable" economies, even when **b** has some zero components.

THEOREM 2.9: Let $\mathbf{b} \geq \mathbf{0}$. Under A1–A4, A6, and stationary expectations, a quasi-reproducible solution exists, for any nonnegative values $W^1, \ldots, W^N$.

Proof: Choose a sequence $\mathbf{b}^\mu \to \mathbf{b}$, where $\mathbf{b}^\mu > \mathbf{0}$. By Theorem 2.5, there is a quasi-reproducible solution $(\mathbf{p}^\mu, \boldsymbol{\alpha}^\mu)$ corresponding to $\mathbf{b}^\mu$. The proof will construct a quasi-reproducible solution at **b**.

(a) $\{\boldsymbol{\alpha}^\mu\}$ possesses a subsequence converging to a vector $\boldsymbol{\alpha} \in P$.

This follows because $\alpha_0^\mu \leq W \; \forall \mu$, and so by the standard convexity argument, $\{\boldsymbol{\alpha}^\mu\}$ is bounded.

(b) $\{\mathbf{p}^\mu\}$ is bounded.

Suppose not. Then for some j, $p_j^\mu \underset{\mu}{\to} \infty$. Because $\mathbf{p}^\mu \mathbf{b}^\mu = 1$, $b_j^\mu \underset{\mu}{\to} 0$ and so $b_j = 0$. Because $\boldsymbol{\alpha}^\mu \to \boldsymbol{\alpha}$ and $\mathbf{b}^\mu \to \mathbf{b}$ and $\hat{\boldsymbol{\alpha}}^\mu \geqq \alpha_0^\mu \mathbf{b}$, it follows that $\hat{\boldsymbol{\alpha}} \geqq \alpha_0 \mathbf{b}$ – that is, $\boldsymbol{\alpha}$ is reproducible at **b**. Decomposing $\boldsymbol{\alpha}^\mu$ into the individual capitalists' profit-maximizing points gives

$$\boldsymbol{\alpha}^\mu = \sum_\nu (\boldsymbol{\alpha}^\nu)^\mu$$

Because $\{\boldsymbol{\alpha}^\mu\}$ is bounded, we can write

$$\boldsymbol{\alpha} = \Sigma\, \boldsymbol{\alpha}^\nu \qquad \text{where } \boldsymbol{\alpha}^\nu = \lim_\mu (\boldsymbol{\alpha}^\nu)^\mu$$

Now, by assumption A6, for some ν, $\underline{\alpha}_j^\nu > 0$, because $b_j = 0$ and $\hat{\boldsymbol{\alpha}} \geqq \alpha_0 \mathbf{b}$. Hence for large μ, $(\underline{\alpha}_j^\nu)^\mu$ are bounded away from zero and positive, because

$$(\underline{\alpha}_j^\nu)^\mu \underset{\mu}{\to} \underline{\alpha}_j^\nu > 0$$

This, however, contradicts the assumption that capitalist ν is always within his capital constraint. For

$$(\alpha_0^\nu)^\mu + \sum_{i=1}^n p_i^\mu (\underline{\alpha}_i^\nu)^\mu \leq W^\nu$$

by definition; however, $p_j^\mu \underset{\mu}{\to} \infty$ and $(\underline{\alpha}_j^\nu)^\mu > 0$ for all large μ and so the inequality fails for large μ.

Hence, by contradiction, $\{\mathbf{p}^\mu\}$ is bounded.

(c) Consequently, $\{\mathbf{p}^\mu\}$ possesses a subsequence converging to a price vector **p**.

By the upper hemicontinuity of the correspondence $\bar{\mathbf{A}}(\mathbf{p})$, it follows that $\boldsymbol{\alpha} \in \bar{\mathbf{A}}(\mathbf{p})$ and hence $(\mathbf{p}, \boldsymbol{\alpha})$ is a QRS at $\mathbf{b}$. Q.E.D.

COROLLARY 2.10: Let $\mathbf{b} \geq \mathbf{0}$. Let $(W^1, \ldots, W^N)$ be any vector of wealths. Under A1–A4, A6, there exists a set of endowments

$$\boldsymbol{\Omega} = \{\boldsymbol{\omega}^1, \ldots, \boldsymbol{\omega}^N\}$$

such that a reproducible solution $(\mathbf{p}, \boldsymbol{\alpha})$ with respect to $\boldsymbol{\Omega}$ exists under stationary expectations, where $\mathbf{p}\boldsymbol{\omega}^\nu = W^\nu$ for all ν.

Proof: The proof is the same as that of Corollary 2.8.

Notice that the reproducible solution shown to exist by these theorems is possibly one of complete inaction, $\boldsymbol{\alpha}^\nu = \mathbf{0}\ \forall\ \nu$. If the total profits $(\mathbf{p}\hat{\boldsymbol{\alpha}} - \alpha_0)$ are zero at the solution, then the solution of complete inaction is reproducible. This motivates the question to be investigated next: What condition will guarantee that the reproducible solutions do not include the trivial one of complete inaction? What guarantees the existence of reproducible solutions with positive profits? This leads us to the generalized fundamental Marxian theorem.

2.4 The fundamental Marxian theorem

Theorems 1.1 and 1.2 show that the necessary and sufficient condition for the profit rate in a linear Leontief economy to be positive is that the rate of exploitation be positive. Morishima generalized this theorem to the linear von Neumann economy under certain assumptions (Morishima, 1974). He called this theorem "fundamental" because it gives a characterization of when the profit rate is positive: From the point of view here, this certainly is a fundamental necessity for reproducibility under stationary expectations, because it is easily seen that a point generating negative social profits cannot be reproducible. (Proof: $\mathbf{p}\hat{\boldsymbol{\alpha}} < \alpha_0 \Rightarrow \mathbf{p}\hat{\boldsymbol{\alpha}} < \mathbf{p}\alpha_0\mathbf{b} \Rightarrow \hat{\boldsymbol{\alpha}} \not\geqq \alpha_0\mathbf{b}$.) The generalization of this theorem to the percent model provides a characterization of economies where the reproducible solutions, known to exist, are nontrivial.

To prove the generalization of this fundamental theorem, we require the following.

A7. (Independence of production)
$(-\alpha_0, -\underline{\boldsymbol{\alpha}}, \bar{\boldsymbol{\alpha}}) \in P$, $\hat{\boldsymbol{\alpha}} \geqq 0$, and $\mathbf{0} \leqq \mathbf{c} \leq \hat{\boldsymbol{\alpha}}$, then $\exists(-\alpha_0', -\underline{\boldsymbol{\alpha}}', \bar{\boldsymbol{\alpha}}') \in P$ such that $\bar{\boldsymbol{\alpha}}' - \underline{\boldsymbol{\alpha}}' \geqq \mathbf{c}$ and $\alpha_0' < \alpha_0$.

Assumption 7 deserves a comment. It says that if a bundle of net outputs $\hat{\boldsymbol{\alpha}}$ can be produced with α_0 labor, then *any* smaller bundle $\mathbf{c}$

can be produced with *strictly less* labor. This is called independence of production because it fails when there is a good that can be produced only as a joint product in fixed proportions with some other good. A7 does not rule out joint products: It does rule out products that are only joint in the most severe sense. An example where A7 fails, and the consequences thereof, is provided later.

The intuition for why independence of production is required to guarantee the validity of the fundamental Marxian theorem is as follows. Suppose that bread and diamonds are not produced "independently"; that is, the production of one loaf of bread, which requires one unit of labor, is always accompanied by the joint product of one diamond. One cannot produce less bread and one diamond with less labor. A worker may require one loaf of bread to subsist. Then his socially necessary labor time is one day, but in the process of producing his daily bread he produces as a "free good," the diamond, which the capitalist gets. Thus, there is zero exploitation and positive profits! This example is worked more carefully later.

We proceed to the theorem.

THEOREM 2.11 (fundamental Marxian theorem): The following statements are equivalent under A1–A7 (and stationary expectations):

(*i*) There exists a point $\boldsymbol{\alpha} \in P$ such that $e(\boldsymbol{\alpha}) > 0$.

(*ii*) There exists a reproducible solution yielding positive total profits.

(*iii*) All reproducible solutions yield positive total profits.

(*iv*) All reproducible solutions yield positive rates of exploitation.

The heart of Theorem 2.11 is the provision of a necessary and sufficient condition for reproducible solutions to be nontrivial: namely, the *possibility* of positive exploitation, in the sense of statement (*i*). The possibility of positive exploitation is the counterpart of the premise that an economy be technically productive, as is captured in a Hawkins–Simons condition on an input–output matrix; positive exploitation is here shown to be the *sine qua non* of capitalist production. Notice that this result is a strong one, because the vector $\boldsymbol{\alpha}$ of statement (*i*) need not be actually producible – it may violate the capital constraint of some capitalists, and its net output vector, $\hat{\boldsymbol{\alpha}}$, may not be nonnegative. Furthermore, Theorem 2.11 states that reproducible solutions either *always* yield positive profits or *always* yield zero profits, even if there are several price vectors at which such solutions exist. This simple social–technological characteristic, of the possibility of exploitation, therefore provides a characterization of economies into those which are unambiguously nontrivial and those which are completely trivial.

The proof of Theorem 2.11 depends on the following lemma.

LEMMA 2.12: If $e(\boldsymbol{\alpha}^*) = 0$ at reproducible solution $(\mathbf{p}^*, \boldsymbol{\alpha}^*)$, then $\mathbf{p}^*\hat{\boldsymbol{\alpha}}^* - \alpha_0^* = 0$.

Proof: Because $\boldsymbol{\alpha}^*$ is reproducible, $\hat{\boldsymbol{\alpha}}^* \geqq \alpha_0^*\mathbf{b}$. $e(\boldsymbol{\alpha}^*) = 0$ means that

$$\min_{\alpha \in \phi(\alpha_0^* \mathbf{b})} \alpha_0 = \alpha_0^*,$$

where

$$\phi(\alpha_0^*\mathbf{b}) = \{\boldsymbol{\alpha} \in P \,|\, \boldsymbol{\alpha} = (-\alpha_0, -\underline{\boldsymbol{\alpha}}, \bar{\boldsymbol{\alpha}}), \hat{\boldsymbol{\alpha}} \geqq \alpha_0^*\mathbf{b}\}$$

Suppose that $\hat{\boldsymbol{\alpha}}^* \geq \alpha_0^*\mathbf{b}$ (i.e., $\hat{\boldsymbol{\alpha}}^* \neq \alpha_0^*\mathbf{b}$). Then, by A7, $\exists \boldsymbol{\alpha}^{**} \in P$, $\boldsymbol{\alpha}^{**} = (-\alpha_0^{**}, -\underline{\boldsymbol{\alpha}}^{**}, \bar{\boldsymbol{\alpha}}^{**})$, $\hat{\boldsymbol{\alpha}}^{**} \geqq \alpha_0^*\mathbf{b}$, and $\alpha_0^{**} < \alpha_0^*$. But $\boldsymbol{\alpha}^{**} \in \phi(\alpha_0^*\mathbf{b})$, thus contradicting that $e(\boldsymbol{\alpha}^*) = 0$ (because α_0^* is evidently not $\min_{\phi} \alpha_0$). Hence $\hat{\boldsymbol{\alpha}}^* = \alpha_0^*\mathbf{b}$. Therefore, $\mathbf{p}^*\hat{\boldsymbol{\alpha}}^* = \mathbf{p}\alpha_0^*\mathbf{b} = \alpha_0^*$.

Proof of Theorem 2.11: Method of proof: (*ii*) ⇒ (*i*) ⇒ (*iii*) ⇒ (*ii*), (*iv*) ⇒ (*i*), (*iii*) ⇒ (*iv*).

(a) Notice (*ii*) ⇒ (*i*) follows from Lemma 2.12, because for any reproducible solution $\boldsymbol{\alpha}$, $e(\boldsymbol{\alpha}) \geq 0$. [$e(\boldsymbol{\alpha}) \geq 0$ because $\hat{\boldsymbol{\alpha}} \geqq \alpha_0\mathbf{b}$ at a reproducible solution.]

(b) (*iii*) ⇒ (*ii*) and (*iv*) ⇒ (*i*) are trivial, because reproducible solutions exist.

(c) (*iii*) ⇒ (*iv*) by Lemma 2.12.

(d) (*i*) ⇒ (*iii*): Let $\boldsymbol{\alpha} = (-\alpha_0, -\underline{\boldsymbol{\alpha}}, \bar{\boldsymbol{\alpha}}) \in P$, $e(\boldsymbol{\alpha}) > 0$. By definition, there is a point $\boldsymbol{\alpha}' = (-\alpha_0', -\underline{\boldsymbol{\alpha}}', \bar{\boldsymbol{\alpha}}') \in P$ such that $\hat{\boldsymbol{\alpha}}' \geqq \alpha_0\mathbf{b}$ and $\alpha_0' < \alpha_0$. Assume that contention (*iii*) is false; then there is a reproducible solution $(\mathbf{p}, \boldsymbol{\beta})$ that produces zero total profits. Each capitalist ν makes zero profits at $\boldsymbol{\beta}^\nu$, where $\boldsymbol{\beta} = \Sigma\, \boldsymbol{\beta}^\nu$. Because $\hat{\boldsymbol{\alpha}}' \geqq \alpha_0\mathbf{b}$ and $\alpha_0 > \alpha_0'$, $\mathbf{p}\hat{\boldsymbol{\alpha}}' > \alpha_0'$. Decompose $\boldsymbol{\alpha}'$ into $\boldsymbol{\alpha}' = \Sigma\, \boldsymbol{\alpha}'^\nu$. Some capitalist ν must make positive profits at $\boldsymbol{\alpha}'^\nu$, because total profits are positive at $\boldsymbol{\alpha}'$. A small positive multiple $\lambda\boldsymbol{\alpha}'^\nu$ of $\boldsymbol{\alpha}'^\nu$ lies in $\mathbf{B}^\nu(\mathbf{p})$, and capitalist ν makes positive profits at $\lambda\boldsymbol{\alpha}'^\nu$; thus $\boldsymbol{\beta}^\nu \notin \mathbf{A}^\nu(\mathbf{p})$, a contradiction. Q.E.D.

We now provide the rigorous formulation of an example showing how Theorem 2.11 fails without independence of production.

EXAMPLE 1: Of where A7 fails, profits are positive, and there is no exploitation.

An example will be constructed of a quasi-reproducible solution, with respect to a certain wealth vector. It will follow that a reproducible solution with respect to an endowment vector can be constructed with the desired property, according to Corollary 2.8.

There are two goods and labor. There is one linear production process, specified by $(-1; 0, 0; 1, 2)$, and one capitalist. The production set is the set of points equal or inferior to a multiple of $(-1; 0, 0; 1, 2)$. The capitalist's capital is 10 units. Notice that A1–A6 are all satisfied but that A7 fails. [For example, as much labor is required to produce $\hat{\boldsymbol{\alpha}} = (1, 1)$ as to produce $\hat{\boldsymbol{\alpha}} = (1, 2)$.] Let $\mathbf{b} = (1, 1)$. It can easily be verified that for any price vector $\mathbf{p}$ in the simplex $\mathbf{pb} = 1$, the profit-maximizing set is

$$A^1(\mathbf{p}) = A(\mathbf{p}) = (-10; 0, 0; 10, 20)$$

The point $\boldsymbol{\alpha} = (-10; 0, 0; 10, 20)$ is a reproducible solution for any such $\mathbf{p}$, because $\alpha_0\mathbf{b} = (10, 10) \leqq (10, 20)$.

Choose $\boldsymbol{p} = (\frac{1}{2}, \frac{1}{2})$. Then profits at $(-10; 0, 0; 10, 20)$ are positive. The rate of exploitation, however, is zero at $\boldsymbol{\alpha}$, because the socially necessary labor required to produce the bundle (10, 10) is 10; that is, one must produce (10, 20) to produce (10, 10).

This example provides more insight into the "positive profits–negative surplus value" debate introduced by Steedman. [For a summary of the discussion, see Steedman (1977, chap. 11).] Steedman pointed out that if one defines labor values additively in a joint production model, positive profits can coexist with negative "surplus value." Morishima's answer to the problem (1973 and 1974) was to define embodied labor in the von Neumann model similar to the way it has been defined in this book. Under various assumptions, Morishima (1974) proved the equivalence of positive profits and positive exploitation.

The above example of a simple von Neumann model shows that if independence of production activities (A7) is not assumed, even the more general definition of embodied labor will not guarantee the equivalence of positive profits and positive exploitation, although, in any case, the perversity of Steedman's negative exploitation cannot occur.

However, not only is independence of production a sufficient condition to generate the FMT 2.11; it is also a necessary condition. Thus, independence of production characterizes production sets for which the FMT is true. That independence of production is a necessary and sufficient condition on technology for the validity of the FMT is shown in Appendix 2 to this chapter.

2.5 Exploitation, labor values, joint products, and scarce inputs

A common criticism of Marxian economics centers on the limited applicability of the labor theory of value as a theory of exchange. If prices are not proportional to labor values, then Marx's classical argument for the existence of exploitation under capitalism does not seem to apply. At this level, the criticism can be countered by showing, as in Theorem 1.1, that prices of production, themselves not proportional to labor values, will yield a positive rate of profit if and only if the rate of exploitation is positive. Thus the nonproportionality of prices and labor values fades as an issue.

A higher level of critique points out that if the technology is not of the Leontief type, but of the von Neumann type, for example, with joint production, then it may be impossible even to define individual labor values. Nevertheless, Morishima (1974) showed that exploitation could be defined independently of individual labor values in the von Neumann model, and the equivalence of a positive profit rate and positive exploitation rate is maintained. The argument of Section 2.4 generalizes Morishima's argument to (reasonably) arbitrary convex production sets.

Yet another level of critique maintains that Marxian value theory is valid only because of the assumption that there is a unique nonproduced factor, labor, and that if we conceive of production as involving various other nonproducibles (such as oil), then the labor theory of value no longer can be specified. We wish to remark that the model of this chapter shows this, too, to be a premature critique. In the model studied here, each producer has access to a different production set, P^ν, and the sets P^ν are convex, which is to say, they exhibit constant or decreasing returns to scale. Both the individuality of the production sets and their convexity can be taken to incorporate the possibility of other nonproduced commodities in production. A's production set may differ from B's because A owns a waterfall that can be used to fire a plant, and B does not; or A may have some skills or information that B lacks. The conventional interpretation of convexity of production as an expression of the presence of some implicit fixed factor (land) is well known. Our version of the fundamental Marxian theorem shows that the presence of these fixed factors and scarce resources does not destroy the equivalence between exploitation and profits.

What is lost with the presence of several nonproduced production inputs is the existence of individual labor values. (That is also lost, as has been pointed out, with joint production, and a single nonproduced factor.) Our effort has been to reconstruct the *conclusions* of Marx's value theory (pertaining to exploitation) on foundations independent of the theory of individual labor values. The above critiques of Marxian value theory apply to the cogency of individual labor values, and as such have no bearing on the conclusions of the theory, if those conclusions can be reconstructed on a different basis. This has been done.

The labor theory of value, for Marx, played a double role – as a theory of exchange and a theory of exploitation. Marx's approach was to use the theory of exchange as a conduit to generate the theory of exploitation. Our approach is to reject the labor theory of value in its role as exchange theory, and reconstruct the theory of exploitation on a different basis. This point is sufficiently important that it is reiterated at some length, and from a somewhat different point of view, in Chapter 7.

These remarks are all to say that as a formal construction the labor theory of exploitation can be preserved even when the production model is more general than the Leontief or von Neumann models, even when other nonproduced factors exist. (This statement is not universal; for instance, I have not discussed how one might preserve the labor theory of exploitation if heterogeneous labor inputs are explicitly enumerated in the specification of production.) What the equivalence of labor exploitation and profits signifies, however, is a deeper question. One cannot maintain, as is frequently done, that labor power is that one special commodity that mysteriously produces more value than is embodied in it, and hence its exploitation is the sole cause of profits. For, as an alternative to labor value, one could choose corn to denominate value, defining the embodied corn values of all commodities, and the following would be true: The economy is productive in the sense of being capable of producing a surplus if and only if the corn value of a unit of corn is less than one, that is, if and only if corn is corn-exploited. An economy is productive if and only if each commodity is exploited when values are denominated in terms of it. Why, then, choose labor power as the privileged commodity with which to denominate exploitation? This question is pursued to some extent in Chapter 10.

2.6 The social determination of the value of labor power

In the model presented, there remains one aspect that is not sufficiently general. The subsistence bundle, **b**, is taken as given. Determining the "value of labor power" (or the bundle **b**) is a problem with a long history. Marx was clear, at least, that the subsistence bundle was not intended as a biologically minimum consumption, but as a level of consumption that was determined by factors including a "historical and moral element." Yet formal models of Marxian economics have made no attempt to include this feature. In Sraffa's model, the question is also left unresolved. It is simply observed that the profit and wage rates are inversely related, so that once one is set, so is the other. No argumentation is provided, however, to determine either rate within his system.

This hiatus is a particularly important one in Marxian value theory. for by assuming workers' consumption to be fixed before the drama of exchange and production – that is, the circuit of capital – occurs, we are assuming workers to be somehow above the social process of production and exchange – and this is a violation of the most fundamental Marxian tenet. Workers' necessary consumption should be socially determined, and not taken as an exogenous datum of the system. To do the latter is to examine a robot economy, where the "factor" labor power might just as well enter production as part of the input–output matrix in the form of commodities that workers consume, eclipsing entirely the conscious element of human work that is at the heart of the Marxian vision. What distinguishes labor power from other inputs into production, at the abstract level of modeling engaged in here, must be that its value [that is, the consumption (**b**)] does not enter as a technological datum, but is determined by social interactions.[2]

We desire, then, to relax the assumption of an exogenously given bundle **b**, but to maintain the Marxian notion of workers' *necessary* consumption. Indeed, the notion of necessity is important to preserve the rationale behind the investigation of *reproducible* solutions, as opposed to some more subjectively specified concept of equilibrium.

There is a straightforward indication in Marx as to how one might proceed to determine the value of labor power. Workers' necessary consumption is determined from two directions: by the consumption necessities that a particular mode of production requires for purely technological reasons, and by the form of consciousness created among workers by a particular mode of production. An example of the first of these causations is that modern technologies require workers to possess certain skills, the education for which thereby becomes a part of the workers' necessary consumption. The second determination is contained in Marx's materialist philosophy: that consciousness is determined primarily by one's relation to the means of production. Because this is a most important point, it is worth quoting Marx and Engels at some length on it.

> Men can be distinguished from animals by consciousness, by religion or anything else you like. They themselves begin to distinguish themselves from animals as soon as they begin to *produce* their means of subsistence, a step which is conditioned by their physical organization. By producing their means of subsistence men are indirectly producing their actual material life.
>
> The way in which men produce their means of subsistence depends first of all on the nature of the actual means they find in existence and have to reproduce. This mode of production must not be considered simply as being the reproduction of the physical existence of the individuals. Rather it is a definite form of activity of these individuals, a definite form of expressing their life, a definite *mode of life* on their part. As individuals express their life, so they are. What they are, therefore, coincides with their production, both with *what* they produce and with *how* they produce. The nature of individuals thus depends on the material conditions determining their production.
>
> This production only makes its appearance with the increase of population. In its turn this presupposes the intercourse of individuals with one another. The form of this intercourse is again determined by production [Marx and Engels, 1963, p. 7].

It seems clear, then, that the value of labor power possesses a complex determination, whose origins are in the method of production. We therefore make the following postulate.

B1. There is a continuous function $\mathbf{b}(\boldsymbol{\alpha}^1, \boldsymbol{\alpha}^2, \ldots, \boldsymbol{\alpha}^N) = \mathbf{b}$ defined on $P^1 \times P^2 \times \cdots \times P^N$. Furthermore, there exist $\mathbf{b}_* > 0$ and $\mathbf{b}^*$ such that $\mathbf{b}_* \leqq \mathbf{b}(\boldsymbol{\alpha}^1, \ldots, \boldsymbol{\alpha}^N) \leqq \mathbf{b}^*$ for any point $(\boldsymbol{\alpha}^1, \ldots, \boldsymbol{\alpha}^N)$.

Necessary consumption **b** is a function of the particular technology adopted. The assumption of continuity is mathematically useful, and is not a harsh assumption, considering the social process that underlies B1. The bounds $\mathbf{b}_*$ and $\mathbf{b}^*$ are not unreasonable: $\mathbf{b}_*$ is a biological minimum necessary for consumption, and there certainly may be assumed to be a vector $\mathbf{b}^*$ that will be an upper bound on necessary consumption under known technologies $P^1, \ldots, P^N$. $\mathbf{b}_* > \mathbf{0}$ is postulated for technical reasons, and can probably be weakened as the analogous assumption was weakened in Section 2.3.

According to B1, all workers have identical necessary consumption, which is a function of the social technology ($\boldsymbol{\alpha}^1, \ldots, \boldsymbol{\alpha}^N$) adopted. This assumption can be generalized so that workers in different "industries" have different, socially determined necessities.

The question becomes: Now that the value of labor power is itself an outcome of the economic process in the above sense, do we have a meaningful economic model – in the sense that reproducible solutions exist? In Appendix 1 to this chapter, the answer is shown to be yes. The analog to Corollary 2.8 is proved. Given any distribution of wealths, there is a set of endowments such that a reproducible solution exists with respect to those endowments, with the subsistence bundle socially determined by technology. The proof of this theorem follows the proof of Corollary 2.8, with the added complication that it uses a technical result of Debreu known as the social equilibrium existence theorem.

Thus, there is no reason that in principle we cannot maintain the notion of reproducible solution, proposed here as the Marxian equilibrium notion, in an environment where workers' consumption is made to depend on technology. Formally, we have introduced a certain kind of externality into the model. There are other ways in which the determination of subsistence could be introduced, perhaps more cogently than this; the purpose here is simply to show the possibility of a more general approach to the question of the social determination of the value of labor power. (One could be even more general by combining neoclassical and Marxian views of consumption in this way: Corresponding to any technology there is a whole map of preferences for workers. Thus, the externality would not specify simply one subsistence bundle as a function of a point in the crossproduct of production sets, but a whole utility function for the worker.) In the next section, we use this general model to illustrate certain interactions between class consciousness and the choice of technique.

2.7 The interaction of class consciousness and the choice of technique

We next seek an analog to the FMT 2.11 for the case of variable consumption bundle **b**, in order to provide a condition for the existence of nontrivial (positive profits) reproducible solutions. First it is necessary to define the rate of exploitation in this case.

Definition 2.7: The rate of exploitation with the value of labor power socially determined is defined on points $\mathbf{a} \in P^1 \times \cdots \times P^N$. Let $\boldsymbol{a}$ be given, $\mathbf{a} = (\boldsymbol{\alpha}^1, \ldots, \boldsymbol{\alpha}^N)$, $\boldsymbol{\alpha} = \Sigma\, \boldsymbol{\alpha}^\nu$. Then

$$e(\mathbf{a}) = \frac{\alpha_0}{\text{l.v.}[\alpha_0 \mathbf{b}(\mathbf{a})]} - 1$$

where $\text{l.v.}[\alpha_0 \mathbf{b}(\mathbf{a})]$ is defined as before.

Notice in this environment that e must be defined on the cross product of the individual capitalists' production sets rather than on the social production set P.

The rate of exploitation continues to be well defined.

Theorem 2.13: Under A1–A5, A7; the rate of exploitation with the value of labor power socially determined is positive at a reproducible solution $\xi = (\mathbf{p}, \boldsymbol{\alpha}^1, \ldots, \boldsymbol{\alpha}^N, \mathbf{b})$ if and only if total profits are positive there. Furthermore, $e(\boldsymbol{\alpha}^1, \ldots, \boldsymbol{\alpha}^N) > 0$ if and only if there exists a point $\boldsymbol{\alpha} \in P$ such that $e_b(\boldsymbol{\alpha}) > 0$, where $e_b(\boldsymbol{\alpha})$ is the rate of exploitation at $\boldsymbol{\alpha}$ evaluated for workers' consumption fixed at $\mathbf{b}$.

Note. It is not necessary for this theorem to assume that the function $\mathbf{b}(\boldsymbol{\alpha}^1, \ldots, \boldsymbol{\alpha}^N)$ is continuous.

Proof: Consider the economy with workers' consumption fixed at $\mathbf{b} = \mathbf{b}(\boldsymbol{\alpha}^1, \ldots, \boldsymbol{\alpha}^N)$. Then surely $(\mathbf{p}, \boldsymbol{\alpha}^1, \ldots, \boldsymbol{\alpha}^N, \mathbf{b})$ is a reproducible solution for this economy; it follows that Theorem 2.11 holds, and in particular, statements (*iii*) and (*iv*) and (*i*) of the theorem are equivalent, which proves the result. Q.E.D.

Theorem 2.13 is weaker than Theorem 2.11. It is nevertheless a "fundamental" Marxian theorem, as it shows that the *sine qua non* for reproducible capitalist production at positive profits is positive exploitation. We proceed to show that Theorem 2.13 is necessarily weaker than Theorem 2.11. There are economies that fulfill all the postulates including B1, yet (1) positive and zero profits can both occur at (different) reproducible solutions, and (2) $e(\boldsymbol{\alpha}^1, \ldots, \boldsymbol{\alpha}^N) > 0$ occurs but all reproducible solutions yield zero profit. This being the case, Theorem 2.13 is evidently the strongest version of Theorem 2.11 that is true when the value of labor power is socially determined.

Example 2: Showing that if the value of labor power is socially determined, reproducible solutions with both positive profits and zero profits can exist.

As in a previous construction, it is sufficient to construct quasi-reproducible solutions with the desired propensities.

There are two linear activities $(-1, 0, 0, 1, 0)$ and $(-1, 0, 0, 0, 1)$, each producing one of two commodities, and one capitalist with $W = 10$. This generates a cone of production:

$$P = [-(x_1 + x_2), 0, 0, x_1, x_2 \mid x_1, x_2 \geq 0]$$

We may assume free disposal as well. If commodity prices are (p_1, p_2), then profit maximization means maximize $(p_1 - 1)x_1 + (p_x - 1)x_2$ subject to $x_1 + x_2 \leqq 10$. If $p_1 = p_2 = 1$, then profit maximization yields zero profits. **b** is defined as a function $\mathbf{b}(x_1, x_2)$. Say $\mathbf{b}(5, 5) = (\frac{1}{2}, \frac{1}{2})$ and so $\mathbf{pb}(5, 5) = 1$. It is clear that (5, 5) is a quasi-reproducible solution yielding zero profits.

Now at $(p_1, p_2) = (2, 2)$, profit maximization yields positive profits. Any activity levels (x_1, x_2) such that $x_1 + x_2 = 10$ yield maximum profits. Say $\mathbf{b}(8, 2) = (\frac{3}{8}, \frac{1}{8})$. Then $\mathbf{pb}(8, 2) = 1$ and $(8, 2) \geq 10\ (\frac{3}{8}, \frac{1}{8})$, so (8, 2) is a reproducible solution yielding positive profits.

It is obviously possible to extend the function **b** continuously to the entire domain P, as it is only defined thus far at two points in P.

Example 3: Showing that even if there is a production point that is feasible for capitalists and yields a positive rate of exploitation, all quasi-reproducible solutions may yield zero profits, where the value of labor power is socially determined.

Let the economy be specified as in the previous example except for the function $\mathbf{b}(x_1, x_2)$. The capitalist's profit-maximization problem is: Given prices (p_1, p_2) choose (x_1, x_2) such that $x_1 + x_2 \leq 10$, to maximize $(p_1 - 1)x_1 + (p_2 - 1)x_2$. Define

$$\mathbf{b}(x_1, x_2) = \begin{cases} (1, 1) \text{ if } x_1 + x_2 = 10 \\ (\frac{1}{3}, \frac{1}{3}) \text{ at } (x_1, x_2) = (2, 2) \\ \text{any continuous extension for other } (x_1, x_2) \geq 0 \end{cases}$$

Notice that no point for which $x_1 + x_2 = 10$ can be a quasi-reproducible solution, because $\hat{\boldsymbol{\alpha}} \geqq \alpha_0\mathbf{b}$ certainly fails at all such points $[(x_1, x_2) \leq (10, 10)]$.

There are various sets $A^1(\mathbf{p})$, depending on **p**. Compute that if $p_i > 1$ for at least one i, then $A^1(\mathbf{p}) \subseteq \{(x_1, x_2) \mid x_1 + x_2 = 10\}$. Hence no such **p** can be viable, for it has been shown that no such (x_1, x_2) can be reproducible because the subsistence requirements are too great along the line $x_1 + x_2 = 10$. But notice that all other price vectors yield at best zero profits. Hence all reproducible solutions have zero profits. Notice, however, that $e(2, 2) > 0$, because the socially necessary bundle at (2, 2) is $4(\frac{1}{3}, \frac{1}{3}) < (2, 2)$.

We now remark upon the significance of these two examples, which are not simply mathematical curiosa, but correspond to important social issues that arise, once workers' necessary consumption is admitted to be socially determined. To see this, it is convenient to emphasize the "subjective" aspect of the social determination of necessary consumption: that some technologies will enable workers to organize themselves to command a larger subsistence bundle than other technologies. That is, class consciousness of workers, and hence their bargaining strength against capital, is determined in part by the technique in use. This theme has been an extensive one in the modern Marxian literature on the labor process – see, for instance, the work of Marglin (1974) and Braverman (1974) and others referred to in Chapter 6. In this light, Example 3 says this: It may be possible for capitalists to choose techniques at which there is exploitation, but if they insist on *maximizing* profits at given prices, they must choose techniques that will alter the balance of class forces to such an extent that subsistence requirements become too great for reproducibility. Exploitation is possible if capitalists limit themselves to suboptimal techniques; but if capitalists choose profit-maximizing techniques, the subsistence wage will be driven up, eliminating profits. In Example 3, this is seen as follows. Suppose that prices are $p = \frac{3}{2}, \frac{3}{2}$, and the capitalist operates at $(x_1, x_2) = (2, 2)$. Then the subsistence requirement of a worker is $b = (\frac{1}{3}, \frac{1}{3})$, and $\mathbf{pb} = 1$. As was shown in the example, enough output is produced to reproduce workers. However, at these prices, capitalists are not profit maximizing: If they profit maximize, they will be driven to operate along the line $x_1 + x_2 = 10$; then workers will force up subsistence requirements to the point that those wage–prices cannot be sustained. [That is, $(\frac{3}{2}, \frac{3}{2}) \cdot (1, 1) > 1$.]

There has been debate in the labor process literature as to whether capitalists choose "efficient" techniques or ones that are not technically efficient but allow them to "control" the workers (see Chapter 6). That is the issue which is captured in this example. It may be that *ex ante* efficient techniques allow very little *ex post* control.

The force of Example 2 is similar. That example shows that there may be different equilibria for the economy in which the relative balance of class forces is different, because of the effect the choice of technique has on workers' organization. In particular, there may be one equilibrium at which there is positive exploitation and another with zero exploitation.

Thus, the fact that Theorem 2.13 takes the form stated, and there is no universal technological condition as in Theorem 2.11, which guarantees that the possibility of exploitation produces profits, is an important consequence of our formulation of the social determination of the value of labor power. When workers are no longer socially inanimate, but react to the technique chosen by capital, the unqualified link (of Theorem 2.11) between exploitation and profits is broken. As we have seen, this might lead to a new specification of capitalists' behavior: that they adopt a strategic profit-maximizing behavior, contingent on evaluating the effect of their choice of technique on workers, rather than a myopic one, which we have postulated in this discussion. We shall not pursue this modification here, but it is clear how such a formulation would lead directly into the type of consideration the labor process literature has dealt with in some historical detail.

This concludes the discussion of social determination of workers' consumption. The model provided is extremely general, and it postulates merely a continuous function $\mathbf{b}(\boldsymbol{\alpha}^1, \ldots, \boldsymbol{\alpha}^N)$ on technology to determine workers' consumption. This generality may also be viewed as a shortcoming of the model; instead of postulating the existence of an exogenous parameter **b**, we have postulated a whole exogenous *function* **b**. Is this in any sense an advance over the simpler formulation? That is, can it be said we have "solved" the problem of closing the Marxian system, by determining the real wage in this functional way?

This question is perhaps best answered by saying that a precise specification of the function $\mathbf{b}(\boldsymbol{\alpha}^1, \ldots, \boldsymbol{\alpha}^N)$ is a historical question. In this sense, the closure of the system is not explicit. Moreover, the neoclassical solution to the consumption problem – of postulating primitive preference orderings or utility functions – seems to be on the same level of generality. The functional determination of workers' consumption from technology does suggest one avenue toward conceiving of materialist determination of the reproduction of the working class. And we have seen that the functional approach allows a formulation of the important interaction of class consciousness and the choice of technique.

Finally, it should be pointed out there is another approach entirely to the determination of workers' consumption, and that is through the nominal, as opposed to real, side of the economy. In the above model, the determination of consumption is entirely real, in the sense that a physical bundle of goods is specified as the consumption bundle, which is determined by technology. The general weakness of this approach is that, in fact, workers and capitalists bargain over money wages; should one not, therefore, specify not a subsistence *bundle* but a subsistence *wage,* and allow workers to determine their individual consumptions in some other way? Another model, in which workers choose goods by maximizing utility functions, is developed in Chapter 7.

2.8 Summary

The aim of this chapter has been to show that the Marxian concepts of equilibrium (reproducible solution) and exploitation are tractable in quite general contexts: In particular, the production sets of the economy do not have to be Leontief, or even activity analysis, or even conical. Moreover, the key relationship of Marxian value theory – that positive profits is synonymous with positive exploitation – remains true in general models of production.

In passing from linear economies to convex economies, one loses one artifact of classical Marxian analysis: individual labor values of commodities. The concept of exploitation is defined *only* socially: We do not define social exploitation as the aggregation of many individual exploitations of workers, but only as an aggregate concept. In general models such as this one, the question does not even arise as to whether prices are proportional to labor values: Labor values play no micro role. In the Leontief economy, labor values can play a micro role, and this has given rise to much obfuscation in Marxian economics concerning the relationship of prices to labor values. Further discussion of this issue will be found in Chapter 7.

Finally, the concept of subsistence needs of workers was generalized to allow for the social determination of workers' consumption. The needs of workers were postulated to be given by a function defined on the technology set. Although it cannot be claimed that this formulation closes the Marxian system in a historically explicit manner, it does provide a model of how the reproduction of workers under capitalism can have a materialist, as opposed to subjective, determination. Some of the important ideas of the labor-process literature can be seen to be contained in this model, in particular, the contradiction between efficiency and control in the choice of technique.

Appendix 1: Existence of reproducible solutions with the value of labor power socially determined

We prove here the analog to Corollary 2.8 for the model of Section 2.6, where the subsistence bundle is a function of the point chosen in the technology.

As before, the main argument runs in terms of quasi-reproducible solutions, defined for a given "wealth" vector $(W^1, \ldots, W^N)$.

DEFINITION 2.8: A quasi-reproducible solution with the value of labor power socially determined is a set $(\mathbf{p}, \boldsymbol{\alpha}^1, \ldots, \boldsymbol{\alpha}^N)$ such that:
(a) $\boldsymbol{\alpha}^\nu \in \mathbf{A}^\nu(\mathbf{p})$; $\nu = 1, N$; $\mathbf{b} = \mathbf{b}(\boldsymbol{\alpha}^1, \ldots, \boldsymbol{\alpha}^N)$
(b) $\Sigma_\nu \alpha_0^\nu \mathbf{b}(\boldsymbol{\alpha}^1, \ldots, \boldsymbol{\alpha}^N) \leqq \Sigma \hat{\boldsymbol{\alpha}}^\nu$, where $\boldsymbol{\alpha}^\nu = \bar{\boldsymbol{\alpha}}^\nu - \underline{\boldsymbol{\alpha}}^\nu$
(c) $\mathbf{p} \cdot \mathbf{b}(\boldsymbol{\alpha}^1, \ldots, \boldsymbol{\alpha}^N) = 1$

We proceed to prove the following theorem.

THEOREM 2.14: Under A1–A4 and B1, there exists a quasi-reproducible solution with the value of labor power socially determined, for any nonnegative values $W^1, \ldots, W^N$.

The proof is accomplished by use of Debreu's social equilibrium existence theorem (Debreu, 1952). We introduce the necessary machinery before stating Debreu's theorem.
Let

$$\mathscr{B}_1 = \{\mathbf{p} \geq 0 \,|\, \mathbf{p}\mathbf{b}_* \leqq 1 \leqq \mathbf{p}\mathbf{b}^*\}$$

$$\mathscr{B}_2 = \{\langle \boldsymbol{\alpha}^1, \ldots, \boldsymbol{\alpha}^N \rangle \,|\, \boldsymbol{\alpha}^\nu \in \bar{P}^\nu\} \qquad \text{where } \bar{P}^\nu = \{\boldsymbol{\alpha}^\nu \in P^\nu \,|\, \alpha_0^\nu \leqq W^\nu\}$$

$$\mathscr{B}_3 = \{\mathbf{b} \,|\, \mathbf{b}_* \leqq \mathbf{b} \leqq \mathbf{b}^*\}$$

Define three correspondences:

$$\beta_1 : \mathscr{B}_2 \times \mathscr{B}_3 \to \mathscr{B}_1$$

$$\beta_2 : \mathscr{B}_1 \times \mathscr{B}_3 \to \mathscr{B}_2$$

$$\beta_3 : \mathscr{B}_1 \times \mathscr{B}_2 \to \mathscr{B}_3$$

by

$\beta_1(\langle \boldsymbol{\alpha}^1, \ldots, \boldsymbol{\alpha}^N \rangle, \mathbf{b}) = \{\mathbf{p} \in \mathscr{B}_1 \,|\, \mathbf{p}\mathbf{b} = 1\}$
$\beta_2(\mathbf{p}, \mathbf{b}) = \mathbf{B}^1(\mathbf{p}) \mathbf{x} \cdots \mathbf{x} \mathbf{B}^N(\mathbf{p})$, where $\mathbf{B}^\nu(\mathbf{p}) \equiv \{\boldsymbol{\alpha}^\nu \in \bar{P}^\nu \,|\, \alpha_0^\nu + \mathbf{p}\underline{\boldsymbol{\alpha}}^\nu \leqq W^\nu\}$
$\beta_3(\mathbf{p}, \langle \boldsymbol{\alpha}^1, \ldots, \boldsymbol{\alpha}^N \rangle) = \mathbf{b}(\boldsymbol{\alpha}^1, \ldots, \boldsymbol{\alpha}^N)$.

Observe image $\beta_i \in \mathcal{B}_i$ as required.

Define three functions:

$$f_i\colon\ \mathcal{B}_1 \times \mathcal{B}_2 \times \mathcal{B}_3 \to \mathbf{R}$$

by

$$f_1(\mathbf{p}; \langle \boldsymbol{\alpha}^1, \ldots, \boldsymbol{\alpha}^N\rangle; \mathbf{b}) = \mathbf{p}\cdot(\alpha_0\mathbf{b} - \hat{\boldsymbol{\alpha}}) \qquad \text{where } \hat{\boldsymbol{\alpha}} = \sum_\nu \hat{\boldsymbol{\alpha}}^\nu,\ \alpha_0 = \sum_\nu \alpha_0^\nu$$

$$f_2(\mathbf{p}; \langle \boldsymbol{\alpha}^1, \ldots, \boldsymbol{\alpha}^N\rangle; \mathbf{b}) = \mathbf{p}\cdot(\hat{\boldsymbol{\alpha}} - \alpha_0\mathbf{b})$$

$$f_3(\mathbf{p}; \langle \boldsymbol{\alpha}^1, \ldots, \boldsymbol{\alpha}^N\rangle; \mathbf{b}) = 1$$

Let ϕ_i be the function that takes on the maximum value of f_i over appropriate domains:

$$\phi_1(\langle \boldsymbol{\alpha}^1, \ldots, \boldsymbol{\alpha}^N\rangle, \mathbf{b}) = \max_{\mathbf{p}\in\beta_1(\langle\alpha^1,\ldots,\alpha^N\rangle,\mathbf{b})} f_1(\mathbf{p}; \langle \boldsymbol{\alpha}^1, \ldots, \boldsymbol{\alpha}^N\rangle; \mathbf{b})$$

$$\phi_2(\mathbf{p}, \mathbf{b}) = \max_{\langle\alpha^1,\ldots,\alpha^N\rangle\in\beta_2(\mathbf{p},\mathbf{b})} f_2(\mathbf{p}; \langle \boldsymbol{\alpha}^1, \ldots, \boldsymbol{\alpha}^N\rangle; \mathbf{b})$$

$$\phi_3(\mathbf{p}, \langle \boldsymbol{\alpha}^1, \ldots, \boldsymbol{\alpha}^N\rangle) = \max_{\mathbf{p}\in\beta_3(\mathbf{p},\langle\alpha^1,\ldots,\alpha^N\rangle)} f_3(\mathbf{p}; \langle \boldsymbol{\alpha}^1, \ldots, \boldsymbol{\alpha}^N\rangle; \mathbf{b})$$

ϕ_1 is defined on $\mathcal{B}_2 \times \mathcal{B}_3$, and so on.

Let sets $M_{x,y}$ be sets of maximizers of the functions f:

$$M_{\langle\alpha^1,\ldots,\alpha^N\rangle,b} = \{\mathbf{p} \in \beta_1(\langle \boldsymbol{\alpha}^1, \ldots, \boldsymbol{\alpha}^N\rangle, \mathbf{b}) \mid f_1(\mathbf{p}; \langle \boldsymbol{\alpha}^1, \ldots, \boldsymbol{\alpha}^N\rangle; \mathbf{b}) = \phi_1(\langle \boldsymbol{\alpha}^1, \ldots, \boldsymbol{\alpha}^N\rangle, \mathbf{b})\}$$

$$M_{\mathbf{p},\mathbf{b}} = \{\langle \boldsymbol{\alpha}^1, \ldots, \boldsymbol{\alpha}^N\rangle \in \beta_2(\mathbf{p}, \mathbf{b}) \mid f_2(\mathbf{p}; \langle \boldsymbol{\alpha}^1, \ldots, \boldsymbol{\alpha}^N\rangle; \mathbf{b}) = \phi_2(\mathbf{p}, \mathbf{b})\}$$

$$M_{\mathbf{p},\langle\alpha^1,\ldots,\alpha^N\rangle} = \{\mathbf{b} \in \beta_3(p, \langle \boldsymbol{\alpha}^1, \ldots, \boldsymbol{\alpha}^N\rangle) \mid f_3(\mathbf{p}; \langle \boldsymbol{\alpha}^1, \ldots, \boldsymbol{\alpha}^N\rangle; \mathbf{b}) = \phi_3(\mathbf{p}, \langle \boldsymbol{\alpha}^1, \ldots, \boldsymbol{\alpha}^N\rangle)\}$$

DEFINITION 2.9: $\xi = (\mathbf{p}, \langle \boldsymbol{\alpha}^1, \ldots, \boldsymbol{\alpha}^N\rangle, \mathbf{b})$ is a social equilibrium point if $p \in \beta_1(\langle \boldsymbol{\alpha}^1, \ldots, \boldsymbol{\alpha}^N\rangle, \mathbf{b})$, $\langle \boldsymbol{\alpha}^1, \ldots, \boldsymbol{\alpha}^N\rangle \in \beta_2(\mathbf{p}, \mathbf{b})$, $\mathbf{b} \in \beta_3(\mathbf{p}, \langle \boldsymbol{\alpha}^1, \ldots, \boldsymbol{\alpha}^N\rangle)$ and $f_i(\xi) = \phi_i(\bar{\xi}_i)$ for $i = 1, 3$, where $\bar{\xi}_i$ is the point ξ with the component ξ_i omitted.

LEMMA (Debreu): If $\mathcal{B}_1$, $\mathcal{B}_2$, $\mathcal{B}_3$ are convex and compact; if correspondences β_i are uhc; if f_i are continuous functions; if ϕ_i are continuous functions; if the sets M are convex for all possible arguments chosen in $\mathcal{B}_2 \times \mathcal{B}_3$, $\mathcal{B}_1 \times \mathcal{B}_3$, $\mathcal{B}_1 \times \mathcal{B}_2$, respectively; then there exists a social equilibrium point.

Proof of Theorem 2.14: We shall first show that a social equilibrium point of Debreu's lemma is a quasi-reproducible solution with the value of labor power socially determined. We then show that all the conditions of the lemma are fulfilled so that a social equilibrium exists.

(a) A social equilibrium is a quasi-reproducible solution with the value of labor power socially determined:

If $(\mathbf{p}, \langle \boldsymbol{\alpha}^1, \ldots, \boldsymbol{\alpha}^N \rangle, \mathbf{b})$ is a social equilibrium, then by definition, $\mathbf{b} = \mathbf{b}(\boldsymbol{\alpha}^1, \ldots, \boldsymbol{\alpha}^N)$; furthermore, $\boldsymbol{\alpha}^\nu \in \mathbf{B}^\nu(\mathbf{p})\ \forall \nu$, and in fact $\boldsymbol{\alpha}^\nu \in \mathbf{A}^\nu(\mathbf{p})\ \forall \nu$ because *total* profits are maximized for prices $\mathbf{p}$. [This follows because $\phi_2(\mathbf{p}; \langle \boldsymbol{\alpha}^1, \ldots, \boldsymbol{\alpha}^N \rangle; \mathbf{b}) = \max_{\langle \alpha^1, \ldots, \alpha^N \rangle \in \mathbf{B}^1(\mathbf{p}) \times \cdots \times \mathbf{B}^N(\mathbf{p})} \mathbf{p} \cdot (\hat{\boldsymbol{\alpha}} - \alpha_0 \mathbf{b})$.] Furthermore, $\mathbf{p} \cdot \mathbf{b} = 1$.

It remains to show $\hat{\boldsymbol{\alpha}} \geqq \alpha_0 \mathbf{b}$. Suppose not; then for some component j, $\hat{\alpha}_j < \alpha_0 b_j$. Choose as price vector $\mathbf{p}^* = \langle 0, 0, \ldots, 0, 1/b_j, 0, \ldots, 0 \rangle$; certainly $\mathbf{p}^*\mathbf{b} = 1$, so $\mathbf{p}^* \in \beta_1(\langle \alpha^1, \ldots, \alpha^N \rangle, \mathbf{b})$. Notice $\mathbf{p}^*(\alpha_0 \mathbf{b} - \hat{\boldsymbol{\alpha}}) > 0$. Now ϕ_1 maximizes the value of f_1 over all possible prices in $\mathcal{B}_1$, so

$$\phi_1(\langle \alpha^1, \ldots, \alpha^N \rangle, \mathbf{b}) \geq \mathbf{p}^*(\alpha_0 \mathbf{b} - \hat{\boldsymbol{\alpha}}) > 0$$

Notice, however, that $\phi_1(\langle \alpha^1, \ldots, \alpha^N \rangle, \mathbf{b})$ is simply the *negative* of total profits at the point $(\mathbf{p}, \langle \boldsymbol{\alpha}^1, \ldots, \boldsymbol{\alpha}^N \rangle, \mathbf{b})$. It follows that total profits must be negative at the given equilibrium. But this is impossible, as it has been shown that $\boldsymbol{\alpha}^\nu \in \mathbf{A}^\nu(\mathbf{p})\ \forall \nu$, and total profits are hence nonnegative. By contradiction, it follows that $\hat{\boldsymbol{\alpha}} \geqq \alpha_0 \mathbf{b}$ and a social equilibrium is a quasi-reproducible solution.

(b) $\mathcal{B}_1, \mathcal{B}_2, \mathcal{B}_3$ are convex and compact; this is easily verified. Notice that compactness of $\mathcal{B}_1$ follows, because $\mathbf{b}_* > 0$, and boundedness of $\mathcal{B}_2$ follows because it has been shown that if the labor component α_0^ν is bounded in a set of vectors in P^ν, then the vectors themselves are bounded. (This uses A1, A2, A3, and A4.)

(c) Correspondences β_i are uhc; this is easily verified.

(d) f_i are continuous functions; this is obvious.

(e) The sets $M_{x,y}$ are convex;

$$M_{\langle \alpha^1, \ldots, \alpha^N \rangle, \mathbf{b}} = \{\mathbf{p} \mid \mathbf{p}\mathbf{b} = 1,\ \mathbf{p}\hat{\boldsymbol{\alpha}} - \alpha_0 \mathbf{b} \text{ is maximized}\}$$

It is obvious that $M_{\langle \alpha^1, \ldots, \alpha^N \rangle, \mathbf{b}}$ is convex.

$$M_{\mathbf{p},\mathbf{b}} = \{\langle \boldsymbol{\alpha}^1, \ldots, \boldsymbol{\alpha}^N \rangle \in \mathbf{B}^1(\mathbf{p}) \times \cdots \times \mathbf{B}^N(\mathbf{p}) \mid \mathbf{p} \cdot \hat{\boldsymbol{\alpha}} - \alpha_0 \mathbf{b} \text{ is maximized}\}$$

$M_{\mathbf{p},\mathbf{b}}$ is convex means that $\mathbf{A}^1(\mathbf{p}) \times \cdots \times \mathbf{A}^N(\mathbf{p})$ is convex, a fact that has been previously verified.

$M_{\mathbf{p}, \langle \boldsymbol{\alpha}^1, \ldots, \boldsymbol{\alpha}^N \rangle}$ is a point and is therefore convex.

(f) ϕ_i are continuous functions.
This follows from the maximum theorem of Berge. (See Debreu, 1973, p. 19.) To have the conditions of Berge's theorem fulfilled, it is sufficient to show the correspondences β_i are lower hemicontinuous (lhc). β_1 is easily shown to be lhc; β_3 is lhc, because it

is in fact a continuous function; and β_2 is lhc by Lemma 2.6, which demonstrates that $\mathbf{B}^\nu(\mathbf{p})$ is lhc.

(g) It follows that a social equilibrium point, which is therefore a quasi-reproducible solution with value of labor power socially determined, exists.

We proceed to the existence of reproducible solutions.

DEFINITION 2.10: A reproducible solution with the value of labor power socially determined, with respect to endowments $\{\boldsymbol{\omega}^1, \ldots, \boldsymbol{\omega}^N\}$, is a set $(\mathbf{p}, \boldsymbol{\alpha}^1, \ldots, \boldsymbol{\alpha}^N, \mathbf{b})$ such that:

(a) $\boldsymbol{\alpha}^\nu \in \mathbf{A}^\nu(\mathbf{p})$, $\mathbf{b} = \mathbf{b}(\boldsymbol{\alpha}^1, \ldots, \boldsymbol{\alpha}^N)$

(b) $\Sigma\, \alpha_0^\nu \mathbf{b} \leqq \Sigma \hat{\boldsymbol{\alpha}}^\nu$

(c) $\mathbf{p} \cdot \mathbf{b} = 1$

(d) $\Sigma(\alpha_0^\nu \mathbf{b} + \boldsymbol{\alpha}^\nu) \leqq \Sigma\, \boldsymbol{\omega}^\nu$

where $\mathbf{A}^\nu(\mathbf{p})$ is defined in terms of the capital constraint $\mathbf{p} \cdot (\alpha_0^\nu \mathbf{b} + \underline{\boldsymbol{\alpha}}^\nu) \leqq \mathbf{p} \cdot \boldsymbol{\omega}^\nu$, as before.

COROLLARY 2.15: Let $(W^1, \ldots, W^N)$ be any vector of wealths. There exists a set of endowments

$$\boldsymbol{\Omega} = \{\boldsymbol{\omega}^1, \ldots, \boldsymbol{\omega}^N\}$$

with respect to which a reproducible solution with value of labor power socially determined, exists; and $\mathbf{p} \cdot \boldsymbol{\omega}^\nu = W^\nu$, for all ν, where $\mathbf{p}$ is the reproducible price vector.

Proof: The proof is the same as for Corollary 2.8.

Appendix 2: Necessary and sufficient conditions for the validity of the fundamental Marxian theorem

2.9 Outline of problem

In Chapter 2 it has been shown that the fundamental Marxian theorem (FMT) holds (Theorem 2.11) if we assume independence of production (A7). An example (bread and diamonds) was given to show that some assumption like A7 is necessary for the validity of the

FMT. In the example, A7 did not hold, and neither did the FMT. In this appendix, we prove that, in fact, A7 is a necessary condition for the truth of the FMT. Thus A7 is a necessary and sufficient condition on technology for the validity of the FMT. We prove the necessity of independence of production by showing that if A7 is false for a production set P, then an economy can be specified with P as its production set, for which reproducible solutions exist with positive profits and zero exploitation. (Note, from an examination of the proof of Theorem 2.11, that positive exploitation implies positive profits even in the absence of A7; thus it is only the possibility of achieving zero exploitation when there are positive profits that is at issue.)

It should be noted that this failure of the FMT has nothing in common with Steedman's positive profits–negative surplus value example. Indeed, our example of zero exploitation and positive profits occurs with the correct general definition of exploitation.

2.10 The model

The model presented here is different in some ways from that of the text. It has been simplified to allow a clear treatment of the question at hand, the characterization of production sets for which the FMT holds.

Here are the elements of the model.

Production

We shall assume, for simplicity, that there is one capitalist who faces a production set P. P consists of vectors of the form $\boldsymbol{\alpha} = (-\alpha_0, \hat{\boldsymbol{\alpha}})$, where α_0 is the direct labor input (a scalar), and $\hat{\boldsymbol{\alpha}}$ is the vector of *net* outputs (in $\mathbf{R}^n$). Labor power is the only nonproduced commodity. We postulate:

A1. P is a closed convex cone.

A2. $\mathbf{0} \in P$.

A3. $\boldsymbol{\alpha} \in P$ and $\hat{\boldsymbol{\alpha}} \nleqq 0$ implies that $\alpha_0 > 0$.

A4. $\forall \mathbf{c} > \mathbf{0}, \mathbf{c} \in \mathbf{R}^n, \exists \boldsymbol{\alpha} \in P$ with $\hat{\boldsymbol{\alpha}} \geqq \mathbf{c}$.

Note that A3 says labor is necessary for any productive activity, although not for disposal activities, and A4 says any desired bundle of commodities can be produced (if enough labor is used).

Because labor is not produced, it is natural to think of production as being labor limited. There is some amount of labor $\bar{L}$ available, and $\boldsymbol{\alpha}$ is only *feasible* if $\alpha_0 \leqq \bar{L}$.

Workers' behavior

Each worker requires a *subsistence bundle* $\mathbf{b} > 0$, $\mathbf{b} \in \mathbf{R}^n$, for a unit of work. The wage must be precisely sufficient to enable workers to purchase this bundle. Thus if $\mathbf{p}$ is the price vector of goods and the wage is taken as unity, $\mathbf{pb} = 1$.

Capitalists' behavior

For a given price vector $\mathbf{p}$, the capitalist maximizes profits subject to the labor constraint. That is, let

$$\mathbf{B} = \{\boldsymbol{\alpha} \in P \mid \alpha_0 \leqq \bar{L}\}$$

$$\mathbf{A}(\mathbf{p}) = \{\boldsymbol{\alpha} \in \mathbf{B} \mid \mathbf{p} \cdot (\hat{\boldsymbol{\alpha}} - \alpha_0 \mathbf{b}) \text{ is maximized}\}$$

Note that $\mathbf{p}(\hat{\boldsymbol{\alpha}} - \alpha_0\mathbf{b})$ is simply profits at the production action $\boldsymbol{\alpha} = (-\alpha_0, \hat{\boldsymbol{\alpha}})$. The capitalist, facing prices $\mathbf{p}$, chooses an action in $\mathbf{A}(\mathbf{p})$.

The simplifying assumption in this model is the existence of one capitalist. This avoids the problem of the aggregate feasibility of different capitalists' production plans. A feasible production plan in this model entails only that labor not in excess of $\bar{L}$ be employed.

A standard convexity argument shows that $\mathbf{A}(\mathbf{p})$ is always non-empty.

LEMMA 2.16: For all $\mathbf{p}$, $\mathbf{A}(\mathbf{p})$ is non-empty.

Proof: Suppose that for $\mathbf{p}$, $A(\mathbf{p})$ is empty. Because P is closed, this can occur only if there is a sequence of feasible production actions for which profits are unbounded:

$$\{\boldsymbol{\alpha}^i\} \text{ such that } \mathbf{p}\hat{\boldsymbol{\alpha}}^i - \alpha_0^i \to \infty \qquad \text{as } i \to \infty$$

Because $\alpha_0^i \leqq \bar{L}$ for all i by hypothesis, we have $\mathbf{p}\hat{\boldsymbol{\alpha}}^i \to \infty$. Hence $\|\hat{\boldsymbol{\alpha}}^i\| \to \infty$, where $\| \ \|$ is the Euclidean norm. Consider the production plans:

$$\boldsymbol{\beta}^i = \frac{\boldsymbol{\alpha}^i}{\|\hat{\boldsymbol{\alpha}}^i\|}$$

By convexity of P and A2, $\boldsymbol{\beta}^i \in P$.

But $\beta_0^i = \alpha_0^i/\|\hat{\boldsymbol{\alpha}}^i\| \to 0$, because $\|\hat{\boldsymbol{\alpha}}^i\| \to \infty$. Because P is closed, $\boldsymbol{\beta}^i \to \boldsymbol{\beta}^* \in P$. But $\beta_0^i \to \beta_0^*$, and so $\beta_0^* = 0$. But $\boldsymbol{\beta}^* \neq \mathbf{0}$, because $\|\hat{\boldsymbol{\beta}}^*\| = 1$. Hence, we have produced a nonzero, nonnegative production action in P that does not require a labor input, a contradiction to A3. Hence $\mathbf{A}(\mathbf{p})$ is non-empty. Q.E.D.

Equilibrium

DEFINITION 2.11: A pair $(\mathbf{p}, \boldsymbol{\alpha})$ is a *reproducible solution* for the economy $(P, \bar{L}, \mathbf{b})$, if:
(a) $\mathbf{pb} = 1$ (subsistence wage)
(b) $\alpha_0 \leqq \bar{L}$ (feasibility)
(c) $\boldsymbol{\alpha} \in \mathbf{A}(\mathbf{p})$ (profit-maximizing capitalists)
(d) $\hat{\boldsymbol{\alpha}} \geqq \alpha_0\mathbf{b}$ (reproducibility)

Exploitation

We define the rate of exploitation $e(\boldsymbol{\alpha})$ at a point in the production set as we have in the body of the chapter:
For any point $\boldsymbol{\alpha} \in P$:

$$e(\boldsymbol{\alpha}) = \frac{\alpha_0 - \text{l.v.}(\alpha_0\mathbf{b})}{\text{l.v.}(\alpha_0\mathbf{b})}$$

2.11 The fundamental Marxian theorem

It is straightforward to observe that reproducible solutions (RS) exist.

THEOREM 2.17: Let $\mathbf{b} > 0$. Under A1–A4, a reproducible solution $(\mathbf{p}, \boldsymbol{\alpha})$ exists.

Proof: Define

$$\mathbf{z}(\mathbf{p}) = \{\alpha_0\mathbf{b} - \hat{\boldsymbol{\alpha}} \mid \boldsymbol{\alpha} = (-\alpha_0, \hat{\boldsymbol{\alpha}}) \in \mathbf{A}(\mathbf{p})\}$$

$\mathbf{z}(\mathbf{p})$ is nonnull by Lemma 2.16, and convex-valued. Furthermore, standard arguments show that $\mathbf{z}(\mathbf{p})$ is upper hemicontinuous. We define $\mathbf{z}$ on the simplex $S = \{\mathbf{p} \mid \mathbf{pb} = 1\}$. (Note the importance of the assumption, here, that $\mathbf{b} > 0$, so that S is a simplex.) Note $\mathbf{pz}(\mathbf{p}) \leqq 0$, because at worst maximal profits are gotten by taking the action $\mathbf{0} \in P$, which exists by A2, and which renders profits zero. Hence, by the fixed point lemma, there exists $\bar{\mathbf{p}}$ and $\alpha_0\mathbf{b} - \hat{\boldsymbol{\alpha}} \in \mathbf{z}(\mathbf{p})$ such that $\alpha_0\mathbf{b} \leqq \hat{\boldsymbol{\alpha}}$.

Recall the assumption of independence of production:
A7. $(-\alpha_0, -\underline{\boldsymbol{\alpha}}, \bar{\boldsymbol{\alpha}}) \in P$, $\hat{\boldsymbol{\alpha}} \geq \mathbf{0}$ and $\mathbf{0} < \mathbf{c} \leq \hat{\boldsymbol{\alpha}}$, then $\exists\ (-\alpha_0', -\underline{\boldsymbol{\alpha}}', \bar{\boldsymbol{\alpha}}') \in P$ such that $\bar{\boldsymbol{\alpha}}' - \boldsymbol{\alpha}' \geqq \mathbf{c}$ and $\alpha_0' < \alpha_0$.

Actually, we have modified A7 a bit here from its first statement in Chapter 2: We require $\mathbf{0} < \mathbf{c}$ instead of $\mathbf{0} \leqq \mathbf{c}$. We shall remark on this later; in fact, at the cost of simplicity, we could state the definition as "$\mathbf{0} \leqq \mathbf{c}$."

It will be useful to relate independence of production to efficiency. An efficient point in P is one having the property that no more outputs can be generated without using more inputs:

DEFINITION 2.12: $\boldsymbol{\alpha} \in P$ is *efficient* if $(\nexists \boldsymbol{\beta} \in P)\ (\boldsymbol{\beta} \geq \boldsymbol{\alpha})$

Now the failure of A7 can be stated in terms of efficiency as follows. We use the symbol (~A7) to mean the negation of A7:

(~A7) $(\exists \mathbf{c} > \mathbf{0})\ (\boldsymbol{\alpha}$ efficient and $\hat{\boldsymbol{\alpha}} \geqq \mathbf{c} \Rightarrow \hat{\boldsymbol{\alpha}} \geq \mathbf{c})$

(~A7) says that there is a strictly positive bundle of net outputs that cannot be exactly produced as the net output bundle of any efficient point in P. Efficient production must produce more than $\mathbf{c}$ if it produces $\mathbf{c}$. Recall, for instance, the bread and diamonds example of Chapter 2. Note that (~A7) is in fact the negation of A7.

It is easy to observe that *if* A7 holds, then positive profits are equivalent to positive exploitation for this model. The proof is identical to that of Theorem 2.11. We proceed to prove the main result of this section, that independence of production is also a necessary condition of the FMT in this model:

THEOREM 2.18: Let P be a production set satisfying A1–A4 and ~A7. Then there exists an economy $(P, \bar{L}, \mathbf{b})$ that supports a reproducible solution with positive profits and zero exploitation.

First it is necessary to choose $\mathbf{b}$ and $\bar{L}$. Let $C = \{\boldsymbol{\alpha} \in P \mid \boldsymbol{\alpha}$ is efficient, $\hat{\boldsymbol{\alpha}} \geq \mathbf{c}\}$. Choose $\boldsymbol{\alpha}^* = (-\alpha_0^*, \hat{\boldsymbol{\alpha}}^*) \in C$ for which the direct labor input is minimized. Such $\boldsymbol{\alpha}^*$ exists by the assumptions on P, and $\alpha_0^* \neq 0$. Define $\mathbf{b} = \mathbf{c}/\alpha_0^* > \mathbf{0}$, because $\mathbf{c} > \mathbf{0}$. Thus $\hat{\boldsymbol{\alpha}}^* \geq \alpha_0^* \mathbf{b}$. Furthermore, by definition of the rate of exploitation, it follows that $e(\boldsymbol{\alpha}^*) = 0$, now that $\mathbf{b}$ is chosen. Choose $\bar{L} \equiv \alpha_0^*$. The economy $(P, \bar{L}, \mathbf{b})$ is now entirely specified, and so a reproducible solution exists, by Theorem 2.17.

We demonstrate:

LEMMA 2.19: Let $\mathbf{p}$ be an equilibrium price vector for the economy $(P, \bar{L}, \mathbf{b})$. Then there exists a reproducible solution $(\mathbf{p}, \boldsymbol{\alpha})$, where $\boldsymbol{\alpha}$ is efficient.

Proof: Because $\mathbf{p}$ is an equilibrium price vector, there exists a RS $(\mathbf{p}, \boldsymbol{\beta})$. Suppose that $\boldsymbol{\beta}$ is not efficient. Then $\exists \boldsymbol{\alpha} = (-\alpha_0, \hat{\boldsymbol{\alpha}}) \geq (-\beta_0, \hat{\boldsymbol{\beta}})$ and $\boldsymbol{\alpha}$ is efficient. It follows that $\boldsymbol{\alpha}$ is feasible and reproducible. But $\mathbf{p}(\hat{\boldsymbol{\alpha}} - \alpha_0 \mathbf{b}) \geq \mathbf{p}(\hat{\boldsymbol{\beta}} - \beta_0 \mathbf{b})$ and so $\boldsymbol{\alpha} \in \mathbf{A}(\mathbf{p})$ also. Hence $(\mathbf{p}, \boldsymbol{\alpha})$ is a RS. Q.E.D.

This lemma allows us to limit our search for reproducible solutions to those actions $\boldsymbol{\alpha} \in P$ that are efficient. That is, if $\boldsymbol{\alpha}$ is a reproducible action that is profit maximizing with respect to prices **p** over the set of *efficient* feasible production points, then α is a reproducible solution.

Proof of Theorem 2.18: Let $V = \{\hat{\boldsymbol{\alpha}} - \alpha_0\mathbf{b} \,|\, (-\alpha_0, \hat{\boldsymbol{\alpha}})$ is feasible, reproducible, and efficient$\}$. Because $(-\alpha_0, \hat{\boldsymbol{\alpha}})$ is reproducible, $V \subset \mathbf{R}^n_+$, the nonnegative orthant. Furthermore, by assumption ~A7 and the choice of **b**, it follows that $\mathbf{0} \notin V$. Hence $V \cap \mathbf{R}^n_- = \emptyset$, where $\mathbf{R}^n_-$ is the nonpositive orthant. Hence, there exists a hyperplane that separates V strictly from $\mathbf{R}^n_-$:

$$(\exists \mathbf{p})\ (\mathbf{p}\mathbf{R}^n_- \leqq 0,\ \mathbf{p}V > 0).$$

Thus, $\mathbf{p} \geq \mathbf{0}$, and because $\mathbf{b} > \mathbf{0}$, we can normalize **p** so that $\mathbf{pb} = 1$. (This is why the assumption $\mathbf{c} > \mathbf{0}$ simplifies the proof.)

By the requirement of feasibility, V is compact. It follows that there is a point $\boldsymbol{\beta}^* = (-\beta_0^*, \hat{\boldsymbol{\beta}}^*) \in V$ that maximizes profits $\mathbf{p}(\hat{\boldsymbol{\alpha}} - \alpha_0\mathbf{b})$ over V. Hence $\boldsymbol{\beta}^*$ is a reproducible solution, by Lemma 2.19. By choice of **p**, profits are positive at $\boldsymbol{\beta}^*$. Furthermore, $\beta_0^* = \bar{L}$: for if $\beta_0^* < \bar{L}$, then the point $(\bar{L}/\beta_0^*)\boldsymbol{\beta}^*$ is in V because P is a cone; and because profits are positive at $\boldsymbol{\beta}^*$, they are even greater at $(\bar{L}/\beta_0^*)\boldsymbol{\beta}^*$ – an impossibility.

Recall, however, that $\beta_0^* = \bar{L} \equiv \alpha_0^*$, and that $e(\boldsymbol{\alpha}^*) = 0$ by choice of $\boldsymbol{\alpha}^*$. Hence, $e(\boldsymbol{\beta}^*) = 0$, because

$$e(\boldsymbol{\beta}^*) = \frac{\beta_0^* - \text{l.v.}(\beta_0^*\mathbf{b})}{\text{l.v.}(\beta_0^*\mathbf{b})} = \frac{\alpha_0^* - \text{l.v.}(\alpha_0^*\mathbf{b})}{\text{l.v.}(\alpha_0^*\mathbf{b})} = e(\boldsymbol{\alpha}^*)$$

Hence, $(\mathbf{p}, \boldsymbol{\beta}^*)$ is the required pair: a reproducible solution exhibiting positive profits and zero exploitation. Q.E.D.

Remark. This theorem can be generalized to include the case where the original vector **c** of ~A7 is simply nonnegative and nonzero: $\mathbf{c} \geq \mathbf{0}$. In this case $\mathbf{b} \geq \mathbf{0}$, and the existence Theorem 2.17 can also be proved for this case. The complication is to guarantee that the normal to the separating hyperplane, **p**, of V and $\mathbf{R}^n_-$, can be normalized so that $\mathbf{pb} = 1$. A version of the separating hyperplane theorem assures us that this can be accomplished with a strictly positive vector **p**, because $\mathbf{0} \notin V$. Because $\mathbf{p} > \mathbf{0}$, it follows that **p** can be normalized so that $\mathbf{pb} = 1$. Hence, the theorem holds when ~A7 is weakened to, say, $\exists \mathbf{c} \geq \mathbf{0}$, although the rigorous demonstration of this generalization is beyond our scope.

2.12 Conclusion

We have characterized production technologies for which the FMT holds as those where independence of production prevails. Note that "independence" is needed only to guarantee the veracity of the statement, "positive profits imply positive exploitation," as the converse is always true.

There are two observations one might wish to make from this fact. One is that it is conceivable for capitalists to make profits without exploiting workers. This can happen only with "dependent" production, in which workers must produce bread for themselves, and they incidentally produce as an unwanted by-product, diamonds, which the capitalists expropriate. Clearly, such a phenomenon is not of major importance in real capitalist economies.

A second observation has to do with the nontriviality of the FMT. The opinion has been frequently voiced that the FMT is "trivial" – because it says simply that there can be profits if and only if there is a surplus produced. The demonstration here shows that the relationship between profits and exploitation is not trivial, in the precise sense that the FMT is not universally true. Statements that must be qualified in a non-obvious way are not trivial statements. We might think of the economics behind the independence criterion in this way: If a production set enjoys independence, then no goods are free in terms of labor. It always costs some labor to increase net output above some specified level. In this classical case of no free lunch, the FMT holds. Only when it is possible to produce an increase in output with no more labor expended can an economy violate the Marxian principle.

The FMT, then, characterizes precisely a certain kind of classical economy (no free lunch of a certain type). It is precisely the no-free-lunch property of production that drives the equivalence of exploitation and profit making. Needless to say, this was not observable in Leontief models of production.

3 The equalization of profit rates in Marxian general equilibrium[1]

3.1 Introduction

It is usually taken as a postulate in Marxian discussions that the rate of profit is equal, at equilibrium, for all capitalists. Such a phenomenon should not, however, be a postulate, but rather a theorem, for what capitalists try to do is maximize profits, and any macroeconomic phenomenon (such as an economy-wide unique rate) should be derived as a consequence of individual capitalist accumulation behavior. In Chapter 1 we showed that for a special linear model where all capitalists face the same Leontief technology, profit rates are equalized at reproducible solutions. It was also shown, in the monopolistic competition model of that chapter, how imperfect entry could prevent the equalization of profit rates.

In the general model of Chapter 2, profit rates are not equalized at reproducible solutions. (Clearly the model of monopolistic competition is a special case of the general model.) This is due to the nonexistence of a market for finance capital: Capitalists are not able to borrow or lend. In this chapter, a finance capital market is appended to the model of Chapter 2, and it is shown that Marxian equilibria continue to exist and, furthermore, profit rates are always equalized at equilibrium.

This sounds like a familiar story – the existence of a capital market will allow investment funds to be efficiently allocated, so that the rate of return on the marginal dollar is everywhere the same. There is, however, another type of profit-rate equalization that is not driven by the existence of a capital market, but rather by the requirement that the system *reproduce* itself. Furthermore, in the general case, the argument here shows that it is not "competition" in some vague sense that equalizes profit rates, but precisely the existence of a capital market. This is a point that has, perhaps, not been made sharply enough in Marxian discussions.

There is another reason to prove theorems that show when a Marxian equilibrium will enjoy profit-rate equalization. Suppose that at given prices **p**, the rates of profit in different sectors differ. A process of capital movement may then begin: We think of capital leaving low-profit-rate sectors and entering high-profit-rate sectors. The presumption has been that such a dynamic process leads to equalization of profit rates, as a consequence of changing prices. Nikaido (1978) claims that such dynamic processes do not necessarily converge. Thus, the dynamic foundations of equal-profit-rate equilibrium seem shaky. It is therefore important to understand precisely which postulates of the Marxian model give rise to a static equilibrium with equal profit rates.

Let us point out the two causes of non-equalization of profit rates in the model of Chapter 2. First, if the production sets P^ν differ among capitalists, the profit rates can differ. This is the case discussed above. Second, if the production set $P = P^1$ is the same for all capitalists and is not a cone (but is convex), then profit rates can differ. This situation arises because of diminishing returns: Capitalists with more capital will operate "farther out" in P^1, thus generating greater total profits but at a lower profit rate. (If, however, all capitalists face the same conical production set, then profit rates will be equalized at equilibrium.) The inefficiencies that can arise then, due to (1) imperfect information or imperfect entry (which is what occurs when capitalists face different production sets), and (2) rents (which can be thought of as case of diminishing returns), are overcome by a finance capital market.

It is worthwhile to review the one important case where profit rates are equalized for all production activities at Marxian reproducible solutions even without a capital market. Suppose that all capitalists face the same conical production set, and it is generated by an indecomposable Leontief technology. Then the only price vector capable of reproducing the system is one that equalizes the profit rates for all production processes, even without a capital market. (See Chapter 1.) Briefly, the argument is this: Capitalists will only invest in maximal profit-rate processes. If all processes do not generate the maximal profit rate, then some processes will not operate. But by indecomposability, the economy cannot reproduce itself unless all processes operate. In this case, then, the requirement of reproducibility drives profit-rate equalization across production activities independent of the existence of a capital market. We shall return to this point later in the chapter.

Finally, the equivalence of positive profits and positive exploitation is proved for the economy with a credit market, which shows the existence of equilibria with positive profits in the model of Chapters 1 and 2 was not due to the lack of a credit market. This, in turn, allows us to evaluate what attribute of the Marxian model is responsible for the existence of positive profits at equilibrium, and requires some discussion of neoclassical theories of profit.

3.2 Marxian equilibrium with finance capital market

As before, there are N capitalists indexed by ν. Capitalist ν possesses an endowment $\boldsymbol{\omega}^\nu \geqq 0$ of goods. He faces a production set P^ν whose points are $(-\alpha_0^\nu, -\underline{\boldsymbol{\alpha}}^\nu, \bar{\boldsymbol{\alpha}}^\nu)$, where $\bar{\boldsymbol{\alpha}}^\nu$, $\underline{\boldsymbol{\alpha}}^\nu \in \mathbf{R}_+^n$, $\alpha_0^\nu \geqq 0$; α_0^ν is the direct labor input, $\underline{\boldsymbol{\alpha}}^\nu$ is the input vector of commodities; $\bar{\boldsymbol{\alpha}}^\nu$ is the output vector of commodities. Assumptions A1–A4 of Chapter 2 hold for P^ν.

Capitalist behavior

A capitalist might borrow funds in amount D^ν. His feasible set, with such borrowing, at prices $\mathbf{p}$, is

$$\mathbf{B}^\nu(\mathbf{p}, D^\nu) = \{\boldsymbol{\alpha}^\nu \in P^\nu \mid \mathbf{p}\underline{\boldsymbol{\alpha}}^\nu + \alpha_0^\nu \leqq \mathbf{p}\boldsymbol{\omega}^\nu + D^\nu\}$$

(Negative borrowing, of course, is lending.)

Capitalists, facing prices $(\mathbf{p}, r)$, where $\mathbf{p}$ is the commodity price vector and r is the interest rate, maximize profits. Profits are the value of what the capitalist possesses at the beginning of the next period minus the value of current endowments. Thus, at borrowings D^ν, profits will be

$$\Pi^\nu(\mathbf{p}, r; D^\nu) = \max_{\alpha^\nu \in \mathbf{B}^\nu(\mathbf{p}, D^\nu)} \{[\mathbf{p}\bar{\alpha}^\nu] + [D^\nu + \mathbf{p}\boldsymbol{\omega}^\nu - (\mathbf{p}\underline{\boldsymbol{\alpha}} + \alpha_0^\nu)] - [(1 + r)D^\nu] - \mathbf{p}\boldsymbol{\omega}^\nu\}$$

where the terms are, respectively, income from production, the value of assets not used in production but held over until next period, the value of borrowing repaid, and the value of today's endowments.

We may simplify:

$$\Pi^\nu(\mathbf{p}, r; D^\nu) = \max_{\alpha^\nu \in \mathbf{B}^\nu(\mathbf{p}, D^\nu)} \{[\mathbf{p}\bar{\boldsymbol{\alpha}}^\nu - (\mathbf{p}\underline{\boldsymbol{\alpha}}^\nu + \alpha_0^\nu)] - rD^\nu\}$$

Let

$$\mathbf{A}^\nu(\mathbf{p}, r; D^\nu) = \{\boldsymbol{\alpha}^\nu \in \mathbf{B}^\nu(\mathbf{p}, D^\nu) \mid \Pi^\nu(\mathbf{p}, r; D^\nu) \text{ is achieved}\}$$

Let

$$\mathcal{D}^\nu(\mathbf{p}, r) = \{D^\nu \mid \Pi^\nu(\mathbf{p}, r; D^\nu) \text{ is maximized}\}$$

[$\mathcal{D}^\nu(\mathbf{p}, r)$ may be empty for some values of $(\mathbf{p}, r)$.]

Let

$$\mathscr{A}^\nu(\mathbf{p}, r) = \bigcup_{D^\nu \in \mathscr{D}^\nu(\mathbf{p},r)} \mathbf{A}^\nu(\mathbf{p}, r; D^\nu)$$

Capitalist behavior, formally, is as follows: Given prices $(\mathbf{p}, r)$, to choose any action in $\mathscr{A}^\nu(\mathbf{p}, r)$. That is, capitalist ν chooses an amount to borrow (lend) at which his profits are maximized at those prices; he then chooses any production action that realizes those maximal profits.

Equilibria

DEFINITION 3.1: $(\mathbf{p}, r)$ is a reproducible solution with finance capital market if:

(a) $(\forall\nu)(\exists D^\nu \in \mathscr{D}^\nu(\mathbf{p}, r)(\Sigma\, D^\nu = 0)$ (feasibility of optimal borrowing)

(b) $[\exists \boldsymbol{\alpha}^\nu \in \mathbf{A}^\nu(\mathbf{p}, r; D^\nu)](\Sigma\, \underline{\boldsymbol{\alpha}}^\nu + \alpha_0^\nu \mathbf{b} \leqq \boldsymbol{\omega})$ (feasibility of production plans)

(c) $\Sigma\, \bar{\boldsymbol{\alpha}}^\nu - \Sigma\, \underline{\boldsymbol{\alpha}}^\nu \geqq \Sigma\, \alpha_0^\nu \mathbf{b}$ (reproducibility)

(d) $\mathbf{pb} = 1$ (subsistence wage)

Conditions (b), (c), and (d) are familiar from before. Condition (a) states that there is a set of individually optimal borrowings for capitalists that is socially feasible: Because capitalists can borrow only from each other, net borrowings must sum to zero.

We summarize the formal definition of a reproducible solution with finance capital market. Facing a price–interest rate pair $(\mathbf{p}, r)$, each capitalist decides what his optimal borrowing (loan) is. The optimal loan is one that allows him to produce affordably at some point that maximizes his profits, after the loan and interest are repaid. (Loans may be negative, of course.) For $(\mathbf{p}, r)$ to be a reproducible solution, four conditions must hold: (1) The capital market must clear; (2) the market for production inputs and wage goods must have no excess demands (feasibility); (3) society must not run down its aggregate endowments (reproducibility); and (4) the subsistence bundle must be precisely affordable. Thus, a reproducible solution with finance capital market is like a reproducible solution of Chapter 2, with one additional market that must clear for all capitalists to be able to optimize.

As was shown in Chapter 2, condition (c) should be thought of as a supplementary condition to the usual notion of general equilibrium. If $(\mathbf{p}, r)$ exists for which (a), (b), and (d) are satisfied, then $(\mathbf{p}, r)$ will be called a *competitive equilibrium* with finance capital market. It will require additional investigation to determine whether reproducible solutions exist.

We next show that a competitive equilibrium exists, and that all capitalists' "profit rates" are equalized at such an equilibrium.

Existence of competitive equilibrium with a finance capital market, and profit-rate equalization

The strategy for showing the existence of a competitive equilibrium with finance capital market is conceptually simple, but notationally difficult, so it is worthwhile to provide a verbal preview of the idea. What a capital market does is produce an allocation of capital among firms that maximizes capitalists' *joint* profits. That is, it allows capital to be allocated in a socially efficient manner, which implies that joint profits will be maximized. Hence, we shall define yet another kind of equilibrium – a joint-profit-maximizing equilibrium. We shall say that a certain distribution of wealths allows a joint-profit-maximizing (JPM) equilibrium if, when capitalists are assigned those wealths and no borrowing is permitted, a joint profit maximum is achieved. (That is, a distribution of capitals, or wealths, that admits a joint-profit-maximing equilibrium is a socially efficient distribution of capitals.) We then show that a JPM competitive equilibrium exists. This is a simple matter: We simply need show that there is a way of allocating total capital to maximize joint profits, which is clearly true. Then, using the idea discussed above, we show that any JPM equilibrium induces a competitive equilibrium with finance capital market. The idea here is also simple: Namely, we assign the νth capitalist a loan that is equal to the difference between his assigned wealth at the JPM equilibrium and his actual, given wealth in the original model. The only trick is to show that there is an appropriate interest rate which will, in fact, make these loans optimal loans for all. But the existence of such an interest rate follows from the JPM nature of the equilibrium. In particular, the reason an equilibrium is JPM is that it equalizes the rate of return on the marginal dollar invested in every line of production (every P^ν). We take this universal rate of return to be the interest rate, and show that it is the required interest rate for the assigned loans to be optimal. This also shows, immediately, that the rate of profit is equalized for all capitalists at the competitive equilibrium with finance capital market, because we have just shown that the individual profit rates are all equal to the economy-wide rate of interest.

So far, we have indicated the argument for the existence of a competitive equilibrium with finance capital market. To deduce the existence of a reproducible solution with finance capital market, we must again introduce the notion of a quasi-reproducible solution. This argument parallels the argument of Chapter 2.

We proceed with this plan by introducing the equilibrium concept of joint profit maximization. What is the distribution of capital values that would produce maximal joint profits at prices $\mathbf{p}$ – *in the absence* of a capital market?

DEFINITION 3.2: Let total endowments $\boldsymbol{\omega}$ be given. Let $\mathbf{p}$ be given. Let a distribution of numbers $(C^1, \ldots, C^N)$ be given, $C^\nu \geq 0$. Define

$$\bar{\mathbf{B}}^\nu(\mathbf{p}, C^\nu) = \{\boldsymbol{\alpha}^\nu \in P^\nu \mid \mathbf{p}\underline{\boldsymbol{\alpha}}^\nu + \alpha_0^\nu \leq C^\nu\}$$

Let

$$\bar{\Pi}^\nu(\mathbf{p}, C^\nu) = \max_{\alpha^\mu \in \bar{\mathbf{B}}^\mu(\mathbf{p}, C^\mu)} \{[\mathbf{p}\bar{\boldsymbol{\alpha}}^\nu] + [C^\nu - (\mathbf{p}\underline{\boldsymbol{\alpha}}^\nu + \alpha_0^\nu)] - C^\nu\}$$

or

$$\bar{\Pi}^\nu(\mathbf{p}, C^\nu) = \max_{\alpha^\mu \in \bar{\mathbf{B}}^\mu(\mathbf{p}, C^\mu)} [\mathbf{p}\hat{\boldsymbol{\alpha}}^\nu - (\mathbf{p}\underline{\boldsymbol{\alpha}}^\nu + \alpha_0^\nu)]$$

[$\bar{\Pi}^\nu(\mathbf{p}, C^\nu)$ is the function that assigns to $(\mathbf{p}, C^\nu)$ the maximum achievable profits with prices $\mathbf{p}$ and wealth endowment C^ν.]

Let

$$\bar{\mathbf{A}}^\nu(\mathbf{p}, C^\nu) = \{\boldsymbol{\alpha}^\nu \in \bar{\mathbf{B}}^\nu(\mathbf{p}, C^\nu) \mid \bar{\Pi}^\nu(\mathbf{p}, C^\nu) \text{ is achieved}\}$$

Define $\bar{\Pi}(\mathbf{p}; C^1, \ldots, C^N) = \Sigma_\nu \bar{\Pi}^\nu(\mathbf{p}, C^\nu)$. Then $\mathbf{p}$ is a joint-profit-maximizing (JPM) competitive equilibrium if:

(a) $(\exists C^\nu)(\Sigma\, C^\nu \leq \mathbf{p}\boldsymbol{\omega})$.

(b) $\bar{\Pi}(\mathbf{p}; C^1, \ldots, C^N)$ is maximized (for $\mathbf{p}$ fixed) over all distributions satisfying condition (a).

(c) $(\forall\nu)(\exists\boldsymbol{\alpha}^\nu \in \bar{\mathbf{A}}^\nu(\mathbf{p}, C^\nu))(\Sigma\, \underline{\boldsymbol{\alpha}}^\nu + \Sigma\, \alpha_0^\nu\mathbf{b} \leqq \boldsymbol{\omega})$.

(d) $\mathbf{pb} = 1$.

This definition says that if capital values are distributed in the manner $(C^1, \ldots, C^N)$, then an individually optimal, socially feasible solution exists, and that joint profits can never be greater at prices $\mathbf{p}$. (*Note:* There is no borrowing in this JPM model.)

By virtue of the next lemma, in our study of the economy with the finance capital market, we shall be able to limit our investigation to JPM equilibria.

LEMMA 3.1: Let $\{(\mathbf{p}, r); D^1, \ldots, D^N\}$ be a competitive equilibrium with finance capital market. Then $\{\mathbf{p}; C^1, \ldots, C^N\}$ is a JPM equilibrium, where $C^\nu \equiv \mathbf{p}\boldsymbol{\omega}^\nu + D^\nu$.

This lemma says that the equilibria with finance capital market are all JPM equilibria – reinterpreted without the capital market. Hence, to find all of the former, we may limit our search to the latter. Conversely, it will be shown below that all JPM equilibria can be reinterpreted as equilibria with a finance capital market.

Proof: Note that joint profits in the two economies $\{(\mathbf{p}, r); D^1, \ldots, D^N\}$ and $\{\mathbf{p}; C^1, \ldots, C^N\}$ are identical. They differ only by the interest and loan charges $\Sigma_\nu (1 + r)D^\nu$, which sum to zero, because by hypothesis $\Sigma D^\nu = 0$.

Suppose, then, that $\{\mathbf{p}; C^1, \ldots, C^N\}$, as defined, were not a JPM equilibrium. Then it is possible to redistribute capital values so that $\{\mathbf{p}; C'^1, \ldots, C'^N\}$ yield greater joint profits. But by the above paragraph, the borrowing induced by

$$D'^\nu \equiv C'^\nu - \mathbf{p}\boldsymbol{\omega}^\nu$$

would yield greater joint profits in the economy with capital market. Hence, for at least one capitalist, borrowing D'^ν must be superior to borrowing D^ν, at prices $(\mathbf{p}, r)$. Hence $\{(\mathbf{p}, r); D^1, \ldots, D^N\}$ was not an equilibrium with finance capital market. Q.E.D.

THEOREM 3.2: A JPM competitive equilibrium $\mathbf{p}$ exists.

Proof (sketch):

(a) We assume, for simplicity, that $\mathbf{b} > 0$. Hence $\mathbf{p}$ may range over the simplex $S = \{\mathbf{p} \mid \mathbf{pb} = 1\}$.

(b) For $\mathbf{p} \in S$, there exists a feasible distribution of capital values $(C^1, \ldots, C^N)$ that maximizes joint profits. This is true because individual maximal profit functions $\Pi^\nu(\mathbf{p}, C^\nu)$ can be shown to be continuous in C^ν, by the assumptions on P^ν. Hence joint profits are a continuous function defined on the compact domain of feasible capital value distributions.

(c) Define the correspondence:

$$\mathbf{Z}(\mathbf{p}) = \{(\Sigma\, \underline{\boldsymbol{\alpha}}^\nu + \Sigma\, \alpha_0^\nu \mathbf{b}) - \boldsymbol{\omega} \mid \boldsymbol{\alpha}^\nu \in \bar{\mathbf{A}}^\nu(\mathbf{p}, C^\nu), \text{ where } (C^1, \ldots, C^N) \text{ maximizes joint profits at } \mathbf{p}\}$$

It follows from the assumptions on P^ν that $\mathbf{Z}(\mathbf{p})$ is upper hemicontinuous and convex valued. Furthermore, $\mathbf{pZ}(\mathbf{p}) \leqq 0$ by the definition of $\bar{\mathbf{A}}^\nu(\mathbf{p}, C^\nu)$.

(d) It follows from the fixed point lemma that $\mathbf{p}$ exists for which

$\mathbf{Z}(\mathbf{p}) \leqq 0$, which provides the required JPM equilibrium. Q.E.D.

THEOREM 3.3: (*i*) A competitive equilibrium with finance capital market exists, $(\mathbf{p}, r)$.

(*ii*) If $(\mathbf{p}, r)$ is any such equilibrium, then r is equal to the marginal rate of profit in production for each capitalist ν for whom the marginal rate of profit is well defined.

We require a well-known result:

LEMMA 3.4: A continuous, concave function f of a real variable possesses right and left derivatives at all points, and $df^+/dx \leq df^-/dx$.

Proof of Theorem 3.3: Let $\xi = (\mathbf{p}; C^1, \ldots, C^N)$ be a JPM equilibrium that exists by Theorem 3.2. Recall that $\bar{\Pi}^\nu(\mathbf{p}; C^\nu)$ is the function that assigns to the value C^ν the maximal profits capitalist ν makes when restricted to his feasible set $\bar{\mathbf{B}}^\nu(\mathbf{p}; C^\nu)$. $\bar{\Pi}^\nu(\mathbf{p}; C^\nu)$ can be shown to be continuous (as has been remarked), and concave, by the convexity of P^ν. We fix $\mathbf{p}$, and from now on speak simply of $\bar{\Pi}^\nu(C^\nu)$.

Because ξ is JPM, it follows that for all sufficiently small positive numbers δ:

$$\forall \mu, \nu \quad \bar{\Pi}^\mu(C^\mu + \delta) - \bar{\Pi}^\mu(C^\mu) \leqq \bar{\Pi}^\nu(C^\nu) - \bar{\Pi}^\nu(C\nu - \delta) \tag{3.1}$$

for if (3.1) failed for some δ, then funds in amount δ could be transferred from capitalist ν to capitalist μ, and joint profits would increase, an impossibility.

Dividing inequality (3.1) by δ and passing to the limit as $\delta \to 0$ gives

$$\frac{d^+\bar{\Pi}^\mu}{dC^\mu} \leq \frac{d^-\bar{\Pi}^\nu}{dC^\nu} \qquad \forall \mu \neq \nu \tag{3.2}$$

where the derivatives are evaluated at C^μ and C^ν (a little notational abuse). (This limit operation is legitimate because, by the lemma, the right and left derivatives exist.)

However, by the lemma also it follows that

$$\frac{d^+\bar{\Pi}^\nu}{dC^\nu} \leq \frac{d^-\bar{\Pi}^\nu}{dC^\nu} \qquad \forall \nu = 1, N \tag{3.3}$$

From (3.2) and (3.3);

$$M \equiv \max_\nu \frac{d^+\bar{\Pi}^\nu}{dC^\nu} \leq \min_\nu \frac{d^-\bar{\Pi}^\nu}{dC^\nu} \equiv m \tag{3.4}$$

Choose r, therefore, so that $r \in [M, m]$.

It is now shown that r is the appropriate interest rate which allows one to reinterpret the existing JPM equilibrium as a competitive equilibrium with finance capital market. Define

$$D^\nu = C^\nu - \mathbf{p}\boldsymbol{\omega}^\nu$$

which will be the borrowings of capitalist ν. Because $r \leq d^-\bar{\Pi}^\nu/dC^\nu$ for all ν, it follows that within a small neighborhood of D^ν, no capitalist wishes to borrow less than he does at D^ν, given prices $(\mathbf{p}, r)$. (That is, profits on his "last" dollar of capital are at least as great as the interest rate.) But because $r \geq d^+\bar{\Pi}^\nu/dC$ for all ν, within a small neighborhood of D^ν, no capitalist wishes to borrow more than he does at D^ν. Because the profit functions are concave, this local argument shows that the borrowings D^ν are in fact a global optimum for the capitalists.

The argument in the last paragraph is slightly intuitive and not formally precise, because it employs the (fictitious) profit functions $\bar{\Pi}^\nu(\mathbf{p}, C^\nu)$ – the actual profit functions for capitalists are $\Pi^\nu(\mathbf{p}, r; D^\nu)$ in the economy with finance capital market. To be formally precise, we observe, from the simplified definitional expressions for $\Pi^\nu(\mathbf{p}, r; D^\nu)$ and $\bar{\Pi}^\nu(\mathbf{p}, C^\nu)$ that

$$\frac{d^\pm\Pi^\nu(\mathbf{p}, r; D^\nu)}{dD^\nu}(C^\nu) \equiv \frac{d^\pm\Pi^\nu(\mathbf{p}, r; D^\nu)}{dD^\nu}(\mathbf{p}\boldsymbol{\omega}^\nu + D^\nu) = \frac{d^\pm\bar{\Pi}^\nu(\mathbf{p}, C^\nu)}{dC^\nu}(C^\nu) - r$$

Hence, from choice of r, it follows that

$$\frac{d^-\Pi^\nu(\mathbf{p}, r; D^\nu)}{dD^\nu}(\mathbf{p}\boldsymbol{\omega}^\nu + D^\nu) \geq 0 \qquad \forall\nu$$

and

$$\frac{d^+\Pi^\nu(\mathbf{p}, r; D^\nu}{dD^\nu}(\mathbf{p}\boldsymbol{\omega}^\nu + D^\nu) \leq 0 \qquad \forall\nu$$

from which it follows rigorously that the point $(\mathbf{p}, r; D^1, \ldots, D^N)$ constitutes an equilibrium.

It has been shown that the JPM equilibrium is an equilibrium with finance capital market. If, in addition, the profit functions are in fact differentiable, then

$$\forall\nu \qquad 0 = \frac{d\Pi^\nu}{dD^\nu}$$

It follows from examination of the definition of $\Pi^\nu(\mathbf{p}, r; D^\nu)$ that the rate of profit from productive activity is equalized to the interest rate for all capitalists at such a point:

$$\frac{d}{dD^\nu}\max_{\alpha^\nu \in B^\nu(\mathbf{p}, D^\nu)}[\mathbf{p}\bar{\alpha}^\nu - (\mathbf{p}\underline{\alpha}^\nu + \alpha_0^\nu)] = r$$

It has, finally, to be shown that *any* equilibrium $(\mathbf{p}, r)$ with finance capital market has the stated property (*ii*) of the theorem. If $\{(\mathbf{p}, r); D^1, \ldots, D^N\}$ is such an equilibrium then by Lemma 3.1, it is a JPM equilibrium also. Hence, by the argument here, inequalities (3.2) and (3.3) hold, and hence the interval $[M, m]$ of (3.4) can be defined. If

$r \notin [M, m]$, then the argument given shows that the equilibrium in question is not a JPM one, because some capitalist could profitably borrow (lend) more. Hence $r \in [M, m]$, and the conclusion follows. Q.E.D.

A remark is due on the statement in Theorem 3.3, part (*ii*), ". . . if the rate of profit is well defined." If the production sets are all differentiable (that is, if the production functions that define the efficient points of the sets are differentiable), then the profit rate at any point is well defined, because the function Π will be differentiable. The only problem arises when the production set has kinks. At a kink, the rate of profit can only be said to lie in an interval between the left- and right-hand slopes. This idea was captured formally above with the notion of left and right derivatives of the profit function. Thus, if the production sets are without kinks, then Theorem 3.3 establishes the equalization of profit rates for all capitalists, in the presence of a finance capital market.

Existence of reproducible solutions with finance capital market

It is now necessary to demonstrate that *reproducible solutions* with finance capital market exist. As in the model without finance capital market, we can show that such solutions exist for any wealth distribution – but *not* for any initial distribution of endowment vectors. We can prove the following theorem.

THEOREM 3.5: Let $(W^1, \ldots, W^N)$ be any vector of wealths. Then there exists a set of initial endowment vectors

$$\boldsymbol{\Omega} = \{\boldsymbol{\omega}^1, \boldsymbol{\omega}^2, \ldots, \boldsymbol{\omega}^N\}$$

such that there exists a reproducible solution with finance capital market $\{(\mathbf{p}, r); D^1, \ldots, D^N\}$ with the property that $\mathbf{p}\boldsymbol{\omega}^\nu = W^\nu$ for all ν.

Because a reproducible solution is a special kind of competitive equilibrium, it follows from Theorem 3.3 that the rates of profit are equalized in all production sets P^ν at the reproducible solution.

A sketch of the method of proving Theorem 3.5 follows.

DEFINITION 3.3: Let W be a positive real number. We define $(\mathbf{p}; C^1, \ldots, C^N)$ to be a quasi-reproducible joint-profit-maximizing solution (QRJPM) if:

(a) $\Sigma\, C^\nu = W$.

(b) Capitalist ν chooses $\boldsymbol{\alpha}^\nu \in P^\nu$ to maximize profits at prices $\mathbf{p}$, subject to the capital constraint

$$\mathbf{p}\underline{\boldsymbol{\alpha}}^\nu + \alpha_0^\nu \leqq C^\nu$$

(c) Profit-maximizing $\{\boldsymbol{\alpha}^\nu\}$ exist that generate reproducibility:

$$\Sigma\, \bar{\boldsymbol{\alpha}}^\nu - \Sigma\, \underline{\boldsymbol{\alpha}}^\nu \geqq \Sigma\, \alpha_0^\nu \mathbf{b}$$

(d) Subject to (a) and (b), $(C^1, \ldots, C^N)$ is the distribution of capital values that maximizes joint profits.
(e) $\mathbf{pb} = 1$.

A QRJPM solution is basically a reproducible solution where feasibility is ignored. [See condition (b) of Definition 3.1. This parallels the construction of quasi-reproducible solutions (QRS) of Chapter 2.]

LEMMA 3.6: For any W, a QRJPM solution $(\mathbf{p}; C^1, \ldots, C^N)$ exists.

Proof: The proof is virtually identical to that for Theorem 2.5.

Proof of Theorem 3.5
(a) Define $W = \Sigma\, W^\nu$. By Lemma 3.6, a QRJPM solution $(\mathbf{p}; C^1, \ldots, C^N)$ exists. Associated with this solution are production points $\{\boldsymbol{\alpha}^\nu\}$ that generate reproducibility, according to condition (c) of Definition 3.3.
(b) Let $\boldsymbol{\omega}$ be any vector of aggregate endowments such that $\boldsymbol{\omega} \geqq \mathbf{b}\, \Sigma\, \alpha_0^\nu + \Sigma\, \underline{\boldsymbol{\alpha}}^\nu$ and $\mathbf{p}\boldsymbol{\omega} = W$. (Such $\boldsymbol{\omega}$ exists by Definition 3.3, because $\mathbf{p}(\mathbf{b}\, \Sigma\, \alpha_0^\nu + \underline{\boldsymbol{\alpha}}^\nu) \leqq W$.) Decompose $\boldsymbol{\omega}$ into $\boldsymbol{\omega} = \Sigma\, \boldsymbol{\omega}^\nu$ in any way so that $\mathbf{p}\boldsymbol{\omega}^\nu = W^\nu$.
(c) Let $\boldsymbol{\omega} = \Sigma\, \boldsymbol{\omega}'^\nu$ be any decomposition of ω such that $\mathbf{p}\boldsymbol{\omega}'^\nu = C^\nu$. By choice of $\boldsymbol{\omega}$, it follows that $\{\mathbf{p}; C^1, \ldots, C^N\}$ is a JPM *competitive equilibrium.*
(d) Let $D^\nu = C^\nu - W^\nu$. Because any JPM competitive equilibrium induces a competitive equilibrium with finance capital market, it follows that a competitive equilibrium with finance capital market $\{(\mathbf{p}, r); D^1, \ldots, D^N\}$ is here induced. Moreover, this equilibrium is a reproducible solution, because the optimal production points satisfy condition (c) of Definition 3.3. Q.E.D.

3.3 Summary: what drives profit-rate equalization in the Marxian model?

It has now been shown that if a finance capital market exists, then Marxian equilibria (reproducible solutions) exist for any given distribution of capital values, and that at these reproducible solutions the following holds: the marginal rate of profit at the chosen production point $\boldsymbol{\alpha}^{\nu}$ in the production set P^{ν} is equalized, for all ν. The capital market thus equalizes profit rates for all production sets, and for all capitalists.

As has been shown, the function of the capital market is to allow joint profits to be maximized: In this sense, the capital market distributes available capital optimally from the point of view of capital as a whole. The inefficiencies that may exist without a capital market are of two types, as we have discussed: (1) where capitalists do not all face the same production set; (2) where capitalists face the same production set, but there are nonconstant returns to scale. The capital market overcomes the inefficiencies due to (1) and (2), in the precise sense that it finds a joint-profit-maximizing solution in those cases – and, consequently, a solution where profit rates are equalized in the sense discussed.

If neither (1) nor (2) is a problem – that is, if all capitalists face the same conical production set – then a capital market is unnecessary to equalize profit rates across capitalists. At any competitive equilibrium, profit rates for all capitalists will be equal.

Finally, for certain special technologies, we can speak about individual production *activities*. In the Leontief or von Neumann models, for instance, we can think of the production cones as being generated by a finite number of discrete activities. As we have discussed, in an indecomposable Leontief model, profit rates are equalized for all activities by the requirement of reproducibility. In a decomposable Leontief model where all capitalists face the same production cone, or in the von Neumann model, reproducible solutions can exist generating different profit rates in different activities, but only the activities with the maximal profit rate will be operated. Thus, profit rates continue to be equalized for capitalists, and in all production sets P^{ν}, but not for all production activities.

We can thus summarize the mechanisms that equalize profit rates in this way:

1. If there is perfect free entry and constant returns to scale, then profit rates are equalized for all capitalists by individual profit maximization in the absence of a capital market; nevertheless, different production activities, if they can be defined, may generate different profit rates.
2. If there is imperfect entry or nonconstant returns, then profit rates for all capitalists are equalized by individual profit maximization and the existence of a capital market.

3. Even if a capital market exists, profit rates for all production activities may not be equalized. In the indecomposable Leontief model, the equalization of profit rates across activities is driven by the requirement of reproducibility.

3.4 Positive profits, positive exploitation, and the theory of profits

It does not come as too much of a surprise that the FMT 2.11 of Chapter 2 remains true in this economy. In fact, Theorem 2.11 is true, *verbatim,* for reproducible solutions with finance capital market, and so the statement of the theorem will not be repeated here.

The proof is simple. In the previous section, it was observed that a reproducible solution with finance capital market always induces a reproducible solution in the economy *without* credit market, where capitalists are assigned wealths or capital values that produce a joint-profit-maximizing (JPM) reproducible solution. That is, let $\boldsymbol{\omega}^1, \ldots, \boldsymbol{\omega}^N$ be the distribution of endowments and let $\mathbf{p}$ be a reproducible solution (without capital market) for those initial endowments, with the property that joint profits are maximized, among all possible endowment distributions whose capital values add up to $\mathbf{p}\boldsymbol{\omega}$. Now this reproducible solution is the type studied in Chapter 2, because there is no capital market at the JPM equilibrium – and so the FMT 2.11 applies: Total profits are positive if and only if there is a point allowing positive exploitation in the aggregate production set P. But total profits in this JPM economy are identical to total profits in the economy *with* capital market, at a reproducible solution. Hence, the theorem remains true in the presence of the capital market. That the other sections of Theorem 2.11 remain true here is easily verified from the existence theorems of the previous section.

That the FMT remains true with a capital market has one implication worth mentioning. What allows an equilibrium with positive profits to exist in a model with constant-returns-to-scale technology? (After all, in neoclassical general equilibrium, profits must be zero at such an equilibrium.) It is the assumption, in the models of the chapter, that capitalists maximize profits constrained by the availability of capital. After all, if a capitalist possessed infinite wealth, he could not maximize profits with a CRTS technology, if positive profits were anywhere possible. It is this assumption of a capital constraint that provides for the existence of equilibria with positive profits in the general case. This said, one might think that if the capital constraint on a capitalist were weakened in some important way, positive-profit equilibria might not occur (again, with CRTS technology). Now the introduction of a capital market apparently weakens the capital constraint – for a capitalist can borrow any amount he wishes on the credit market, or lend any amount he wishes. Because the capital constraint is weakened one might expect positive-profit reproducible solutions not to exist.

However, because the FMT holds for the economy, this is not the case. In fact, by that theorem, for any linear technology (for instance) for which the rate of exploitation is positive, a reproducible solution with positive profits exists, even in the presence of the capital market. Thus, the existence of positive-profit equilibria is not to be associated with the institution of internal financing of capitalist production; rather, it is to be associated with the necessity of time in production, that capitalists must advance the costs of production before they receive the revenues from production. It is this temporal structure of production that gives rise to the economic necessity of a capital constraint, whether or not funds for production are limited to internal finance or are available on a capital market.

It may appear to be a small step from the position that has been developed to this point to the neoclassical/Austrian position, which says that *because* of the temporal structure of production, profits are a return to the capitalist for providing the factor capital, or that interest is the reward for waiting. This position, however, certainly does not follow from the model here. All that has been proved is that the interest rate will be positive if and only if workers are exploited, in the sense of receiving in value terms less than the value of their labor. If one wishes to interpret the interest rate as a "return to the capitalist" or a "price of waiting," one would need some additional structure that a Marxian model does not possess. For instance, for the interest rate to be a price of waiting, one would need to endow capitalists with some utility function that made them suffer from lending out their capital. As Marx pointed out in *Capital,* it is more appropriate to think of capitalists as suffering while abstaining from accumulating, rather than while abstaining from consuming.

The second feature of capitalist economy, together with the temporal structure of production, that accounts for positive profits and exploitation is the differential distribution of produced assets. Some producers enter the economy with stocks of goods, and others have only their labor power to sell. To reproduce themselves, the disenfranchised producers have no option but to sell their labor power to those who possess capital.[2] If there are sufficient numbers of workers competing for employment by a limited stock of capital, the real wage will be bid sufficiently low to sustain a positive rate of interest or profit. Some bourgeois explanations or justifications of profits, therefore, attempt to justify the original differential distribution of endowments. Perhaps producers had different rates of time preference; some accumulated endowments and others ate them up. Marx's historical study of the primitive or original accumulation of capital (*Capital,* Volume I) attacks this suggestion. The precondition for capitalism was the forced disenfrachisement of petty producers (for example, the enclosure movement in England). Plunder, robbery, and power are more appropriate categories than rates of time preference for explaining why producers enter our model with different stocks.

Other endogenous characteristics of agents are sometimes held to explain the differential endowment distribution: the possession of different skills, or different attitudes toward the acquisition of skills and different attitudes toward risk. Suppose, for example, that entreprenurial ability is a scarce skill, and suppose as well that the accumulation of the great capitalist fortunes is explainable by entrepreneurship – a not uncontested claim. (In the models of this book, entrepreneurship could be the factor that differentiates the production sets to which different capitalists have access.) Then profits can be viewed as a rent to entreprenurial ability. Workers are exchanging their "surplus" labor time for the benefits that accrue to them from the exercise of entreprenurial talent that they do not possess. The language of "profits are the return to entreprenurial talent" implies, however, something in addition: either that profits are the just return to entrepreneurship, or, less grandly, that they are the *necessary* return for eliciting it. There is no good justification for the first claim, and there is evidence that the necessary return to entrepreneurship is considerably less than profits. For in modern capitalism, entrepreneurship is exercised by hired managers who presumably are paid the necessary, competitive wage for their skill, while capitalists are, in principle, the coupon clippers who at best exercise the "skill" of choosing the most competent manager. Pressing the point still further, it can be argued that although profits are not entirely exhausted by the necessary payments to entrepreneurship, still profits are necessary, for the capitalist coupon clippers will not seek or authorize new investment projects that are risky without the expectation of profits. But, if this is so, it need not be taken as proof that capitalist profits are necessary, but rather as evidence that capitalism is a poor mechanism for organizing investment activity, as contrasted with a socialist investment mechanism. The correct statement is, at best, that profits are the necessary return to risky investment activity *given the constraint* of private ownership of the means of production. Clearly this statement cannot be taken to justify what qualifies it, namely those private ownership relations.[3]

In summary, the key assumptions that bring about positive profits in equilibrium in the models of this book are: the temporal structure of production; the differential endowments of produced assets; and the abundance of a class of agents, relative to the capital stock which can employ them, who do not have sufficient endowments to reproduce themselves without selling labor power to other asset holders. It does not follow, however, that profits are, therefore, a just or even necessary return to capitalists for advancing their assets in production. Wage payments in real form must go to workers for the factor labor power to be reproduced. Payments for capital, however, need not go to capitalists to reproduce capital; that is, capitalists need not be reproduced to reproduce social investment funds. Profits are a genuine social surplus in the precise sense that their distribution is determined by property relations, which are guaranteed ultimately by institutions of power and authority, and not by some objectively necessary economic law.

4 Viable and progressive technical change and the rising rate of profit

4.1 Introduction

Before beginning the technical discussion of the theory of the falling rate of profit, it is worthwhile recalling Marx's intellectual project in proposing his theory. Falling-rate-of-profit theories were a standard part of the armor of classical economics. The theories of Ricardo and Malthus were driven by diminishing returns in the natural productivity of the earth: As society was forced to adopt inferior land for agriculture, an increasing part of the economic surplus would be absorbed as rent, with a correspondingly smaller part available for profits. Hence, the rate of profit would fall as a natural, immutable consequence of a growing population, independent of what social and economic system prevailed.

Marx's aim was to show, on the contrary, that the rate of profit would fall as a consequence of the specific laws of motion of *capitalist* economy. As with so many other questions, he spurned general laws (that is, laws that purported to apply to all modes of production) and sought to locate developments such as a falling rate of profit in a historically specific context. Thus Marx proposed a falling-rate-of-profit theory that was driven by the specific form of technical change he conceived of as taking place under capitalism. There is no diminishing returns aspect to the argument. Although it will be shown in this chapter and the following one that Marx's theoretical conjecture was incorrect, his general methodological insight – that any crisis theory should be specific to the mode of production it seeks to describe – still stands. Furthermore, his skepticism of the diminishing returns argument has proved correct. At least so far in history, technology has succeeded in making obsolete all theories of diminishing returns.

Indeed, the general insight of the Marxian falling-rate-of-profit theory can fruitfully be applied today. In our generation, a host of new neo-Ricardian – Malthusian "falling-rate-of-profit" arguments have arisen. I refer to the gamut of theories that view continued progress of mankind as resource limited. This takes various forms: The rate of population growth is too high, there is not enough food to feed the world, there is not enough energy to run our technology, we shall strangle ourselves in pollution. What these theories all have in common is a tendency to locate the "crisis" in a natural phenomenon, natural in the sense that it is quite independent of the social system. This world view is corollary to the neoclassical characterization of economics as the study of scarcity – that is, of how to allocate scarce resources among competing projects. (The scarcity approach casts the economic problem as independent of social system.)

A Marxist does not deny that population growth, food production, and lack of oil are genuine problems. But, taking Marx's cue, one should not locate the problem in natural causes. In fact, to turn the usual accusation around, this approach of bourgeois social scientists is technologically determinist (or vulgar materialist) in the worst sense. The working postulate should be that crises are a consequence of the laws of motion of late capitalist society. They can be resolved by changing the social and economic system. It is not our purpose here to defend this viewpoint in any detail, but rather to point out the ideological controversy concerning the question of global resources that exists today and parallels the controversy that prompted Marx to propose his specifically capitalist theory of the falling rate of profit. It is the historical–materialist posture that is the deep contribution of Marx to crisis theory, and that has still not made sufficient impact on social science.[1]

It is, in a sense, a shame that we must spend so much effort in the next several chapters criticizing the specific mechanism that Marx proposed for bringing about a falling rate of profit under capitalism, as such a discussion can distract attention from the important Marxian methodological approach discussed above. Yet it is mandatory that this critique be made in depth, because among Marxists, the specific falling-rate-of-profit mechanism of Marx is still largely accepted as true. To the extent that investigators remain wedded to this incorrect theory, creative research into a capitalist theory of crisis is stymied. Indeed, the dogmatism that has been associated with the theory of the "rising organic composition of capital" has been one of the heaviest palls on the development of a creative Marxian project to study the laws of motion of modern capitalist society. It is obviously correct that economic crises are endemic to capitalism, and to advanced capitalism. Neoclassical economics has its own blindfold on this question – the inability to explain satisfactorily unemployment in a market economy – and Marxian economics has its chalice, the rising-organic-composition–falling-rate-of-profit theory. Before progress can be made, at least for Marxists, the chalice must be cast aside.

Marx's formulation of the mechanism of the falling rate of profit is, briefly, this: The rate of profit is given by $\pi = S/(C + V) = eV/(C + V)$, where C and V are the values of constant and variable capital, S is surplus value, and e is the (uniform) rate of surplus value. Hence, $\pi = e/(k + 1)$, where $k = C/V$ is the social organic composition of capital. Now if technical change has the effect of increasing k – as capital is substituted for labor because of class struggle, innovation, and competition – then over time, π decreases, if e remains unchanged. However, e may increase, due to the cheapening (in labor-value terms) of the workers' subsistence bundle as a result of technological advance, and hence the increase in k may be offset. The fall in π, then, remains only a tendency. In fact, we shall show that the increase in k is *always* offset by the simultaneous increase in e.

On an even vaguer, more intuitive level, the insight behind the falling-rate-of-profit mechanism is this: Profits come from the exploitation of living labor. Technical change replaces living labor with machines (the rising organic composition of capital). With less living labor to exploit, the rate of profit should fall. What the argument avoids is a precise treatment of what happens to the rate of exploitation as a consequence of the technical change.

As several authors have pointed out, there is no reason to believe that the various "countervailing factors" (such as the cheapening of the wage bundle) do not offset the rise in k. [See, for instance, Sweezy (1942).] The discussions of the falling rate of profit, moreover, frequently fail to distinguish between the rate of profit in price terms and the value rate of profit, the latter being $S/(C + V)$. When the value rate of profit is used, there is little or no concern with the problem that the value rate of profit changes with the output mix. (That is, S, C, and V are aggregate value quantities, aggregated at a particular set of sectoral outputs.) Marx's discussion, and the discussions of many (though not all) writers since then, are concerned with movements in the value rate of profit; any conclusions concerning the viability or efficiency of capitalism must ultimately consider the price rate of profit, which is the measure of the system's efficiency in *realizing* surplus value. It is this aspect of the transformation problem that is muddied.

In the next section, the relationship between the value rate of profit and the price rate of profit will be clarified. It will then be possible to ask if movements in the value rate of profit as a result of technical change mirror movements in the price rate of profit – if so, then the confusion alluded to in ignoring the transformation problem is of no great import. Then, the effects of various types of technical change on the price rate of profit will be assessed. We shall show that if the real wage remains constant then the technical changes which capitalists will introduce always produce a rise in the rate of profit. There are, however, types of "socially desirable" technical change that will not be introduced by capitalists, and some of these would produce a fall in the rate of profit. This classification between technical changes that are "viable" under capitalism and that are "progressive" is arrived at by evaluating technologies with respect to prices of production and labor values, respectively.

In this chapter, we make the argument as simple as possible by postulating a pure circulating capital, Leontief model like the one studied in Chapter 1. This model has been the traditional environment for studying the Marxian falling rate of profit. In the next chapter, we show that the same theorem holds for a von Neumann technology; hence the rate of profit will rise, in a competitive fixed-wage model, even in the presence of fixed capital, joint products, differential turnover times, and all the general aspects of production that can be captured in the von Neumann model.

Finally, we shall assume that the real wage remains unchanged as a consequence of the technical change under discussion. This is also the traditional postulate to make in this discussion. In Chapter 6 we weaken this assumption, and investigate a falling-rate-of-profit model where the real wage adjusts as a consequence of technical change.

Several mathematical results on eigenvalues of positive matrices are needed for the development here, as well as a formula developed by Morishima–Seton. These are presented in an appendix to the chapter.

4.2 The value and price rates of profit

The model is specified thus: Let there be m commodities, the first n of which are capital goods (department I). Only capital goods and direct labor enter into production of capital goods and wage goods. (The wage goods, department II, are commodities $n + 1$ through m.) Let:

A_{I} be the $n \times n$ matrix of input–output coefficients for department I

A_{II} be the $n \times (m - n)$ matrix of input–output coefficients for department II

$\mathbf{L}_I$ be the n row vector of direct labor inputs, measured in worker-days, for department I

$\mathbf{L}_{II}$ be the $(m - n)$ row vector of direct labor inputs for department II

$\mathbf{b}$ be the $(m - n)$ column vector that is each worker's daily consumption bundle of wage goods

π be the price rate of profit

It is assumed that there are no alternative production techniques, no joint products, and that all capital circulates in the unit time of production, which is the same for all commodities. It is clear, then, that the row vectors of labor values $\mathbf{\Lambda}_I$ and $\mathbf{\Lambda}_{II}$ for the two departments are defined by

$$\mathbf{\Lambda}_I = \mathbf{\Lambda}_I A_I + \mathbf{L}_I \tag{4.1}$$

$$\mathbf{\Lambda}_{II} = \mathbf{\Lambda}_I A_{II} + \mathbf{L}_{II} \tag{4.2}$$

and the vectors of wage–prices, $\mathbf{p}_I$ and $\mathbf{p}_{II}$, and rate of profit satisfy

$$\mathbf{p}_I = (1 + \pi)(\mathbf{p}_I A_I + \mathbf{L}_I) \tag{4.3}$$

$$\mathbf{p}_{II} = (1 + \pi)(\mathbf{p}_I A_{II} + \mathbf{L}_{II}) \tag{4.4}$$

[For a development of this standard model, see Morishima (1973).]

We adopt the usual assumptions that A_I is productive and indecomposable, thus assuring that values are positive and that there is a positive profit rate satisfying (4.3), (4.4), and the budget constraint

$$1 = \mathbf{p}_{II} \cdot \mathbf{b} \tag{4.5}$$

(Note that the workers' daily wage is unity.)

In addition, we adopt the assumption that there are no luxury goods; that is, $\mathbf{b} > 0$. This assumption can be dropped without drastically changing the results; however, the assumption makes the proofs somewhat simpler.

At this point, it might be mentioned that the specific structure of a two-department technology, which has been assumed here, is not at all necessary for a study of this problem. Indeed, the whole argument is algebraically simpler if we simply assume one technology $(A, \mathbf{L})$ as in Chapter 1. The main result, in that case, becomes that if A is an indecomposable matrix, then the rate of profit must rise as a consequence of competitive technological change; if A is decomposable, the rate of profit may stay the same; but in no case will it fall. Nevertheless, despite the elegance gained by assuming the model $(A, \mathbf{L})$, it is thought advisable, in this chapter, to display the more conventional two-department model, thereby adhering closely to the original Marxian formulation. This, then, is a small concession to the long debate that has existed on the question of the falling rate of profit. The effort is to treat the problem in as classical a framework as possible.

Let the $m \times m$ matrix M be defined as

$$M = \begin{pmatrix} A_{\mathrm{I}} & A_{\mathrm{II}} \\ \mathbf{bL}_{\mathrm{I}} & \mathbf{bL}_{\mathrm{II}} \end{pmatrix} \tag{4.6}$$

M is the matrix of "augmented input coefficients." The ith column of M specifies the capital inputs and wage good inputs that must enter the production of the ith commodity, the wage good inputs entering through consumption of workers "used" in production. The assumption of no luxury goods, along with the indecomposability of A_{I}, enables us to conclude that M is indecomposable.[2]

The row vectors of constant and variable capital are defined as

$$\begin{aligned} \mathbf{C} &= \langle \mathbf{\Lambda}_{\mathrm{I}} A_{\mathrm{I}}, \mathbf{\Lambda}_{\mathrm{I}} A_{\mathrm{II}} \rangle \\ \mathbf{V} &= \langle (\mathbf{\Lambda}_{\mathrm{II}} \mathbf{b}) \mathbf{L}_{\mathrm{I}}, (\mathbf{\Lambda}_{\mathrm{II}} \mathbf{b}) \mathbf{L}_{\mathrm{II}} \rangle \\ \mathbf{S} &= e\mathbf{V} \end{aligned} \tag{4.7}$$

where the rate of exploitation is given by

$$e = \frac{1 - \mathbf{\Lambda}_{\mathrm{II}} \mathbf{b}}{\mathbf{\Lambda}_{\mathrm{II}} \mathbf{b}} \tag{4.8}$$

These preliminaries stated, how is the value rate of profit defined? It must be defined at a particular set of output levels, to be used as aggregators.

DEFINITION 4.1: The value rate of profit for an economy at an output (column) vector $\mathbf{x}$ is

$$\nu(\mathbf{x}) = \frac{\mathbf{S} \cdot \mathbf{x}}{\mathbf{C} \cdot \mathbf{x} + \mathbf{V} \cdot \mathbf{x}} \tag{4.9}$$

Let us also define the value rate of profit in the ith sector.

DEFINITION 4.2: The value rate of profit in the ith sector is

$$\nu_i = \frac{S_i}{C_i + V_i}$$

where C_i, V_i, S_i are components of the vectors **C, V, S.**

It is then possible to express the value rate of profit as follows:

THEOREM 4.1: The value rate of profit $\nu(\mathbf{x})$ is the harmonic mean of the sectoral value rates of profit, with sectoral weights given by the fraction of society's total direct labor time expended in that sector under production vector **x**. This is,

$$\nu(\mathbf{x}) = (\Sigma\, a_i \nu_i^{-1})^{-1}$$

where

$$a_i = \frac{l_i x_i}{\mathbf{L} \cdot \mathbf{x}}$$

Proof: By definition of $\nu(\mathbf{x})$,

$$\nu(\mathbf{x}) = \frac{e}{k(\mathbf{x}) + 1} \tag{4.10}$$

where $k(\mathbf{x}) = (\mathbf{C} \cdot \mathbf{x})/(\mathbf{V} \cdot \mathbf{x})$. $k(\mathbf{x})$ is the social organic composition of capital. Let $k_i = C_i/V_i$ be the sectoral organic composition of capital. Then

$$k(\mathbf{x}) = \frac{\Sigma\, C_i x_i}{\Sigma\, V_i x_i} = \frac{\Sigma\, k_i V_i x_i}{\Sigma\, V_i x_i} = \Sigma\, k_i \left(\frac{V_i x_i}{\Sigma\, V_j x_j}\right) \tag{4.11}$$

Let $a_i = V_i x_i / \Sigma\, V_j x_j$. Then, from (4.10) and (4.11),

$$\nu(\mathbf{x}) = \frac{e}{\Sigma\, a_i k_i + 1} = \frac{e}{\Sigma\, a_i (k_i + 1)} \tag{4.12}$$

this last following because $\Sigma\, a_i = 1$. From (4.12),

$$\frac{1}{\nu(\mathbf{x})} = \Sigma\, a_i \left(\frac{k_i + 1}{e}\right) = a_i \nu_i^{-1} \tag{4.13}$$

from which it follows that

$$\nu(\mathbf{x}) = (\Sigma\, a_i \nu_i^{-1})^{-1} \tag{4.14}$$

Finally,

$$a_i = \frac{V_i x_i}{\mathbf{V} \cdot \mathbf{x}} = \frac{l_i x_i}{\mathbf{L} \cdot \mathbf{x}},$$

by (4.7), and the result is shown. Q.E.D.

COROLLARY 4.2: The price rate of profit is given by

$$\pi = [a_i(\mathbf{y}) \nu_i^{-1}]^{-1}$$

where **y** is the von Neumann "golden age" output vector, and

$$a_i(\mathbf{y}) = \frac{l_i y_i}{\mathbf{L} \cdot \mathbf{y}}$$

Proof: The proof follows directly from Theorem 4.1 and the Morishima–Seton transformation formula (Theorem 4.15, in the appendix to this chapter).

The theorem and corollary illustrate how any particular value rate of profit and the price rate of profit can be viewed as certain harmonic means of the sectoral value rates of profit. The question arises as to whether the price rate of profit, π, occupies any special position in the range of possible value rates of profit. To specify this question more precisely we define the following:

DEFINITION 4.3: An output vector $\mathbf{x}$ is feasible if and only if $\mathbf{x} \geqq 0$ and $M\mathbf{x} \leqq \mathbf{x}$. Let the set of feasible outputs be called $X = \{\mathbf{x} \mid \mathbf{x} \geq 0, M\mathbf{x} \leqq \mathbf{x}\}$.

Because $M\mathbf{x}$ is the vector of inputs consumed in the process of producing $\mathbf{x}$, an output vector is feasible if it generates a nonnegative vector of final demands, $\mathbf{x} - M\mathbf{x}$. We limit ourselves to such output vectors, as the reasonable output vectors to examine in a stationary state. Notice that X is a convex cone. As the function $\nu(\mathbf{x})$ ranges over $X - \{0\}$, it achieves a maximum and minimum. This follows because $\nu(\mathbf{x})$ is constant along any ray, hence it is sufficient to examine the values along some hyperplane cutting X; that is, a compact set such as $X \cap \{\mathbf{x} \mid \mathbf{L}\mathbf{x} = \mathbf{L}_0\}$. Denote the max and min values that $\nu(\mathbf{x})$ achieves on $X - \{0\}$ as ν_{max} and ν_{min}.

THEOREM 4.3: If the sectoral organic compositions are all equal, then $\nu_{min} = \pi = \nu_{max}$. Otherwise, $\nu_{min} < \pi < \nu_{max}$.

Proof: The first statement is easily verified by Theorem 4.1. So we suppose that the ν_i are not all the same. Notice that the eigenvector $\mathbf{y}$ is in the interior of X; this follows from Theorem 4.15, because $y = (1 + \pi)M\mathbf{y}$ and $\mathbf{y} > 0$, so $\mathbf{y} > M\mathbf{y}$.

$$\text{Recall that } k(\mathbf{x}) = \frac{\mathbf{C}\mathbf{x}}{\mathbf{V}\mathbf{x}} = \frac{\Lambda_I A_I \mathbf{x}_I + \Lambda_I A_{II} \mathbf{x}_{II}}{\mathbf{L}\mathbf{x}} \tag{4.15}$$

If $\nu(\mathbf{x})$ possesses an extremum in the interior of X, at $\mathbf{x}^*$, then we must have

$$\frac{\partial k}{\partial \mathbf{x}}(\mathbf{x}^*) = 0.$$

Differentiating (4.15),

$$\frac{\partial k}{\partial x_i} = \begin{cases} \dfrac{(\mathbf{Lx})(\Lambda_I A_I)_i - (\Lambda A\mathbf{x})l_i}{(\mathbf{Lx})^2} & \text{for } i = 1, n \\[2ex] \dfrac{(\mathbf{Lx})(\Lambda_I A_{II})_i - (\Lambda A\mathbf{x})\mathbf{l}_i}{(\mathbf{Lx})^2} & \text{for } i = n+1, m \end{cases} \tag{4.16}$$

from which it follows that $(\partial k/\partial \mathbf{x})(\mathbf{x}^*) = 0$ if and only if

$$(\mathbf{Lx}^*)\Lambda_I A = (\Lambda A\mathbf{x}^*)\mathbf{L} \tag{4.17}$$

But (4.17) means that the vector of constant capitals, $\Lambda_I A$, is proportional to the vector of labor inputs, $\mathbf{L}$; that is, all sectors have the same organic composition of capital. Because we have assumed this not to be the case, $k(\mathbf{x})$ cannot achieve an extremum in the interior of X; hence, $\nu(\mathbf{y}) = \pi$ cannot be an extremum of $\nu(\mathbf{x})$ on X, because $\mathbf{y} \in$ interior X. Q.E.D.

Theorem 4.3 adds to the characterization of the relationship between the price and value rates of profit: The value rate of profit can be greater or smaller than the price rate. A further implication will be discussed presently.

We next answer the question whether the value rate of profit and the price rate of profit necessarily move in the same direction as a result of technical change.

THEOREM 4.4: Let a technology be specified $\{A_I, A_{II}, \mathbf{L}_I, \mathbf{L}_{II}, \mathbf{b}\}$, with an associated profit rate π_0. Then there is a perturbed technology $A_I^*, A_{II}^*, \mathbf{L}_I^*, \mathbf{L}_{II}^*, \mathbf{b}$ with associated profit rate π^* such that $\pi^* < \pi_0$ but $\nu^*(\mathbf{x}) > \nu(\mathbf{x})$, where $\nu^*(\mathbf{x})$, $\nu(\mathbf{x})$ are the value rates of profit for the two technologies calculated at some output vector $\mathbf{x}$ that is feasible for both technologies.

Proof: We begin by perturbing only $\mathbf{L}_{II}$ and asking: What is the set of vectors $\mathbf{L}_{II}^*$ that will render the profit rate in the perturbed technology $\{A_I, A_{II}, \mathbf{L}_I, \mathbf{L}_{II}^*, \mathbf{b}\}$ unchanged at π_0? That is, define:

$$\Psi_{\pi_0} = \{\mathbf{L}_{II}^* \mid \pi(\mathbf{L}_{II}^*) = \pi_0\}$$

(We denote π as a function of $\mathbf{L}_{II}^*$ because all other parameters in the determination of π are fixed. See Equations 4.3, 4.4, 4.5.) From Equation 4.3, the solution $\mathbf{p}_I$ does not vary with $\mathbf{L}_{II}^*$ as long as π remains fixed; that is, $\mathbf{p}_I = \mathbf{p}_I(\pi)$. From Equations 4.4 and 4.5, $\mathbf{L}_{II}^* \in \Psi_{\pi_0}$ if and only if:

$$(1 + \pi_0)[\mathbf{p}_I(\pi_0)A_{II} + \mathbf{L}_{II}^*]\mathbf{b} = 1 \tag{4.18}$$

from which it follows that

$$\Psi_{\pi_0} = \{\mathbf{L}_{\text{II}}^* \mid \mathbf{L}_{\text{II}}^*\mathbf{b} = \mathbf{L}_{\text{II}}\mathbf{b}\} \tag{4.19}$$

Notice, now, that $\mathbf{\Lambda}_{\text{I}}$ remains unchanged as $\mathbf{L}_{\text{II}}$ varies, by (4.1); hence, by (4.2) and (4.19), $\mathbf{\Lambda}_{\text{II}}\mathbf{b}$ remains unchanged as $\mathbf{L}_{\text{II}}^*$ varies over Ψ_{π_0}, because

$$\mathbf{\Lambda}_{\text{II}}^*\mathbf{b} = \mathbf{\Lambda}_{\text{I}}A_{\text{II}}\mathbf{b} + \mathbf{L}_{\text{II}}^*\mathbf{b} = \mathbf{\Lambda}_{\text{I}}A_{\text{II}}\mathbf{b} + \mathbf{L}_{\text{II}}\mathbf{b} = \mathbf{\Lambda}_{\text{II}}\mathbf{b} \tag{4.20}$$

Hence, the rate of exploitation, e, remains unchanged as $\mathbf{L}_{\text{II}}^*$ varies over Ψ_{π_0} [see (4.8)].

Now

$$\nu(\mathbf{x}) = \frac{e}{(\mathbf{Cx}/\mathbf{Vx}) + 1} = \frac{e}{(e + 1)\,(\mathbf{Cx}/\mathbf{Lx}) + 1} \tag{4.21}$$

As $\mathbf{L}_{\text{II}}$ varies, the vector $\mathbf{C}$ remains fixed. The vector $\mathbf{L} = \langle \mathbf{L}_{\text{I}}, \mathbf{L}_{\text{II}} \rangle$, of course, changes. If $\mathbf{L}_{\text{II}}$ is perturbed slightly to $\mathbf{L}_{\text{II}}^*$, then the cone $X(\mathbf{L}_{\text{II}})$ is perturbed slightly to a new feasible cone $X(\mathbf{L}_{\text{II}}^*)$ for the new technology. It is clear that $\mathbf{x} \in X(\mathbf{L}_{\text{II}}) \cap X(\mathbf{L}_{\text{II}}^*)$ can be chosen so that $\nu^*(\mathbf{x}) > \nu(\mathbf{x})$, by (4.21). (That is, e and $\mathbf{C}$ remain fixed, as has been shown, so we need only choose $\mathbf{L}_{\text{II}}^*$ and $\mathbf{x}$ such that $\mathbf{L}_{\text{II}}^*\mathbf{x}_{\text{II}} > \mathbf{L}_{\text{II}}\mathbf{x}_{\text{II}}$.)[3]

We have, at this point, a perturbed augmented input coefficient matrix

$$M' = \begin{pmatrix} A_{\text{I}} & A_{\text{II}} \\ \mathbf{bL}_{\text{I}} & \mathbf{bL}_{\text{II}}^* \end{pmatrix}$$

Now increase some component of A_{I} to form a new matrix M^*. Because M^* is indecomposable (by assumption $\mathbf{b} > 0$), by Theorem 4.13 (see appendix), the eigenvalue $\lambda^* > \lambda'$. Because $\lambda = 1/(1 + \pi) = \lambda'$ and $\lambda^* = 1/(1 + \pi^*)$, by Theorem 4.15, $\pi^* < \pi$. Furthermore, the perturbation of M' to M^* can be made small enough so that the new $\nu^*(\mathbf{x})$ remains larger than $\nu(\mathbf{x})$ and $\mathbf{x}$ remains feasible, because $\nu(\mathbf{x})$ varies continuously with the technology. Thus the original technology $\{A_{\text{I}}, A_{\text{II}}, \mathbf{L}_{\text{I}}, \mathbf{L}_{\text{II}}\}$ has been perturbed to a technology $\{A_{\text{I}}^*, A_{\text{II}}, \mathbf{L}_{\text{I}}, \mathbf{L}_{\text{II}}^*\}$ in such a way that $\pi^* < \pi$ and $\nu^*(\mathbf{x}) > \nu(\mathbf{x})$. Q.E.D.

The implications of Theorem 4.3 and 4.4 can now be summarized. Theorem 4.4 says that one cannot infer the direction of movement of π from the direction of movement of $\nu(\mathbf{x})$, as a consequence of technical change. However, Theorem 4.3 says that if technical change is sufficient to shift the whole *range* of values $[\nu_{\min}, \nu_{\max}]$ to a new range $[\nu_{\min}^*, \nu_{\max}^*]$ such that $\nu_{\min}^* \geqq \nu_{\max}$, then certainly $\pi^* > \pi$. In particular, we have according to the harmonic mean formula (Theorem 4.1) that $\nu_{\min} \geqq \min \nu_i$ and $\nu_{\max} \leqq \max \nu_i$. Thus, if technical change is sufficiently great to render $\min \nu_i^* \geq \max \nu_i$, then in fact $\pi^* > \pi$. In summary, for small technical changes, the profit rate and the value rate of profit may move differently; for sufficiently dramatic (long-run?) technical change, however, the two rates of profit move in the same direction. In this light, one can evaluate the various arguments on the falling rate of profit that restrict themselves to an analysis of the value rate of profit alone.

4.3 The effect of technical change on the rate of profit

There is considerable disagreement on the effect of technical change on the rate of profit. Morishima (1973) shows that for a certain category of technical change, the price rate of profit must fall (see later); Samuelson claims that for any kind of technical change that profit-maximizing capitalists would introduce, the rate of profit rises (1972, p. 54); and Okishio, in a little-known paper (1961), shows that the price rate of profit must rise for a certain class of reasonable technical changes. In this section, the result of Okishio is resurrected and extended, and it is shown when technical changes generate a rise or a fall in the equilibrium price rate of profit.

First, a rather obvious proposition is shown: that if the technology after technical change does not use more of any input for any process than it did before, the profit rate for the economy increases.

THEOREM 4.5: Let M be the augmented input coefficient matrix before technical change, and M^* the matrix after technical change, and $M^* \leq M$. Then $\pi^* > \pi$.

Proof: M is indecomposable, as has been shown. By Theorem 4.13 (see the appendix to this chapter), $\lambda^* < \lambda$ and hence, by Theorem 4.15, $\pi^* > \pi$. Q.E.D.

This sort of technical change is not very interesting. Okishio (1961) has posited a more reasonable criterion for technical innovation. Capitalists will introduce a new technology if it is cost-reducing, at current prices. Such a technical change is called *viable.*

THEOREM 4.6: If technical change is introduced by capitalists only when it is cost reducing at current prices, then the equilibrium rate of profit will rise.

Notice that this theorem is not obvious. Clearly, if a capitalist introduces a cost-reducing technical change, his short-run rate of profit rises. This, however, produces a disequilibrium; what the theorem says is that after prices have readjusted to equilibrate the rate of profit again, the new rate of profit will be higher than the old rate.

Proof of Theorem 4.6: Before technical change, the current equilibrium prices are a vector $\mathbf{p} > \mathbf{0}$ such that:

$$\begin{aligned} \mathbf{p}M &= \lambda \mathbf{p} \\ &= \frac{1}{1+\pi}\mathbf{p} \end{aligned} \tag{4.22}$$

Let $\mathbf{m}_i$ be the ith column of M. Then, by definition,

$$\frac{\mathbf{p} \cdot \mathbf{m}_i}{p_i} = \lambda \qquad i = 1, m \tag{4.23}$$

The new technology for a particular sector, $\mathbf{m}_{i_0}^*$, is cost-reducing at current prices, then, if and only if:

$$\frac{\mathbf{p} \cdot \mathbf{m}_{i_0}^*}{p_{i_0}} < \lambda \tag{4.24}$$

(The cost of operating the ith process is $\mathbf{p}\mathbf{m}_i$.) Let M^* be the matrix M with $\mathbf{m}_{i_0}$ replaced by $\mathbf{m}_{i_0}^*$. (Rename the columns of M^* as $\mathbf{m}_i^*$.) By Theorem 4.14 in the appendix to this chapter, the eigenvalue λ^* of M^* obeys

$$\min_i \frac{\mathbf{p} \cdot \mathbf{m}_i^*}{p_i} < \lambda^* < \max_i \frac{\mathbf{p} \cdot \mathbf{m}_i^*}{p_i} \tag{4.25}$$

Since we know

$$\min_i \frac{\mathbf{p} \cdot \mathbf{m}_i^*}{p_i} = \frac{\mathbf{p} \cdot \mathbf{m}_{i_0}^*}{p_{i_0}} < \frac{\mathbf{p} \cdot \mathbf{m}_{i_0}}{p_{i_0}} = \max_i \frac{\mathbf{p} \cdot \mathbf{m}_i^*}{p_i} = \lambda \tag{4.26}$$

it follows that $\lambda^* < \lambda$, and hence $\pi^* > \pi$. Q.E.D.

Theorem 4.6 settles, in a fundamental way, the Marxian conjecture of a falling rate of profit due to competitive innovations by price-taking capitalists. It is essentially the end of the classical story. We shall continue, nevertheless, to discuss other points that have appeared in the literature on the question.

Another type of technical change is suggested by Morishima (1973, p. 142). He assumes that technical change is *capital-using* ($a_{ij}^* \geq a_{ij}$) and *labor-saving* ($l_j^* \leq l_j$). There is some basis for thinking that this was the type of technical change Marx foresaw, and indeed, the type of technical change that does in fact occur. Morishima furthermore posits that technical change be *neutral* in the sense of leaving values (Λ_{I}, Λ_{II}) unchanged. Morishima shows that such neutral technical change necessarily implies a fall in the rate of profit when all department I sectors have equal organic compositions, and all department II sectors have equal organic compositions. The next proposition shows this to be true in general.

THEOREM 4.7: Let capital-using, labor-saving (CU–LS), neutral technical change occur: $A_I^* \geq A_I$, $A_{II}^* \geq A_{II}$, $\mathbf{L}_I^* \leq \mathbf{L}_I$, $\mathbf{L}_{II}^* \leq \mathbf{L}_{II}$, $\mathbf{\Lambda} = \mathbf{\Lambda}^*$. Then $\pi^* < \pi$.

This result, to say the least, is quite different from that of Theorem 4.6. In fact, we conclude: Neutral technical change is not viable! That is, competitive capitalists will never introduce neutral technical changes. Hence, the falling rate of profit of Theorem 4.7 is not very interesting. It is on these grounds that Samuelson (1972, p. 68) chides Morishima – the type of technical change the latter posits will never occur in a profit-maximizing world where capitalists treat prices as given.[4]

Proof of Theorem 4.7: Let M be the augmented input coefficient matrix for the original technology and

$$\mathbf{p}M = \lambda\mathbf{p} \tag{4.27}$$

Because values remain unchanged, we have

$$\begin{aligned} \lambda_i &= \mathbf{\Lambda}_I\mathbf{a}_i + l_i \\ \lambda_i &= \mathbf{\Lambda}_I\mathbf{a}_i^* + l_i^* \end{aligned} \tag{4.28}$$

where $\mathbf{a}_i$, $\mathbf{a}_i^*$ are columns of A_I, A_I^*. From (4.28) it follows that

$$l_i - l_i^* = \mathbf{\Lambda}_I(\mathbf{a}_i^* - \mathbf{a}_i) \tag{4.29}$$

Let M^* be the augmented input coefficient matrix for the * technology. Then

$$\begin{aligned} \mathbf{pm}_i &= \mathbf{p}_I\mathbf{a}_i + \mathbf{p}_{II}\mathbf{b}l_i = \mathbf{p}_I\mathbf{a}_i + l_i \\ \mathbf{pm}_i^* &= \mathbf{p}_I\mathbf{a}_i^* + l_i^* \end{aligned} \tag{4.30}$$

Hence

$$\mathbf{pm}_i^* - \mathbf{pm}_i = \mathbf{p}_I(\mathbf{a}_i^* - \mathbf{a}_i) + (l_i^* - l_i) \tag{4.31}$$

Substituting from (4.29) into (4.31) yields

$$\mathbf{pm}_i^* - \mathbf{pm}_i = (\mathbf{p}_I - \mathbf{\Lambda}_I)(\mathbf{a}_i^* - \mathbf{a}_i) \tag{4.32}$$

Now it is well known that $\mathbf{p}_I > \mathbf{\Lambda}_I$, as long as $\pi > 0$, and we are given $\mathbf{a}_i^* \geq \mathbf{a}_i$ (let us assume that technical change has taken place in sector i, so that $\mathbf{a}_i^* \neq \mathbf{a}_i$). Then, from (4.32),

$$\mathbf{pm}_i^* > \mathbf{pm}_i \tag{4.33}$$

and so

$$\frac{\mathbf{pm}_i^*}{p_i} > \frac{\mathbf{pm}_i}{p_i} \tag{4.34}$$

From this argument, it follows that $\mathbf{pm}_i^*/p_i > \mathbf{pm}_i/p_i$ in all sectors where technical change took place, and, of course, $\mathbf{pm}_i^*/p_i = \mathbf{pm}_i/p_i$ in the others. Because $\lambda = \mathbf{pm}_i/(p_i)$ (Equation 4.27), it follows by Theorem 4.14 that $\lambda^* > \lambda$, where λ^* is the eigenvalue associated with M^*. Hence $\pi^* < \pi$. Q.E.D.

There is a third type of technical change that must be examined. It is reasonable to inquire into the types of technical change that reduce values of commodities – this, indeed, is what we might describe as technical progress, that less of society's available labor time must be expended in the production of commodities. (A more precise discussion of "progress" follows in Section 4.3.) We now summarize these definitions of technical change:

Definition 4.4: Technical change from initial technology $\{A, \mathbf{L}\}$ will be called:

(a) Viable if and only if it is cost-reducing at initial prices ($\mathbf{pA} + \mathbf{L} \geq \mathbf{pA}^* + \mathbf{L}^*$)
(b) Progressive if and only if $\mathbf{\Lambda}^* \leq \mathbf{\Lambda}$
(c) Neutral if and only if $\mathbf{\Lambda}^* = \mathbf{\Lambda}$
(d) [5]Retrogressive if and only if $\mathbf{\Lambda}^* \geq \mathbf{\Lambda}$

We next investigate the relationship among these types of technical change. Let the technical change occur in the first sector, and be characterized by a vector

$$\boldsymbol{\delta} = \langle l_1^* - l_1, a_{11}^* - a_{11}, a_{21}^* - a_{21}, \ldots, a_{n1}^* - a_{n1}\rangle$$

Let $\bar{\mathbf{p}}$ be the price vector augmented by the wage:

$$\bar{\mathbf{p}} = \langle 1, p_1, p_2, \ldots, p_n\rangle \equiv \langle 1, \mathbf{p}\rangle$$

and $\bar{\mathbf{\Lambda}}$ be the value vector augmented thus:

$$\bar{\mathbf{\Lambda}} = \langle 1, \mathbf{\Lambda}\rangle$$

Then Theorem 4.8 follows.

Theorem 4.8: The technical change described by $\boldsymbol{\delta}$ is

(*i*) Viable if and only if $\bar{\mathbf{p}} \cdot \boldsymbol{\delta} < 0$
(*ii*) Neutral if and only if $\bar{\mathbf{\Lambda}} \cdot \boldsymbol{\delta} = 0$
(*iii*) Progressive if and only if $\bar{\mathbf{\Lambda}} \cdot \boldsymbol{\delta} < 0$

Proof: (In this proof we cease distinguishing between A_I and A_{II}. More generally, we let A be the global input–output matrix, which is assumed to be productive but not necessarily indecomposable. Thus $(I - A)^{-1}$ exists and is nonnegative.)

Statement (*i*) is seen to be simply the definition of viability.

Statement (*ii*): If the change is neutral, then

$$\mathbf{\Lambda} = \mathbf{\Lambda}A + \mathbf{L} = \mathbf{\Lambda}A^* + \mathbf{L}^*$$

and so

$$\mathbf{\Lambda}(A - A^*) + (\mathbf{L} - \mathbf{L}^*) = 0$$

from which $\bar{\mathbf{\Lambda}} \cdot \boldsymbol{\delta} = 0$ immediately follows.

$\bar{\mathbf{\Lambda}} \cdot \boldsymbol{\delta} = 0$ implies that $\mathbf{\Lambda}A + \mathbf{L} = \mathbf{\Lambda}A^* + \mathbf{L}^*$ and so $\mathbf{\Lambda} = \mathbf{\Lambda}A^* + \mathbf{L}^*$, from which it follows that $\mathbf{\Lambda} = \mathbf{\Lambda}^*$.

Statement (*iii*): Define the transformation

$$T(\mathbf{\Lambda}) = (\mathbf{\Lambda}A^* + \mathbf{L}^*) - \mathbf{\Lambda} = \mathbf{L}^* - \mathbf{\Lambda}(I - A^*) \tag{4.35}$$

If $\bar{\mathbf{\Lambda}} \cdot \boldsymbol{\delta} < 0$, then, by definition, $T(\mathbf{\Lambda}) \le 0$. Apply $(I - A^*)^{-1}$ to (4.35), yielding

$$T(\mathbf{\Lambda})(I - A^*)^{-1} = \mathbf{L}^*(I - A^*)^{-1} - \mathbf{\Lambda} = \mathbf{\Lambda}^* - \mathbf{\Lambda} \tag{4.36}$$

Now $(I - A^*)^{-1}$ is a nonnegative matrix, and thus the left-hand side of (4.36) is a nonpositive vector. $T(\mathbf{\Lambda})(I - A^*)^{-1}$ cannot be the zero vector, because $(I - A^*)^{-1}$ is invertible and $T(\mathbf{\Lambda}) \neq 0$. Consequently, $T(\mathbf{\Lambda})(I - A^*)^{-1}$ is nonpositive and nonzero, and so, by (4.36), $\mathbf{\Lambda}^* \le \mathbf{\Lambda}$ and the technical change is progressive.

Suppose that the change $\boldsymbol{\delta}$ is progressive but that $\bar{\mathbf{\Lambda}} \cdot \boldsymbol{\delta} \ge 0$. By statement (*ii*) of the theorem, we must have $\bar{\mathbf{\Lambda}} \cdot \boldsymbol{\delta} > 0$. Now decrease l_1^* and the $\{a_{i1}^*\}$ to new values l_1^{**}, $\{a_{i1}^{**}\}$ and form a new vector

$$\boldsymbol{\delta}^{**} = \langle l_1^{**} - l_1, a_{11}^{**} - a_{11}, \ldots, a_{n1}^{**} - a_{n1}\rangle$$

such that $\bar{\mathbf{\Lambda}} \cdot \boldsymbol{\delta}^{**} = 0$. (This is clearly possible, because if $l_1^{**} = a_{i1}^{**} = 0$, we would have $\bar{\mathbf{\Lambda}} \cdot \boldsymbol{\delta}^{**} < 0$.) Thus, by statement (*ii*), the change described by $\boldsymbol{\delta}^{**}$ is neutral; however, $\boldsymbol{\delta}^{**}$ must certainly be progressive, as it is a strict improvement in value terms over the change $\boldsymbol{\delta}$. This contradiction proves the theorem. Q.E.D.

Theorem 4.8 enables us to characterize the different types of technical change in a convenient geometric way. For simplicity, let us consider the case when there is only one commodity and labor, so that the vector characterizing technology is $\langle l_1, a_{11}\rangle$. In Figure 3, this vector is drawn. The vectors $\bar{\mathbf{\Lambda}}$ and $\bar{\mathbf{p}}$ are appended to $\langle l_1, a_{11}\rangle$; notice that $\bar{\mathbf{p}}$ will always lie above $\bar{\mathbf{\Lambda}}$ as shown, because it is well known that $\mathbf{p} > \mathbf{\Lambda}$ for $\pi > 0$. A technical change $\boldsymbol{\delta}$ is depicted by appending the vector $\boldsymbol{\delta}$

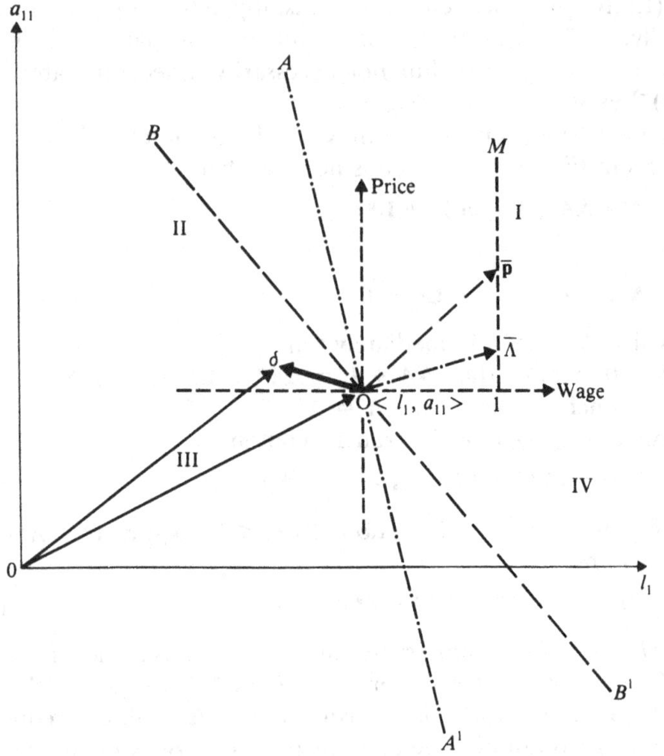

Figure 3. Viable and progressive technical changes from initial technology $O\ \langle l_1, a_{11} \rangle$.

at origin O as well. By Theorem 4.8, a change $\boldsymbol{\delta}$ is progressive if and only if it lies below the line AA' orthogonal to $\bar{\boldsymbol{\Lambda}}$; it is viable if and only if it lies below the line BB' orthogonal to $\bar{\mathbf{p}}$; and it is neutral if and only if it lies on the line AA'. (Furthermore, it is easily seen to be retrogressive if and only if it lies above AA'.)

Examine the four quadrants of technical change (with origin O) that can occur. It is clear that changes that are strictly resource-saving (quadrant III) are always viable and progressive, and changes that are resource-using (quadrant I) are always retrogressive and nonviable. Quadrants II and IV are the only interesting changes, and we have the following theorem.

THEOREM 4.9

(*i*) All CU–LS (quadrant II) technical changes that are viable are progressive; but there are CU–LS progressive changes that are not viable.

(*ii*) All CS–LU (quadrant IV) technical changes that are progressive are viable; but there are CS–LU changes that are viable but not progressive.

This theorem is clearly true from Figure 3 in the two-dimensional case; the proof for the general case follows.

Proof: [We prove only part (*i*). Part (*ii*) of Theorem 4.9 is identical and requires no separate proof.] $\boldsymbol{\delta}$ is CU–LS means that

$$\boldsymbol{\delta} = \langle -\delta_0, \delta_1, \ldots, \delta_n \rangle$$

where $\delta_i \geq 0$. Because $\boldsymbol{\delta}$ is viable,

$$\bar{\mathbf{p}} \cdot \boldsymbol{\delta} < 0$$

and thus

$$\sum_1^m p_i \delta_i < \delta_0$$

Hence

$$\sum_1^m \lambda_i \delta_i < \sum_1^m p_i \delta_i < \delta_0 \qquad \text{(because } \lambda_i < p_i \ \forall i\text{)}$$

and so $\bar{\boldsymbol{\Lambda}} \cdot \boldsymbol{\delta} < 0$, which demonstrates that $\boldsymbol{\delta}$ is progressive.

To show that there are CU–LS progressive changes that are not viable, it is only necessary to construct a vector $\boldsymbol{\delta}$ such that

$$\Sigma \lambda_i \delta_i < \delta_0 \quad \text{and} \quad \Sigma p_i \delta_i > \delta_0$$

Because it is required that $\delta_i \geq 0 \ \forall i$, this is easily done using the fact that $p_i > \lambda_i$. Q.E.D.

Thus, if cost-reducing innovations that are developed are CU–LS, then we are guaranteed that retrogressive changes will never be introduced. To this extent, the invisible hand operates. There remain, however, some progressive (socially desirable) CU–LS innovations that will not be introduced; and if we discard the assumption of CU–LS changes, we have the perverse situation that capitalists may introduce retrogressive changes (which lie in the cone $A'OB'$).

An economic motivation for the viability of changes in quadrants II and IV can be seen by thinking of the real wage bundle as variable and decreasing it to the zero bundle. We hold the technology fixed. In this case the profit rate π increases to a maximum value, which is a function of the dominant eigenvalue of matrix A. As π increases, the vector $\bar{\mathbf{p}}$ travels up the line $1M$, becoming vertical in the limit, and its orthogonal line BB' approaches the horizontal. (As π decreases to zero, $\bar{\mathbf{p}}$ moves down $1M$, becoming coincidental with the $\bar{\boldsymbol{\Lambda}}$ at $\pi = 0$.)

Table 1[6]

e \ π	Increases	Decreases
Increases	$\boldsymbol{\delta} \in A'OB$	$\boldsymbol{\delta} \in AOB$
Decreases	$\boldsymbol{\delta} \in A'OB'$	$\boldsymbol{\delta} \in AOB'$

Let $\boldsymbol{\delta}$ be any CU–LS progressive change; it is seen by the above argument that $\boldsymbol{\delta}$ will be viable only (i.e., below line BB') for profit rates sufficiently *small.* Let $\boldsymbol{\delta}$, now, be *any* CS–LU (quadrant IV) change; it is seen that $\boldsymbol{\delta}$ will be viable only for profit rates sufficiently *large.* Thinking of the profit rate as a price of capital makes economic sense of this – i.e., the capital-using changes are adopted only if capital is sufficiently cheap, and labor-using changes are adopted only if labor is sufficiently cheap. We see from this argument (and Figure 3) that neutral changes are the "least" feasible from among the class of CU–LS progressive and neutral changes, as they are furthest away from the viable set. Summarizing, we have Theorem 4.10:

THEOREM 4.10

(*i*) Let $\boldsymbol{\delta}$ be a CU–LS, progressive change. Then for sufficiently large wage bundles **b**, $\boldsymbol{\delta}$ is viable. (Recall, however, that CU–LS neutral changes are not viable at any positive profit rate.)

(*ii*) Let $\boldsymbol{\delta}$ be any CS–LU change. Then for sufficiently small wage bundles **b**, $\boldsymbol{\delta}$ is viable.

The proof of Theorem 4.10 is a straightforward continuity argument and has been spelled out in its essentials in the preceding paragraph.

This analysis is easily related to questions of the falling rate of profit. It has been established that viable changes increase the profit rate; thus, there are retrogressive changes (quadrant IV) that increase the profit rate. The obverse to this statement applies to quadrant II: There are socially desirable (progressive) changes that decrease the rate of profit. We can easily show the relationship between the changes in the rate of profit and rate of exploitation induced by technical innovation, as is summarized in Table 1.

Thus, there is no necessary relationship between innovation-induced changes in the two classical Marxian variables, π and e. In particular, even among the class of viable changes, the rate of exploitation may rise or fall. All viable changes that are CU–LS, however, increase the rate of exploitation (Theorem 4.9).

An important remark concerning Theorem 4.10 must now be made. A major insight of neoclassical economics is that competition, in suitably tranquil environments, leads to socially desirable outcomes. In particular, competitively generated technical innovations should be socially desirable. According to Theorem 4.10, this is not necessarily the case. What is wrong? The answer is that the Marxian equal-profit-rate equilibrium prices, **p**, are *not* the neoclassical competitive prices, unless $\pi = 0$. (Under constant returns to scale, profits must be zero for prices to be neoclassical competitive equilibrium prices.) When $\pi = 0$, the Marxian prices are equal to labor values, and it is then true that competitive innovations are socially desirable. Or, as we see in the next section, if the profit rate is equal to the growth rate then viable and progressive changes coincide.

4.4 Progressive and viable technical change in steady-state growth

In the stationary state, the criterion for socially desirable technical change is the labor-value criterion of progressivity of Section 4.3. However, in the case of steady-state growth, the rational "prices" to use in choosing the optimal production technique are what have been called "synchronized labor costs": We compound dated labor by the growth factor (see Definition 4.5 below). This has been shown by von Weizsäcker and Samuelson (1971) and Wolfstetter (1973). In this section, we extend Theorem 4.9 to the case of steady-state growth, using synchronized labor costs.

Definition 4.5: The vector of synchronized labor costs at growth rate g for technology $\{A, \mathbf{L}\}$ is $\mathbf{\Lambda}(g) \equiv (1 + g)\mathbf{L}[I - (1 + g)A]^{-1}$.

Definition 4.6: An innovation $\{A, \mathbf{L}] \rightarrow [A^*, \mathbf{L}^*\}$ is progressive at growth rate g if $\mathbf{\Lambda}^*(g) \leq \mathbf{\Lambda}(g)$.

Theorem 4.11: If $\pi > g$, then:

(*i*) All CU–LS technical changes that are viable are progressive at rate g; but there are CU–LS changes that are progressive at rate g and not viable.

(*ii*) All CS–LU technical changes that are progressive at rate g are viable; but there are CS–LU changes that are viable but not progressive at rate g.

Proof: (As in Theorem 4.9, it is sufficient to prove part (*i*), as the second statement follows with like reasoning.)

Let $\{A, \mathbf{L}\} \rightarrow \{A^*, \mathbf{L}^*\}$ be a viable change such that $A^* \geq A$, $\mathbf{L}^* \leq \mathbf{L}$. By viability,

$$\mathbf{p}A^* + \mathbf{L}^* \leqq \mathbf{p}A + \mathbf{L}$$

Notice that $\mathbf{p} = \boldsymbol{\Lambda}(\pi)$; because $\pi > g$, $\mathbf{p} \equiv \boldsymbol{\Lambda}(\pi) \geq \boldsymbol{\Lambda}(g)$. Because $A^* - A \geq 0$, it follows that

$$\boldsymbol{\Lambda}(g)(A^* - A) + \mathbf{L}^* \leq \mathbf{p}(A^* - A) + \mathbf{L}^* \leq \mathbf{L}$$

or

$$\boldsymbol{\Lambda}(g)A^* + \mathbf{L}^* \leq \boldsymbol{\Lambda}(g)A + \mathbf{L}$$

and hence

$$(1 + g)\,[\boldsymbol{\Lambda}(g)A^* + \mathbf{L}^*] \leq (1 + g)\,[\boldsymbol{\Lambda}(g)A + \mathbf{L}] \equiv \boldsymbol{\Lambda}(g) \tag{4.37}$$

Define $T(\mathbf{v}) = (1 + g)\,[\mathbf{v}A^* + \mathbf{L}^*] - \mathbf{v}$ for row vectors $\mathbf{v}$; by definition of T, (4.37) can be written

$$T[\boldsymbol{\Lambda}(g)] \leq 0$$

Observe that

$$T(\mathbf{v})\,[I - (1 + g)A^*]^{-1} = \boldsymbol{\Lambda}^*(g) - \mathbf{v}$$

from which it follows that

$$T[\boldsymbol{\Lambda}(g)][I - (1 + g)A^*]^{-1} = \boldsymbol{\Lambda}^*(g) - \boldsymbol{\Lambda}(g) \tag{4.38}$$

Because $T[\boldsymbol{\Lambda}(g)] \leq 0$ and $[I - (1 + g)A^*]^{-1} \geq 0$, it immediately follows that the left-hand side of (4.38) is nonpositive, and so

$$\boldsymbol{\Lambda}^*(g) \leqq \boldsymbol{\Lambda}(g)$$

Moreover, it is known that $T[\boldsymbol{\Lambda}(g)] \neq 0$; because $[I - (1 + g)A^*]^{-1}$ is obviously invertible, it follows that $\boldsymbol{\Lambda}^*(g) \neq \boldsymbol{\Lambda}(g)$ and hence $\boldsymbol{\Lambda}^*(g) \leq \boldsymbol{\Lambda}(g)$.

To prove that there are CU–LS progressive changes at rate g that are not viable, we must generalize Theorem 4.8 to the case of synchronized labor costs.

THEOREM 4.12: The technical change described by $\boldsymbol{\delta}$ is
(*i*) Neutral at rate g if and only if $\bar{\boldsymbol{\Lambda}}(g) \cdot \boldsymbol{\delta} = 0$
(*ii*) Progressive at rate g if and only if $\bar{\boldsymbol{\Lambda}}(g) \cdot \boldsymbol{\delta} < 0$
[Note: As before, $\bar{\boldsymbol{\Lambda}}(g) \equiv \langle 1, \boldsymbol{\Lambda}(g)\rangle$.]

Proof of Theorem 4.12
(*i*) Neutrality at rate g means that $\boldsymbol{\Lambda}(g) = \boldsymbol{\Lambda}^*(g)$, which implies that $(1 + g)[\boldsymbol{\Lambda}(g)A + \mathbf{L}] = (1 + g)\,[\boldsymbol{\Lambda}(g)A^* + \mathbf{L}^*]$, which implies that

$\bar{\mathbf{\Lambda}}(g) \cdot \boldsymbol{\delta} = 0$. Conversely, $\bar{\mathbf{\Lambda}}(g) \cdot \boldsymbol{\delta} = 0$ implies that $\mathbf{\Lambda}(g)A^* + \mathbf{L}^* = \mathbf{\Lambda}(g)A + \mathbf{L}$ and so $\mathbf{\Lambda}(g) = (1 + g)[\mathbf{\Lambda}(g)A + \mathbf{L}] = (1 + g)[\mathbf{\Lambda}(g)A^* + \mathbf{L}^*]$. Inverting this last equation gives $\mathbf{\Lambda}(g) = (1 + g)\mathbf{L}^* [I - (1 + g)A^*]^{-1}$, which means that $\mathbf{\Lambda}(g) = \mathbf{\Lambda}^*(g)$.

(*ii*) Suppose that $\bar{\mathbf{\Lambda}}(g) \cdot \boldsymbol{\delta} < 0$. Then $(1 + g)\bar{\mathbf{\Lambda}}(g) \cdot \boldsymbol{\delta} < 0$, which implies that

$$(1 + g)\,[\mathbf{\Lambda}(g)A^* + \mathbf{L}^*] \leq (1 + g)\,[\mathbf{\Lambda}(g)A + \mathbf{L}] = \mathbf{\Lambda}(g) \tag{4.39}$$

But (4.39) is identical to (4.37); hence, it follows by the argument above that $\mathbf{\Lambda}^*(g) \leq \mathbf{\Lambda}(g)$ and $\boldsymbol{\delta}$ is progressive.

Conversely, suppose that $\bar{\mathbf{\Lambda}}(g) \cdot \boldsymbol{\delta} \geq 0$ and $\boldsymbol{\delta}$ is progressive at rate g. Following the proof of Theorem 4.8, a contradiction is arrived at, using statement (*i*) above. Q.E.D.

The characterization of progressive changes $\boldsymbol{\delta}$ as those such that $\bar{\mathbf{\Lambda}}(g) \cdot \boldsymbol{\delta} < 0$ allows us to construct CU–LS progressive changes at rate g that are not viable. It is only necessary to produce a vector $\boldsymbol{\delta} = \langle -\delta_0, \delta_1, \ldots, \delta_n \rangle$, $\delta_i \geqq 0$, such that

$$\sum_1^n \lambda_i(g)\,\delta_i < \delta_0 \quad \text{and} \quad \sum_1^n p_i\delta_i > \delta_0$$

Because $\mathbf{\Lambda}(g) \leq \mathbf{\Lambda}(\pi) = \mathbf{p}$ (because $g < \pi$ and $\mathbf{\Lambda}(g)$ is an increasing vector-valued function of g), such a change $\boldsymbol{\delta}$ is easily constructed. Q.E.D.

4.5 Summary

It has been shown that an evaluation of the falling rate of profit must consider the effects of technical change on the price rate of profit, not simply the value rate of profit, as the two rates can move in different directions as a consequence of technical innovation. There are two interesting types of technical change to consider: viable ones, which are the only kind capitalists will introduce; and progressive ones, which simultaneously reduce the labor values of all commodities.

Under the assumption of a stationary state, the implications of the above propositions may be summed up as follows:

1. In a competitive economy, the rate of profit will not fall due to technical change alone.
2. If technical innovations are capital-using and labor-saving, then those that are introduced by capitalists are also socially desirable; if innovations are not CU–LS, they may be at once competitively introduced and socially undesirable.

3. In a market socialist economy, the rate of profit may fall as a consequence of a rational (socially desirable) technical change.

The market socialist economy works like this: Central planners impose progressive technical changes, and then allow the market to equilibrate prices and profit rate. The falling rate of profit afflicts certain Lange-type economies but not capitalist ones.

If the economy is not in stationary state, but in steady-state growth at positive rate g, the same qualitative results hold, as long as the rate of growth is not equal to the profit rate. If $\pi > g$, then competitive prices will differ from synchronized labor costs; capitalists will make decisions about innovations based on prices, whereas rational planners would minimize the synchronized labor costs. The three conclusions above hold as long as $\pi > g$. Only in the golden age case $g = \pi$, where capitalists dispose of all surplus products in just such a way as to employ the growing labor force and feed all the workers what they need, does the dichotomy between the two pricing systems disappear.

Clearly, then, the fact that the profit rate rises due to competitively introduced innovations does not vindicate the price mechanism, if we adopt the criterion of progressiveness (at growth rate zero or $g > 0$) as the measure of social improvements.

Finally, it should be emphasized that changes in the subsistence vector **b** resulting from technological "progress," class struggle, and the growth of the reserve army have not been taken into account. When this, and the various deviations from the ideal model posited here are considered, the story becomes less definitive. What has been shown here is that if the rate of profit does fall under competitive capitalism, it must be due to an increase in the real wage. Further discussion of this question is pursued in Chapter 6.

As a historical remark, it is worth observing that Marx appeared to have in mind the process that has been modeled here. His description of the relationship between the rate of profit and technical change reads:

> No capitalist ever voluntarily introduces a new method of production, no matter how much more productive it may be, and how much it may increase the rate of surplus-value, so long as it reduces the rate of profit. Yet every such new method of production cheapens the commodities. Hence, the capitalist sells them originally above their prices of production, or, perhaps, above their value. He pockets the difference between their costs of production and the market-prices of the same commodities produced at higher costs of produc-

> tion. He can do this, because the average labour-time required socially for the production of these latter commodities is higher than the labour-time required for the new methods of production. His method of production stands above the social average. But competition makes it general and subject to the general law. There follows a fall in the rate of profit – perhaps first in this sphere of production, and eventually it achieves a balance with the rest – which is, therefore, wholly independent of the will of the capitalist [Marx, 1966, p. 264].

Notice that the first sentence in this quotation states that technical changes are introduced only if they are cost-reducing at current prices. The second, third, and fourth sentences state that in the disequilibrium situation thus created, the capitalist reaps superprofits, a higher profit rate than is made in other sectors. In the fifth and sixth sentences, Marx states that the new technique is in fact progressive, an insight that we have shown is true under the assumption that innovations are CU–LS. The seventh sentence points out that eventually, through competition, a new equilibrium is established. And, finally, the transitory rate of profit falls to achieve a new equilibrium. It is not clear in this passage whether Marx expected the new rate of profit π^* to be less than the original π. On this point Marx is ambivalent. Finally, one might note that the mathematical heart of the correct argument, the Frobenius-Perron theorem, was not discovered until a generation after Marx's death.

As was discussed in the opening section of this chapter, it is hoped that students of the falling-rate-of-profit mechanism of Marx will not concentrate on the fallacy of Marx's *particular* theory, but on the insight of his *general* project: to locate a tendency for crisis in the nature of the economic relations between people (i.e., the mode of production), not in natural phenomena. In any case, it would be a great fallacy to make a theory of the eventual demise of capitalism rest on *any* theory of the falling rate of profit. It is hoped that one effect of the argument presented here will be to rectify the "economist" position of many Marxists that socialism necessarily follows from capitalist crisis, which necessarily follows from the decline in the rate of profit. Social revolution depends on processes much more political and intricate than enter into the usual discussions of the falling rate of profit.

Appendix: Frobenius-Perron eigenvalue theorems

In this appendix, the key theorems used in this chapter are quoted.

THEOREM 4.13 (Frobenius–Perron): Let A be an indecomposable, nonnegative matrix. Then A possesses a unique nonnegative eigenvector $\mathbf{x}$ (up to a scalar), and its associated eigenvalue, λ, is positive (and real). Furthermore, $\mathbf{x} > 0$. λ is called the Frobenius root of A. If $A^* \geq A$, then $\lambda^* > \lambda$. λ is a continuous function of A.

Proof of this theorem may be found in many sources, for example, Schwartz (1961).

THEOREM 4.14: Let A be nonnegative, indecomposable and λ its Frobenius root. Let $\mathbf{z} > 0$. Then either

$$(i)\quad \min_i \frac{(A\mathbf{z})_i}{z_i} < \lambda < \max_i \frac{(A\mathbf{z})_i}{z_i}$$

or

$$(ii)\quad \min_i \frac{(A\mathbf{z})_i}{z_i} = \lambda = \max_i \frac{(A\mathbf{z})_i}{z_i}$$

Proof: Case (*ii*) clearly occurs if and only if $\mathbf{z}$ is the associated eigenvector of λ. So assuming that this is not the case, we must show that case (*i*) holds.

Suppose that

$$A\mathbf{z} \leq \lambda\mathbf{z} \tag{4.40}$$

Now it is easy to show (see, for instance, Schwartz, 1961) that A' (the transpose of A) has the same Frobenius root as A. Hence, there exists a positive row vector $\mathbf{y}$ such that

$$\mathbf{y}A = \lambda\mathbf{y} \tag{4.41}$$

Premultiplication of (4.40) by $\mathbf{y}$ yields

$$\mathbf{y}A\mathbf{z} < \lambda\mathbf{y}\mathbf{z} \tag{4.42}$$

On the other hand, post-multiplication of (4.41) by $\mathbf{z}$ yields

$$\mathbf{y}A\mathbf{z} = \lambda\mathbf{y}\mathbf{z} \tag{4.43}$$

(4.43) contradicts (4.42); hence, (4.40) cannot hold.

In like manner, it can be shown that

$$A\mathbf{z} \geq \lambda\mathbf{z} \tag{4.44}$$

cannot hold.

But the impossibility of (4.40) and (4.44) are equivalent to the impossibility of

$$\lambda \geqq \frac{(A\mathbf{z})_i}{z_i} \qquad \forall i \tag{4.40'}$$

and

$$\lambda \leqq \frac{(A\mathbf{z})_i}{z_i} \qquad \forall i \tag{4.44'}$$

From the impossibility of (4.40′) follows

$$\max_i \frac{(A\mathbf{z})_i}{\mathbf{z}_i} > \lambda$$

and from the impossibility of (4.44′),

$$\min_i \frac{(A\mathbf{z})_i}{z_i} < \lambda \quad \text{Q.E.D.}$$

THEOREM 4.15 (Morishima–Seton): Let

$$M = \begin{pmatrix} A_{\mathrm{I}} & A_{\mathrm{II}} \\ \mathbf{bL}_{\mathrm{I}} & \mathbf{bL}_{\mathrm{II}} \end{pmatrix}$$

be the augmented input coefficient matrix. Then M possesses an eigenvalue and a positive column eigenvector $\mathbf{y}$: $M\mathbf{y} = \lambda\mathbf{y}$. Furthermore,

$$\lambda = \frac{1}{1 + \pi}$$

where π is the competitive rate of profit, and the formula

$$\pi = \frac{\mathbf{S} \cdot \mathbf{y}}{\mathbf{C} \cdot \mathbf{y} + \mathbf{V} \cdot \mathbf{y}}$$

holds, where **C, V, S** are the vectors of constant capital, variable capital, and surplus value per unit of the various commodities, respectively. That is, **C, V,** and **S** are row vectors defined by:

$$\mathbf{C} = \langle \mathbf{\Lambda}_{\mathrm{I}} A_{\mathrm{I}},\ \mathbf{\Lambda}_{\mathrm{I}} A_{\mathrm{II}} \rangle$$
$$\mathbf{V} = \langle \mathbf{\Lambda}_{\mathrm{II}} \mathbf{bL}_{\mathrm{I}},\ \mathbf{\Lambda}_{\mathrm{II}} \mathbf{bL}_{\mathrm{II}} \rangle$$
$$\mathbf{S} = \langle (1 - \mathbf{\Lambda}_{\mathrm{II}} \mathbf{b}) \mathbf{L}_{\mathrm{I}},\ (1 - \mathbf{\Lambda}_{\mathrm{II}} \mathbf{b}) \mathbf{L}_{\mathrm{II}} \rangle$$

For proof of this theorem, see Morishima (1973, Chapter 6).

5 Continuing controversy on the falling rate of profit: fixed capital and other issues

5.1 The need for microfoundations: methodology

For the most part, discussion of the Marxian falling rate of profit (FRP) theory is marked by lack of attention to microeconomic detail. Precisely, how do the anarchic actions of atomistic capitals give rise to a falling rate of profit? Marx's discussion of this issue in *Capital,* Volume III, was formulated in a microeconomic way, as we pointed out in the last chapter. Briefly, the profit-maximizing urge of capitalists directs them to replace workers with machinery, which raises the organic composition of capital, which lowers (or produces a tendency to lower) the profit rate. Whether or not this argument is correct, it must be admitted that it is microeconomic in this sense: It claims to deduce a macroeconomic phenomenon, itself quite beyond the ability of any individual capitalist to realize, from the anarchic (competitive) behavior of atomized economic units. This type of economic reasoning, of deducing aggregate economic effects from the behavior of individual economic units, was employed by economists of all ideological bents in the nineteenth century. It is, indeed, one of the hallmarks of why Marxism is scientific socialism. The outcome of socialism (and of capitalist crisis) was argued, by Marx and Engels, not to be a utopian solution (and crisis fortuitous), but the predictable outcome of social forces that eventually were reducible to the actions of individuals and classes of individuals. That Marx determined individual behavior as a consequence of the social context and imperatives, while the neoclassical school postulated a hegemonic, ahistorical position for the individual, in no way weakens the claim that Marx's theory possesses a microeconomic foundation.

Weaknesses have been pointed out in Marx's FRP theory by various authors, presented originally in a formal way in the theorem of Okishio (1961) discussed in Chapter 4. The argument is briefly this: If capitalists introduce technical innovation when and only when it is cost-reducing, then the equilibrium rate of profit will rise, in a situation when prices are determined by competition and the real wage does remain fixed. Although the real wage in fact does not remain fixed, the problem has been to understand whether a FRP can be construed to be due to technical innovation itself, independent of changes in the real wage.

Responses to this claim, of Okishio and others, have been of three types. These are, first, what Fine and Harris (1976) call fundamentalist positions on FRP. These consist, essentially, of postulating FRP as part of the definition of capital. Somehow, FRP is inherent in capital, hence the proposition is not a proposition, is not falsifiable. Although this position may have been adopted as an invincible counter to critiques of the theory, it renders the theory completely uninteresting and powerless. Second are empirical discussions of whether or not the organic composition of capital is indeed rising. Although this sort of investigation may be useful, it does not bear upon the theoretical issue of whether or not the rate of profit falls due to technical change. That is, either such investigation will be consistent with the Okishio conclusion, or it will not be; in the latter case, it would show the need for a different microeconomic argument of capitalist technical innovation; it would not, however, show Okishio's *argument* to be wrong. The empirical investigations, then, are certainly necessary, but they cannot provide refutation of a theory. To some extent, they appear to be carried out without sufficient consciousness of the microeconomic arguments that exist. That is, if one believes Okishio's model, then there is no increase possible in the organic composition of capital so great as to reduce the rate of profit. What, then, is the point of tracking the organic composition, unless one first consciously questions the postulates of the Okishio model? Third are arguments that argue for FRP, against the Okishio model, but on the same analytical level; that is, by postulating microeconomic behavior of capitalist technical innovation that will (may) lend to a falling rate of profit. Papers that contain elements of this position are Persky and Alberro (1978), Shaikh (1978a, 1978b) and Fine and Harris (1976). One common claim of these arguments is that if one takes fixed capital into account, as Okishio did not, then the rate of profit can be shown to fall (always, *ceteris paribus,* independent of wage changes).

It is the intent of this chapter to examine more carefully the microeconomic foundations of the rising-rate-of-profit position. In a word, the conclusion is this: Capitalist technical innovation, even in the presence of fixed capital, will produce a rising rate of profit, *ceteris paribus.* (As in all discussions of this type the *ceteris paribus* assumption includes real wages and realization of surplus value.) It is imperative to emphasize from the outset what this conclusion *does not* claim. First, it does not say that the rate of profit does not fall. If one includes as part of a theory of technical change how the real wage responds to innovation, the rate of profit can be shown systematically to fall, under various realistic hypotheses. (See Chapter 6.) Second, it does not say there *cannot* exist a microeconomic theory of FRP: It says, more narrowly, that the *usual* competitive assumptions do not produce such a theory. [Indeed, Persky and Alberro (1978) put forth a theory of FRP, with microeconomic foundations.]

Because the technique of exploring the "micro foundations" of economic behavior may seem to many Marxists to be a neoclassical (and hence forbidden) methodology, it should be emphasized that this is not the case. Indeed, this approach is one of the attributes of Marxist analysis that render it scientific and not utopian. To put this point a little differently, an avoidance of microeconomic analysis can lead to functionalism. If one does not investigate the mechanism by which decisions are made and actions carried out, one can too easily fall into the error of claiming that what is good or necessary for the preservation of the economic order comes to prevail. Or, somewhat perversely, whatever is necessary for the demise of the system – such as a falling rate of profit – must come to prevail. This latter sort of functionalism serves the end of justifying the demise of the capitalist mode of production, which is viewed as historically necessary. The sort of fundamentalism that this chapter criticizes takes the study of capitalism back to the level of Marx's utopian predecessors.

5.2 Miscellaneous arguments against Okishio's theorem

In this section, various arguments that have been advanced in reply to Okishio's argument against a FRP are discussed. For this purpose, a pure circulating capital model is sufficient. In the next section, problems peculiar to models with fixed capital are discussed.

Okishio's theorem

A brief review of Okishio's theorem is appropriate. The original reference is Okishio (1961); a more general treatment is in Chapter 4.

We posit a pure circulating "capital" model, where

A is the $n \times n$ input matrix

L is the n row vector of direct labor coefficients in worker days

b is the n column vector that is the worker's daily subsistence bundle

π is the equilibrium rate of profit
p is the n row vector of prices of production

The equations that specify equilibrium in the model are

$$\mathbf{p} = (1 + \pi)(\mathbf{p}A + \mathbf{L}) \tag{5.1}$$

$$1 = \mathbf{pb} \tag{5.2}$$

where the daily wage is taken as unity. These can be written as

$$\frac{1}{1 + \pi}\mathbf{p} = \mathbf{p}M \tag{5.3}$$

where $M = A + \mathbf{bL}$. M is the input–output matrix obtained by viewing all commodities as being produced by commodities, the augmented input coefficient matrix. If M is a productive matrix, then a positive solution π and nonnegative solution **p** exist to (5.3); if M is in addition indecomposable, then $(\pi, \mathbf{p})$ is uniquely determined. (This is a consequence of the Frobenius–Perron theorems.)

Suppose, now, that we are in such an equilibrium, and a technical innovation appears, which can be characterized as a new column $\mathbf{A}^{i*}$ for the matrix A, and a new coefficient L^{i*}. We say the innovation $(\mathbf{A}^{i*}, L^{i*})$ is *viable* if capitalists can cut costs, at current equilibrium prices, by using it; that is, if and only if:

$$\mathbf{pA}^{i*} + L^{i*} < \mathbf{pA}^{i} + L^{i} \tag{5.4}$$

If and only if the innovation is viable, it will be introduced. After its introduction there will, for the time being, be a higher rate of profit earned by the innovators in sector i; eventually, through entry and price cutting, a new equilibrium will be arrived at which we call $(\pi^*, \mathbf{p}^*)$:

$$\mathbf{p}^* = (1 + \pi^*)(\mathbf{p}^*A^* + \mathbf{L}^*) \tag{5.5}$$

$$\mathbf{p}^*\mathbf{b} = 1 \tag{5.6}$$

where A^* is the old matrix A with column $\mathbf{A}^i$ replaced by the innovation $\mathbf{A}^{i*}$, and similarly for $\mathbf{L}^*$. Notice the real wage **b** is assumed to remain constant. Question: Can we say anything about the relative sizes of π^* and π? Answer: π^* will be greater than π, if M is indecomposable. (If M is decomposable, π^* may equal π.) This, in brief, is the crucial argument: Viable technical changes at constant real wages raise the equilibrium profit rate.

The maximum rate of profit

One of the arguments that has been advanced in an attempt to mollify the impact of the above argument is that although the actual rate of profit rises, the *maximal* rate of profit falls. This position has been put forth by Fine and Harris (1976) and Shaikh (1978a, 1978b) as significant – the claim being that if the maximal rate of profit falls over time, the system becomes more and more hemmed in, so to speak, and crisis-prone. To quote Shaikh: "The proposition that mechanization lowers the maximum rate of profit would appear to imply that *sooner or later* the actual rate of profit must necessarily fall. And indeed this is exactly how it has been interpreted by many Marxists. The basic logic of Marx's argument therefore, seems to emerge unscathed" (1978b, p. 240). I will argue that the conclusions here do not follow from the premises.

By the maximal rate of profit is meant the rate of profit that would prevail under a given technology if the wage were reduced to zero; that is, what return capitalists would get if they had no direct labor costs. From our Equation 5.1, this is seen to be that number $\bar{\pi}$, such that a price vector $\bar{\mathbf{p}}$ exists such that:

$$\bar{\mathbf{p}} = (1 + \bar{\pi})\bar{\mathbf{p}}A \tag{5.7}$$

That is, $1/(1 + \bar{\pi})$ is the eigenvalue of the matrix A. Let us demonstrate very simply how the maximum rate of profit can fall with viable technical innovation.

Suppose that an innovation $(\mathbf{A}^{i*}, \mathbf{L}^{i*})$ is capital-using and labor-saving (CU–LS):

$$\mathbf{A}^{i*} \geq \mathbf{A}^{i}, L^{i*} < L^{i}$$

All material input coefficients increase or stay the same, and direct labor input decreases. This is the kind of technical change we think of as being common. There certainly exist viable, CU–LS technical changes. Clearly, with such innovations, $A^* \geq A$. Because the *maximal* rates of profit before and after the innovation are $\bar{\pi}$ and $\bar{\pi}^*$, defined by

$$\frac{1}{1 + \bar{\pi}} \text{ is the eigenvalue of } A$$

$$\frac{1}{1 + \bar{\pi}^*} \text{ is the eigenvalue of } A^*$$

it follows immediately that $\bar{\pi}^* < \bar{\pi}$, because it is well known (Frobenius–Perron) that if $A^* \geq A$, then the eigenvalue of A^* is greater than the eigenvalue of A. However, by Okishio's thereom, the *actual* rate of profit rises, as long as the change is viable: $\pi^* > \pi$.

Suppose, now, that we have an infinite sequence of such viable CU–LS technical changes, one after the other. In each case the actual rate of profit must rise (always holding constant real wages **b**) and the maximal rate of profit must fall. We have

$$\pi^1 < \pi^2 < \pi^3 < \cdots < \pi^t < \cdots < \bar{\pi}^t < \bar{\pi}^{t-1} < \cdots < \bar{\pi}^3 < \bar{\pi}^2 < \bar{\pi}^1$$

Certainly the $\{\bar{\pi}^t\}$ decrease, but they never cause the *actual* rate of profit to fall. In particular, *any* actual rate of profit π^* is a lower bound for *all* maximal rates of profit $\{\bar{\pi}^t\}_{t=1,\infty}$. In particular, the sequence of maximal rates of profit $\bar{\pi}^t$ does not converge to zero, but rather to some "large" positive number – large in the sense that it is larger than any actual rate of profit the system ever achieved in the hypothetical history.

Another writer who discusses the "falling maximal rate of profit" phenomenon is Schefold (1976). It must be pointed out that Schefold is careful not to draw any false inferences from his demonstration; it is worth discussing here, however, for his mathematical model is sufficiently complex that readers might think the falling maximal rate of profit in that model does imply something about what happens to the actual rate. Schefold's model includes fixed capital. He demonstrates that "mechanization" leads to a falling maximal rate of profit. By "mechanization," Schefold means a technical innovation that uses at least the same amount of circulating capital (what he calls raw materials) as the old technique, an increased amount of fixed capital, and less direct labor. Because, in computing the maximal rate of profit, the direct labor has no impact since the wage is assumed to be zero, it is obvious that if we increase fixed capital and do not decrease circulating capital, the maximal rate of profit will fall. The economic intuition remains the same as the one given above for the pure circulating capital case, although the model with fixed capital is mathematically more complex. Hence, the fall in the maximal rate of profit is of no consequence for what happens to the actual rate.

Clearly, what does happen in the infinite history that has been proposed is that the actual and maximal rates of profit get closer to each other. As long as the real wage remains nonzero at **b**, however, the two sequences cannot converge to the same limit. If, in addition, we wish to allow the real wage to vary with technical changes, then the actual rate of profit will not increase so fast, or may even decrease. That is, suppose that $\mathbf{b}^t$ is the real wage bundle associated with the technology $(A^*, \mathbf{L}^*)^t$ extant at time t. Let us say that workers succeed in raising the real wage with each viable innovation: $\mathbf{b}^t \geq \mathbf{b}^{t-1}$. Then we shall certainly have that the sequence $\{\pi^*(\mathbf{b}^t)\}$ of actual rates of profit (viewed as a function of the contemporary real wage) will increase less fast than the sequence $\{\pi^*(\mathbf{b})\}$ would have; and we may even have $\{\pi^*(\mathbf{b}^t)\}$ to be a decreasing sequence in periods when the real wage rises sufficiently rapidly. In this case, of variable real wage, the maximal rates of profit (which remain the same as before) become even less "constraining" than they were before.

Another version of the falling maximal rate of profit theory is put forth by Okishio (1977). Using the Marxian categories S, C, V, and L, he observes:

$$\text{value rate of profit} = \frac{S}{C+V} < \frac{S+V}{C+V} = \frac{L}{C+V} < \frac{L}{C} \tag{5.8}$$

Hence, if $L/C \to 0$ with technical change, then $S/(C + V)$ must approach zero. In particular, L/C is an upper bound for the rate of profit.

It may be intuitively pleasing to think of L/C approaching zero under advanced mechanization. Recall, however, that the *value* of constant capital, C, will get small if total direct labor L in the system gets small. So mechanization does not necessarily mean that $L/C \to 0$. More to the point, however, there are no micro foundations for the argument that $L/C \to 0$. Note that $S/(C + V)$ is a weighted harmonic mean of the sectoral value rates of profit, where the weights are given by a measure of the particular sector's labor share in total labor (Theorem 4.1). Hence $L/C \to 0$ only if a rather special condition obtains: that those sectors for which the value rate of profit does not approach zero are of vanishing significance in the economy! But regardless of whether $L/C \to 0$ or not, we have shown that the price rate of profit, π, does not approach zero, but in fact increases, under the assumption of a fixed real wage. Hence, under the fixed-wage assumption, observations of the behavior of L/C are irrelevant for falling-rate-of-profit concerns.

Hence, the inferences that are frequently drawn concerning the actual rate of profit from the decrease in the maximal rate of profit are without foundation.

Rising organic composition of capital arguments

These arguments go back to Marx. Briefly they are based on this:

$$\rho = \frac{S}{C+V} = \frac{S/V}{C/V+1} = \frac{e}{C/V+1}$$

If the organic composition of capital (OCC) C/V rises over time as a consequence of technical change, then, "all other things being equal," ρ, the value of rate profit, falls. The argument is fallacious, under the assumption that the real wage remains fixed, because in that case e will *always* rise sufficiently to more than offset the rise in C/V, under the competitive scenario we are assuming. (Actually, the *value* rate of profit may fall as a consequence of viable technical changes, although the *price* rate of profit will never fall. Furthermore, because the price rate of profit is always an average of the sectoral value rates of profit, it is clear that the value rates of profit cannot fall too much; this was discussed in Chapter 4.)

It should probably be reiterated that I am not opposed to measuring the OCC over time – precisely because whether or not the rate of profit has fallen is an empirical question, as it rests entirely on the relation between technological change and the rate of change of the wage. We can, of course, put forth theories of the relation between technical change and changing real wages and examine the consequences for the rate of profit. Verification of such theories must be empirical. But the argument here is addressed to those who conclude that technical change itself (that is, in the absence of real wage change) can bring about a falling rate of profit in consequence of a rising OCC. There is no reason to examine the OCC either to demonstrate such an argument or to rebut it, unless one questions the competitive, cost-cutting theory of technical innovation.

5.3 The rising rate of profit with fixed capital: a special case

Shaikh (1978b) has claimed that in a model with fixed capital, the rate of profit may fall due to rational, competitive capitalist innovation. Because the version of Okishio's theorem that is appropriate to the case of fixed capital does not appear in the literature, it is appropriate to present such a theorem here. In this section a special case of a fixed-capital model is presented; it is assumed that there are no joint products, and that all fixed capital lasts forever. (These assumptions are related: Because fixed capital does not wear out, it does not have to be considered a joint product of a process in which it is used. The only process that "produces" an item of fixed capital is the one that manufactures it originally.) In the next section, we treat the general problem of fixed capital by examining the von Neumann model. However, it is worthwhile to treat the special case of nondepreciating fixed capital first, for several reasons: (1) It appears as a straightforward generalization of the pure circulating capital model, and the economic ideas embedded in the equations are therefore quite transparent; and (2) it is the polar opposite of the pure circulating capital case. That is, if the rate of profit can be shown to rise as a consequence of technical innovation in a model when fixed capital lasts forever, *a fortiori* it should rise when fixed capital wears out, this latter case being in some sense an average between the two polar cases.

Production, as before, consists of n processes producing n commodities. We define:

A is the $n \times n$ input matrix of circulating capital coefficients
L is the n row vector of direct labor coefficients
b is the n column vector of worker's subsistence
$\mathbf{\Phi}$ is the $n \times n$ input matrix of fixed capital coefficients

In this case, the capital inputs into process i consist of a column $\mathbf{A}^i$ of inputs which are consumed in the process, and a column $\mathbf{\Phi}^i$ that are used but not consumed. Notice no distinction has been made in labeling "fixed capital" goods and "circulating capital" goods and "consumption" goods. In general, we would therefore expect many components of $\mathbf{A}^i$ and $\mathbf{\Phi}^i$ to be zero. [This formulation of the fixed capital model is due, first, to Schwartz (1961).]

What is the equilibrium price vector $\mathbf{p}$ and profit rate π in this model? It is that pair $(\mathbf{p}, \pi)$ which makes the present discounted value (PDV) of the revenue stream, from operating each process at unit level, equal to zero. That is,

$$-(\mathbf{p}\Phi + \mathbf{p}A + \mathbf{L}) + \sum_{1}^{\infty} \frac{\mathbf{p} - (\mathbf{p}A + \mathbf{L})}{(1 + \pi)^i} = 0 \tag{5.9}$$

Let us consider one component of this matrix equation (5.9) obtained by examining process i. The first term, $-(\mathbf{p}\mathbf{\Phi}^i + \mathbf{p}\mathbf{A}^i + L^i)$, is the cost incurred in the first period of operation, when fixed capital to operate the process must be purchased $(\mathbf{p}\mathbf{\Phi}^i)$ as well as circulating capital $(\mathbf{p}\mathbf{A}^i + L^i)$. There is no revenue in the first period, because output appears only in the second period. In the second period, gross revenue is p^i, from selling the output made last period, and gross costs are the circulating capital laid out for next period, $(\mathbf{p}\mathbf{A}^i + L^i)$. There is no fixed capital cost, as the fixed capital set up in the first period works forever. For all subsequent periods, net revenue is $[p^i - (\mathbf{p}\mathbf{A}^i + L^i)]$; hence Equation 5.9.

Using the identity

$$\sum_{1}^{\infty} \left(\frac{1}{1 + \pi}\right)^i = \frac{1}{\pi}$$

we can rewrite (5.9) as

$$\mathbf{p} = \pi\mathbf{p}\Phi + (1 + \pi)(\mathbf{p}A + \mathbf{L}) \tag{5.10}$$

from which the economic interpretation is clear. In equilibrium, price consists of three components: costs of materials used ($\mathbf{p}A + \mathbf{L}$), the markup on materials used $\pi(\mathbf{p}A + \mathbf{L})$, and the markup on fixed capital used $\pi\mathbf{p}\mathbf{\Phi}$. There are no costs in consuming fixed capital, because depreciated over its infinite lifetime, zero fixed capital is used up each period. Equation 5.10 is, therefore, the straightforward generalization of Equation 5.1.

Now suppose that an innovation appears in sector i – that is, a new technique ($\mathbf{\Phi}^{i*}$, $\mathbf{A}^{i*}$, L^{i*}). What is the capitalists' innovation criterion? They will adopt it if at current prices and rate of return π, the stream of discounted net revenues, is positive with the new technique. That is, the rational capitalist treating prices as given, adopts the new technique if and only if:

$$-(\mathbf{p}\mathbf{\Phi}^{i*} + \mathbf{p}\mathbf{A}^{i*} + L^{i*}) + \sum_{1}^{\infty} \frac{\mathbf{p}^i - (\mathbf{p}\mathbf{A}^{i*} + L^{i*})}{(1 + \pi)^i} > 0 \tag{5.11}$$

This is equivalent to

$$\mathbf{p}^i > \pi\mathbf{p}\mathbf{\Phi}^{i*} + (1 + \pi)(\mathbf{p}\mathbf{A}^{i*} + L^{i*}) \tag{5.12}$$

If (5.12) holds, and the innovation is adopted, a new equilibrium ($\mathbf{p}^*$, π^*) must be reached under the new technique ($\mathbf{\Phi}^*$, A^*, $\mathbf{L}^*$), which consists of the old technique ($\mathbf{\Phi}$, A, $\mathbf{L}$) with column i replaced with the innovation ($\mathbf{\Phi}^{i*}$, $\mathbf{A}^{i*}$, L^{i*}). The generalization of Okishio's theorem becomes as follows:

THEOREM 5.1: Let ($\mathbf{p}$, π) be the equilibrium for technique ($\mathbf{\Phi}$, A, $\mathbf{L}$), satisfying:

$$\begin{aligned} \mathbf{p} &= \pi\mathbf{p}\mathbf{\Phi} + (1 + \pi)(\mathbf{p}A + \mathbf{L}) \\ 1 &= \mathbf{p}\mathbf{b} \end{aligned} \tag{5.10}$$

Let an innovation satisfy Inequality 5.12. Then, if ($\mathbf{p}^*$, π^*) is the new equilibrium,

$$\begin{aligned} \mathbf{p}^* &= \pi^*\mathbf{p}^*\hat{\mathbf{\Phi}} + (1 + \pi^*)(\mathbf{p}^*A^* + \mathbf{L}^*) \\ 1 &= \mathbf{p}^*\mathbf{b} \end{aligned} \tag{5.13}$$

it follows that $\pi^* > \pi$, where $\hat{\mathbf{\Phi}}$ is the matrix $\mathbf{\Phi}$ with column i replaced by $\mathbf{\Phi}^{i*}$. (It is assumed that the matrix $A^* + \mathbf{b}\mathbf{L}^* + \mathbf{\Phi}$ is indecomposable.)

Proof: It is not proved here that a unique equilibrium exists. That is a consequence of the Frobenius theorem in the usual way.

Let $M \equiv A + \mathbf{bL}$ be the augmented circulating input coefficient matrix. Then (5.10) can be rewritten as

$$\mathbf{p} = \mathbf{p}[M + \pi(M + \Phi)] \tag{5.10'}$$

Similarly, let $M^* \equiv A^* + \mathbf{bL}^*$, where the matrix A^* (and vector $\mathbf{L}^*$) are obtained, recall, by replacing the ith column (component) of $A(L)$ with $\mathbf{A}^{i*}(L^{i*})$.

According to (5.10) and (5.12), we have

$$\begin{aligned} p_i &> \mathbf{p}[\mathbf{M}^{i*} + \pi(\mathbf{M}^{i*} + \hat{\mathbf{\Phi}}^i)] \\ p_j &= \mathbf{p}[\mathbf{M}^{j*} + \pi(\mathbf{M}^{j*} + \hat{\mathbf{\Phi}}^j)] \quad \text{for } j \neq i \end{aligned} \tag{5.14}$$

Consider the matrix $[M^* + \pi(M^* + \hat{\Phi})] \equiv \mathbf{\Omega}(\boldsymbol{\pi})$. According to (5.14), $\mathbf{p}$ is a nonnegative vector that has the property

$$\mathbf{p} \geq \mathbf{p}\Omega(\pi)$$

It is well known that the existence of such a nonnegative vector implies that the Frobenius eigenvalue of $\mathbf{\Omega}(\pi)$ is smaller than unity (Frobenius theorem). It is also well known that increasing the components of $\mathbf{\Omega}(\boldsymbol{\pi})$ will increase the matrix's Frobenius eigenvalue; this follows because $M^* + \Phi$ is indecomposable, and therefore so is $M^* + \pi(M^* + \hat{\Phi})$. Hence, increasing $\boldsymbol{\pi}$, which increases the components of $\mathbf{\Omega}(\pi)$, eventually produces a matrix $\mathbf{\Omega}(\pi^*)$ with eigenvalue of unity, because an equilibrium exists. For π^*, there exists a positive eigenvector $\mathbf{p}^*$ such that:

$$\mathbf{p}^* = \mathbf{p}^*\Omega(\pi^*) \tag{5.15}$$

But (5.15) is equivalent to (5.13). It has been shown that $\pi^* > \pi$. Q.E.D.

It is now necessary to remark on Shaikh's (1978b) observation that in the presence of fixed capital the equilibrium rate of profit may fall, a statement which is incompatible with Theorem 5.1. Shaikh maintains that under a Marxian criterion, capitalists simply evaluate whether the new technique permits lower circulating costs of production than the old one. If so, they innovate. Shaikh defines the *profit margin* as the ratio of profits to circulating capital (including depreciation), and the *profit rate* as the ratio of profits to total capital advanced. He tries to rescue the FRP theory by claiming that competitive innovations will, indeed, cause the profit margin to rise, but the profit rate will fall if large amounts of fixed capital are involved. But the criterion of innovation with which Shaikh burdens his capitalists is completely irrational and ad hoc: they ignore the costs of fixed capital (except for depreciation)! Any capitalist considering an innovation that involves fixed capital must amortize the costs of fixed capital, as the procedure of Theorem 5.1 requires him to do. Capital costs are real costs: They take the form of interest payments. Shaikh's invented criterion is not a competitive one.

To reject the procedure of Theorem 5.1 is precisely equivalent to rejecting that Equation 5.10 captures the correct notion of equilibrium prices and profit rate in a model with fixed capital. Thus, adherents to Shaikh's position must confront Equation 5.10 and propose an alternative notion of equilibrium prices in the presence of fixed capital.

A final note should be appended to this argument. Saying that capitalists seek to maximize the internal rate of return is *not* tautologically the same as saying the general rate of profit increases in the economy. A theorem is required to prove this (Theorem 5.1). Maximizing the internal rate of return is the relevant notion of cutting costs in the fixed capital model. Hence, it is not being said that the economy naturally gravitates to the furthest wage–profit curve "because it's there"; rather, that competitive cost cutting pushes the economy to the frontier.

It is appropriate at this juncture to mention the interesting paper of Persky and Alberro (1978). Suppose that an innovation appears, which should be introduced, according to Inequality 5.12. The new rate of return is π^*. Then, two years later, another innovation appears, which is *again* profitable to introduce, even considering that the two-year-old machines must be scrapped. (The new innovation yields an equilibrium profit rate $\pi^{**} > \pi^*$.) But then the *actual* rate of return for the two-year period in which the first innovation operated was considerably less than π^*, for the infinite stream of positive net revenues never materialized. In this way, we see how a sequence of innovations can occur, each one of which will be adopted as it leads to a higher *expected* rate of return; but then, due to the truncated lifetimes of these innovations because of the unforeseen obsolescence, the *actual* rate of return falls. The most extreme case is when the innovations occur every year, so the capitalist is every period incurring the large costs of new fixed capital, and receiving only the small revenue of last period's output. A rising expected profit rate is, therefore, consistent with a falling actual profit rate.

This is, indeed, a theory of the falling rate of profit with microfoundations. It depends, however, on an assumption that is of dubious validity: that there is a series of *unforeseen* technical innovations. Capitalists are, for some reason, consistently underestimating the speed of technical progress. It is certainly possible that this may happen for a short period, but after a while capitalists will adjust their expectations, and assume that innovations will occur at a reasonable rate. Mathematically, this takes the form of truncating the expected economic lifetime of a technique. They will, for instance, not sum Σ_1^∞ in Inequality 5.12, but Σ_1^5, say; they will demand that an innovation pay for itself at the going rate of return in five years to pass the test for adoption. Furthermore, when most innovations today come from huge R&D labs, and are the result of planned and concerted development on a mass scale, it is reasonable to suppose that capitalists can forecast quite accurately the speed of innovation.

The Persky–Alberro proposal, then, does provide a story of a falling rate of profit. At best, it seems to work only for a short period; it cannot support a secular falling rate of profit. It depends on an unanticipated rate of technical change. It may be convenient to say that the anarchy of capitalist production is captured in this unanticipated rate of innovation; it seems more realistic, however, to believe that capitalists are not caught unaware for long, especially given the institutional environment for successful technical development today.

5.4 The general case of fixed capital: the von Neumann model

In the previous section, a special model of fixed capital was considered where all fixed capital lasts forever, and there is no joint production. In this section, we treat the general von Neumann model, where fixed capital can wear out at different rates, joint production occurs, and production processes can have different periods of production. It will be our aim to examine what happens to the rate of profit following the introduction of a cost-reducing technical change, with the real wage, as always, fixed.

To review the von Neumann model, there are n commodities, and m processes, each of which uses some inputs and labor and produces some outputs. We represent the technology by a set $\{B, A, \mathbf{L}, \mathbf{b}\}$, where

B is an $n \times m$ matrix of output coefficients
A is an $n \times m$ matrix of input coefficients
$\mathbf{L}$ is an m-row vector of direct labor inputs
$\mathbf{b}$ is an n-column vector of subsistence wage

The ith column $\mathbf{B}^i$ and $\mathbf{A}^i$ of the matrices B and A give the outputs and inputs of operating process i at unit level. We call $M \equiv A + \mathbf{bL}$ the augmented input coefficient matrix, and refer to the technology from now on as $\{B, M\}$. Recall that old machines are joint products themselves, which is why the joint-product framework is so convenient for analyzing the general model with fixed capital. [For a more complete discussion of fixed capital as a joint product see, for instance, Morishima (1969, chap. 6).]

An equilibrium price vector and profit rate $(\mathbf{p}, \pi)$ must satisfy

$$\mathbf{p}B \leqq (1 + \pi)\mathbf{p}M \tag{5.16}$$

We shall call *the von Neumann profit rate* the minimum π for which there exists a price vector $\mathbf{p} \geq 0$ satisfying (5.16). (This is, however, not a sufficient characterization of what constitutes an equilibrium, as will be discussed in the following section.)

An example: fixed capital that lasts forever

It may be useful, in making the transition from the special case of Section 5.3 to the general formulation of fixed capital here, to show how the case of the previous section looks if modeled in the von Neumann way. To this end, assume that we have a technology in which the only joint products are the fixed capital used in production. Otherwise, each process produces a single output. Furthermore, because fixed capital does not depreciate in that model, there are no new processes for producing the commodities using old fixed capital (because old fixed capital does not exist). Consequently, the output matrix B, in this case, is a square matrix given by

$$B = I + \Phi$$

where Φ, as in Section 5.3, is the matrix of fixed capital coefficients. The input matrix is $M + \Phi$. Inequality 5.16 becomes

$$\mathbf{p}(I + \Phi) \leqq (1 + \pi)\mathbf{p}(M + \Phi)$$

or

$$\mathbf{p} \leqq \mathbf{p}[M + \pi(M + \Phi)] \tag{5.17}$$

Now, by the Frobenius–Perron theorem, it is known that the minimum π for which there exists a nonnegative vector $\mathbf{p}$ such that (5.17) holds is, in fact, the value π such that

$$\mathbf{p} = \mathbf{p}[M + \pi(M + \Phi)] \tag{5.18}$$

If the matrix M is indecomposable, then the value π is unique, as is the price vector $\mathbf{p}$, and in fact $(\mathbf{p}, \pi)$ is the equilibrium discussed in Section 5.3. Equation 5.18 is precisely Equation 5.10.

Hence, the von Neumann formulation readily reduces to the characterization of equilibrium obtained by our present-discounted-value formulation of Section 5.3, in the special case dealt with there.

Marxian equilibrium in the von Neumann model

In the case of a simple Leontief model with no fixed capital, no joint production, and unit periods of production, we have the nice situation, assuming that the technology is indecomposable, that a unique price–profit rate equilibrium exists. Indeed, it is unnecessary to consider at what levels the various outputs are produced; one need only look at the price equations of the economy. This is because at equilibrium, all processes operate at the same (and therefore maximal) profit rates, and consequently capitalists can operate all processes, and produce any desired output combination. In the von Neumann case this is not necessarily so, because some processes will not be operated at an equilibrium described in Equation 5.16, as they do not produce the maximum attainable profit rate. It is necessary, then, to define an equilibrium in such a way that it is guaranteed extended reproduction is possible, while operating only those processes that produce a maximum profit rate. There are various ways of doing this. To avoid a lengthy treatment here, we take a modified von Neumann formulation:

Definition 5.1: A price vector and profit rate $(\mathbf{p}, \pi)$ are an *equilibrium* for the von Neumann system (B, M) if:
(a) $\mathbf{p}B \leqq (1 + \pi)\mathbf{p}M$
(b) $\exists \mathbf{x} \geqq 0$ such that $B\mathbf{x} \geqq (1 + \pi)M\mathbf{x}$
(c) $\mathbf{p}B\mathbf{x} > 0$

This definition states that it is possible for the system to reproduce itself (at growth rate π) by operating only those processes that achieve the maximal profit rate, π, from among the various processes. One might note that if (B, M) is an indecomposable Leontief system (I, M), then the unique von Neumann equilibrium is the usual equal-profit-rate price vector. Hence, this definition is a generalization of "Marxian equilibrium" to the joint production context.

It may, in general, be the case that there are many equilibria $(\mathbf{p}, \pi)$ in the sense of Definition 5.1. To avoid an extended discussion, we postulate that the system (B, M) is *irreducible* (see Gale, 1960, p. 314). Irreducibility is a weak generalization of indecomposability in Leontief models. If (B, M) is irreducible, then Gale (1960) shows there is a *unique* π associated with von Neumann equilibrium.

For our purposes, this suffices to define the equilibrium profit rate associated with a joint production economy – in particular, for an economy with fixed capital of all kinds.

The change in rate of profit in the von Neumann model in the presence of viable innovations

Given the von Neumann technology (B, M) as specified earlier, we define an *optimal price vector* as any semipositive price vector that minimizes the profit factor for the economy.

DEFINITION 5.2: The minimal profit factor for (B, M) is that number $\rho = 1 + \pi$ that is minimal in the set

$$\{\rho \geqq 0 \mid (\exists \mathbf{p} \geq 0)(\mathbf{p}B \leqq \rho\mathbf{p}M)\}$$

Any vector $\mathbf{p} \geq 0$ satisfying

$$\mathbf{p}B \leqq \rho\mathbf{p}M$$

is an optimal price vector.

Gale (1960) shows that if $\mathbf{p}$ is an optimal price vector, then $(\mathbf{p}, \pi)$ is a von Neumann equilibrium (Definition 5.1). Hence it is precisely the optimal price vectors, in this sense, that are the equilibrium prices with which we are concerned.

An innovation in this economy is a new process that can be characterized as a new pair of columns to be added to the B and M matrices. Call the innovation $(\mathbf{B}^{m+1}, \mathbf{M}^{m+1})$, where $\mathbf{B}^{m+1}$ and $\mathbf{M}^{m+1}$ are the two new column vectors. Notice that we do not *replace* columns of the production matrices with the innovations, as was the procedure in the simple Leontief model; rather, we append them to the old technology. In general, there are many alternative processes already in (B, M). Also, we may append many columns at once to (B, M).

We follow the same procedure for investigating changes in the rate of profit under innovation as is followed in the Leontief model of Chapter 4.

DEFINITION 5.3: Let $(\mathbf{p}, \pi)$ be an optimal price vector at the minimal profit rate π for economy (B, M). An innovation $(\mathbf{B}^{m+1}, \mathbf{M}^{m+1})$ will be called viable with respect to $\mathbf{p}$ if and only if:

$$\mathbf{p}\mathbf{B}^{m+1} > (1 + \pi)\mathbf{p}\mathbf{M}^{m+1} \tag{5.19}$$

If an innovation is viable, it upsets the old equilibrium, because it is more profitable than any process currently in operation at existing prices. (If a process is not viable, it does not upset the existing price equilibrium, and there is no question of a change in equilibrium.) Thus, we consider the appended technology $(\bar{B}, \bar{M})$, where $\bar{B} = (B, \mathbf{B}^{m+1})$, $\bar{M} = (M, \mathbf{M}^{m+1})$, which includes the new viable innovation, and ask: What happens to the minimal profit factor of $(\bar{B}, \bar{M})$? Does it necessarily rise or fall from π?

THEOREM 5.2: Let (B, M) be an irreducible von Neumann technology with equilibrium profit rate π and optimal price vector **p**. Let $(\mathbf{B}^{m+1}, \mathbf{M}^{m+1})$ be a viable innovation at prices **p**. Then:

(*i*) If the optimal price vector **p** is unique for (B, M), the equilibrium profit rate, $\bar{\pi}$, of the appended technology $(\bar{B}, \bar{M})$ is greater than π.

(*ii*) If **p** is not unique, then there can always be constructed viable innovations $(\mathbf{B}^{m+1}, \mathbf{M}^{m+1})$ that leave the equilibrium profit rate unchanged.

(*iii*) The equilibrium profit rate can never fall due to viable innovations.

This theorem completely resolves the issue of what happens to the rate of profit in fixed-capital, joint-production, alternative-process models in consequence of the introduction of new techniques – subject to the caveats of what the definition of a Marxian equilibrium *is* in such general models. For our purposes here, the theorem makes this general point: No matter how one complicates the technology, the "competitive" profit rate can rise only as a result of technical innovation, if the real wage remains unchanged. Note that Theorem 5.2, part (*iii*), is the generalization of the "Okishio theorem" to the von Neumann world.

Proof of Theorem 5.2

Part (*iii*). It is clear that the minimal profit can never fall in the appended technology. For let $(\bar{\mathbf{p}}, \bar{\pi})$ be an optimal price vector – minimal profit rate for $(\bar{B}, \bar{M})$. Then $\bar{\mathbf{p}}\bar{M} \leqq (1 + \bar{\pi})\bar{\mathbf{p}}M$. Thus $\bar{\pi} \geqq \pi$ by definition of π. But, Gale shows (1960) that the *minimal* profit rate is in fact the unique *equilibrium* profit rate for the irreducible von Neumann economy. Hence $\bar{\pi}$ is the new equilibrium profit rate, and the claim is proved.

Part (*i*). Let **p** be the *unique* optimal price vector for (B, M). Suppose that the minimal profit rate for $(\bar{B}, \bar{M})$ were π – that is, it did not rise. Then:

$$\text{there exists } \bar{\mathbf{p}} \geq 0 \text{ such that } \bar{\mathbf{p}}\bar{B} \leqq (1 + \pi)\bar{\mathbf{p}}\bar{M} \tag{5.20}$$

In particular, $\bar{\mathbf{p}}B \leqq (1 + \pi)\bar{\mathbf{p}}M$. But by the unicity of **p**, we must therefore have $\bar{\mathbf{p}} = \mathbf{p}$. This, however, is impossible, because by the assumption of viability, $\mathbf{pB}^{m+1} > (1 + \pi)\mathbf{pM}^{m+1}$; but according to (5.20), $\bar{\mathbf{p}}\mathbf{B}^{m+1} \leqq (1 + \pi)\bar{\mathbf{p}}\mathbf{M}^{m+1}$. Hence the minimal profit factor must rise in the appended technology.

Part (ii). Let $\mathbf{p}^*$ and $\mathbf{p}^{**}$ be two optimal price vectors for (B, M). Because $\mathbf{p}^* \neq \mathbf{p}^{**}$, there can be chosen a vector $\mathbf{C}$ such that

$$\mathbf{p}^*\mathbf{C} < 0 \qquad \mathbf{p}^{**}\mathbf{C} \geqq 0 \tag{5.21}$$

(This is a result of the so-called separating hyperplane theorem.) We can always find nonegative vectors called $\mathbf{B}'$ and $\mathbf{M}'$ such that

$$\mathbf{C} = (1 + \pi)\mathbf{M}' - \mathbf{B}' \tag{5.22}$$

Because $\mathbf{B}'$ and $\mathbf{M}'$ are nonnegative, they qualify as a conceivable technical process, with inputs and outputs specified by $\mathbf{M}'$ and $\mathbf{B}'$, respectively.

By (5.21) and (5.22), it follows that the innovation $(\mathbf{B}', \mathbf{M}')$ is viable with respect prices $\mathbf{p}^*$; however, from (5.21) we also have

$$\mathbf{p}^{**}\mathbf{B}' \leqq (1 + \pi)\mathbf{p}^{**}\mathbf{M}' \tag{5.23}$$

which means that in the appended technology $\bar{B} = (B, \mathbf{B}')$, $\bar{M} = (M, \mathbf{M}')$ we have $\mathbf{p}^{**}\bar{B} \leqq (1 + \pi)\mathbf{p}^{**}\bar{M}$. Hence the minimal profit rate of $(\bar{B}, \bar{M})$ remains unchanged at π^*.

It is worthwhile to notice the apparent simplicity of the proof of part *(iii)* of this theorem. Notice that this includes as a special case the "Okishio theorem" for the Leontief technology which was proved by use of eigenvalue properties in Chapter 4 (Theorem 4.6). In fact, the proof of part *(iii)* is not trivial: It is a consequence of the von Neumann existence theorem – that is, the existence of an equilibrium for the von Neumann model. (The statement that the *minimal* profit rate is in fact an *equilibrium* profit rate for the von Neumann model is the von Neumann existence theorem.) Thus, the rising-rate-of-profit theorem in the general case is a simple corollary to the von Neumann existence theorem.

A comment is worthwhile on the assumption of uniqueness of the optimal price vector $\mathbf{p}$. If the optimal price vector $\mathbf{p}$ is not unique, then the theorem tells us that the profit rate might stay the same after innovation. This is the generalization of what occurs in decomposable Leontief economies with no joint production: If an innovation occurs in a "luxury-goods" process, the rate of profit will not be affected. If we are willing to assume that the proper specification of the economy has sufficient structure to guarantee unicity of equilibrium prices, then the profit rate must rise, unambiguously, with the innovation of a viable process – according to Theorem 5.2, part *(i)*. The question naturally arises: Is there a condition on the von Neumann technology, such as indecomposability in the Leontief economy, that will guarantee unicity of the optimal price vector in the von Neumann model? The answer is yes. There is a natural type of indecomposability for the von Neumann model that guarantees the uniqueness of the price vector. A study of this question can be found in Roemer (1980b).

Hence, if real wages are assumed fixed, then rational innovation *never* leads to a falling rate of profit, regardless of complications introduced by fixed capital, differential turnover times, and so on.

Some miscellaneous points on technical innovations

Two assumptions on the nature of technical change have been made in this chapter, which are almost ubiquitous, it appears, in Marxian discussions of the falling rate of profit. One is that innovations take the form of inventing new *processes,* but not new *commodities;* the second is that innovations fall costlessly from the sky. A brief evaluation of what occurs upon relaxation of these assumptions follows.

One can introduce the concept of the invention of new commodities into the von Neumann model. Recall that each column of the matrix B (or M) is an n-vector of goods that appear as outputs (or inputs) from (or into) a particular process. Suppose that a process is invented which produces a new commodity – the $(n + 1)$st commodity. The process is characterized by two $(n + 1)$-column vectors $\mathbf{B}^{m+1}$, $\mathbf{M}^{m+1}$, where the $(n + 1)$st components of the vectors are the outputs and inputs of the new commodity in the new process. We simply adjust the old technology (B, M) to the new commodity space by adding a zero component to each column of B and M – because the old processes involve the new commodity as neither input nor output. Hence the appended technology is

$$(\bar{B}, \bar{M}) = \left(\begin{matrix} B \\ \mathbf{0} \end{matrix}, \mathbf{B}^{m+1}\right)\left(\begin{matrix} M \\ \mathbf{0} \end{matrix}, \mathbf{M}^{m+1}\right)$$

where the symbol $\mathbf{0}$, in both places, is a row vector of zeros m components long.

An optimal price vector for $\{\bar{B}, \bar{M}\}$ is in $\mathbf{R}^{n+1}$. Let $\bar{\mathbf{p}}$ be such an optimal price vector. Write $\bar{\mathbf{p}} = (\mathbf{p}, \bar{p}_{n+1})$, where $\mathbf{p}$ is the vector consisting of the first n components of $\bar{\mathbf{p}}$ and $\bar{p}_{n+1}$ is the $(n + 1)$st component. Now

$$\bar{\mathbf{p}}\bar{\mathbf{B}} \leqq (1 + \bar{\pi})\bar{\mathbf{p}}\bar{M} \tag{5.24}$$

which holds by definition of $\bar{\mathbf{p}}$, where $\bar{\pi}$ is the minimal profit rate for $(\bar{B}, \bar{M})$, implies that

$$\mathbf{p}B \leqq (1 + \bar{\pi})\mathbf{p}M \tag{5.25}$$

(This is easily seen from the definitions of $\bar{\mathbf{p}}$, $\mathbf{p}$, B, M, $\bar{B}$, $\bar{M}$.) Hence, by (5.25), as long as $\mathbf{p} \neq \mathbf{0}$, $\bar{\pi}$ must be at least as large as π, the minimal profit rate for the old technology (B, M). But it is certainly reasonable to assume that $\mathbf{p} \neq \mathbf{0}$, for if $\mathbf{p} = \mathbf{0}$, that is a statement that a price equilibrium exists in the new technology in which *all* old commodities become free goods. Let us rule out such an occurrence as economically unrealistic. Hence an innovation that introduces a new commodity cannot but raise the minimal profit rate of the economy.

After the new good exists, it will gradually become used as input into many more processes; this phenomenon takes the form of adding many new columns to the technology $(\bar{B}, \bar{M})$ – the dynamics of which have already been discussed. Eventually all the original processes of (B, M) may become obsolete; but at each step the von Neumann profit rate rises or stays the same, according to Theorem 5.2.

We take up next the issue of costly innovation. It is certainly un-Marxian to assume that innovation falls costlessly from the sky. Innovations are socially determined. Indeed, as has been remarked before, in discussing the Persky–Alberro paper, technical change in modern capitalism is a costly and deliberate process, emerging out of huge R&D centers. How does this alter the FRP discussion?

We shall not engage in a thorough analysis of this question here; for even if such an analysis did give rise to a theory of falling rates of profit, that would be a genuinely new theory, and not a theory of the type this chapter concentrates on.

Several general comments can be made, however. Let us view the process of innovation as itself an activity, that is, it can be characterized by a set of inputs, and a set of outputs (new, improved techniques). Suppose that there is a fair degree of certainty in what "outputs" will emerge from this process, for given input expenditure. Then capitalists can rationally allocate resources to the R&D process in such a way as to maximize total expected present discounted value – which is to say, they will never engage in R&D to such an extent as to lower the expected rate of profit.

Suppose, however, that there is uncertainty in the operation of the R&D activity. This opens a Pandora's box, akin to the phenomenon pointed out by Persky and Alberro (1978). In this case, capitalists may commit large expenditures to R&D, which do not pan out, and actual profit rates fall (while expected rates rise, due to capitalists' misestimates). Although this does generate a FRP "theory," one must ask: Can such a theory explain secular or even cyclic falling rates of profit on an economy-wide level? Certainly not. Research and development has itself become such a large business, and so systematized and "rationalized" through division of labor, that the outputs are not random and subject to elements of individual genius, but quite predictable. One cannot appeal to uncertainty in the innovation process as a source for endemic falling rates of profit in capitalist economies.

5.5 Conclusion

For at least a generation, various writers have pointed out that there is no necessity for the rate of profit to fall as a consequence of technical change considered by itself (Robinson, 1942; Sweezy, 1942; Dobb, 1945). Okishio (1961) demonstrated in a simple and compelling model that the rate of profit would rise as a consequence of competitive innovation. In recent years, other writers have attempted to resurrect FRP theories, by posing more complicated, but still competitive, models. The argument of this chapter is that there is no hope for producing a FRP theory in a competitive, equilibrium environment with a constant real wage.

It must be reiterated that this does not mean that the rate of profit does not fall; it does not mean that there cannot exist a theory of a falling rate of profit in capitalist economies. One must, however, relax some of the assumptions of the stark models discussed here to achieve such a FRP theory. Perhaps the most natural change to make concerns behavior of the real wage. If the real wage increases as a consequence of technical innovations, then a FRP may result, as is shown in the next chapter. The general point is this: If the rate of profit falls in such a changing real wage model, it is a consequence of the class struggle that follows technical innovation, not because of the innovation itself. A second possibility for producing a FRP theory is to produce a theory of rising state expenditures, which eat into before-tax profits, thus rendering a fall in the after-tax profit rate. This, indeed, is the suggestion of much recent Marxist work on the state (see Wright, 1975; O'Connor, 1973). An example of such a model is presented in Chapter 9. A third possibility, suggested by Rowthorn (1976), is that the increase in bargaining power of the LDCs vis-à-vis the imperialist countries may have shifted the terms of trade against the latter, resulting in a lower rate of profit for imperial capital.

Clearly this list does not pretend to be exhaustive; the general point is that many FRP theories can exist if the pure competitive model is abandoned. The general attack by the "fundamentalists" on these attempts is this: The "new" theories of FRP do not deduce a falling rate of profit from the development of capital itself, but from various ad hoc phenomena, such as class struggle (rising real wages), increased role of state, and so on. A favorite quotation, from Marx, is this: "The real barrier of capitalist production is *capital itself*." But if one wishes to construct an exegesis of FRP based on the implied theory of the development of capital from this quote, one can reply that the fundamentalists have taken far too narrow a definition of what "capital itself" is. Capital itself is a social relation, as we are so often reminded, and as such its development must include such phenomena as class struggle around the real wage, the increasing role of the state, uneven development of capitals (shifting terms of trade), and all the various influences that appear as ad hoc modifications of the rising organic composition model. These new theories are also called "profit-squeeze" theories. It is only the most narrow view of capital that classifies profit-squeeze theories as abandoning the view that capitalism develops according to its internal contradictions, and therefore that the fundamental barrier to capitalist production is capital itself.

Finally, a comment is necessary concerning the political positions that are frequently said necessarily to coexist with the positions taken in the FRP debate. The fundamentalists often say or imply that the profit-squeeze theories lead to reformist politics, as the fall, if any, in the rate of profit becomes completely contingent on ad hoc and subjective elements. The rising OCC theories, on the other hand, imply capitalist crisis independent of the subjective wills of men/women and lead, therefore, to a more revolutionary politics. A profit-squeeze theorist, however, could reply the supposed deduction that a FRP and capitalist crisis occurs independently of the intervention of class struggle, as in the rising OCC theories, can give rise to an economist and mechanistic theory of politics, where the necessity for conscious organization is dissipated. Neither of these theories of political action follows logically from its respective premises; the connection between economic theory and political practice is considerably more circuitous and subtle. The point of the examples, then, is to call for a more dispassionate discussion of the issues. One should not have to fear advocating a particular position in the discussion, or in scientific work in general, because of consequential branding as a political heretic. Were the discussions conducted on this dispassionate basis, whatever myths remain could be more easily cast aside, and progress would be made in developing a Marxian theory of crisis.

6 Changes in the real wage and the rate of profit

6.1 Introduction

In the preceding two chapters, we have shown that the rate of profit will not fall as a consequence of rational, competitive technical change if the real wage is held constant. It is clear that if the real wage rises, however, the equilibrium rate of profit may fall. To develop a full theory of a dynamic rate of profit, one would require a theory of how the real wage changes as a consequence of technical change. From the Marxian point of view, such a theory cannot be entirely "economic," in the usual sense, as what wage the workers succeed in receiving depends on subjective elements that become realized in class struggle. In this chapter we investigate one simple model which posits a relationship between technical change and the real wage. Briefly, we shall assume that real wages adjust after the innovation so that the relative shares of labor and capital remain unchanged.

In recent discussions of the labor process by the Marxian economists, there has been some controversy as to whether technical change is introduced by capitalists because it is *efficient,* or because it allows capitalists better to *control* workers and hence extract surplus value. [See, for instance, the writings of Marglin (1974), Stone (1974), Braverman (1974), Gordon (1976), Edwards (1979), and Gintis (1976).] In the final section of this chapter, we shall indicate how the model presented can be used to discuss this dichotomous aspect of technical change. Hence the classical issue of the falling rate of profit is resurrected in the modern discussions of the nature of technical change and the labor process under capitalism.

6.2 Technical change with constant relative shares

Because the model of the present chapter is offered as an example rather than as a general theory, we descend from the heights of generality of the previous chapters and confine the discussion to a two-sector linear, Leontief model. Sector 1 is the capital-goods sector, sector 2 the consumption-goods sector. To operate sector i at unit level uses as inputs direct labor in amount l_i and the capital good in amount a_i. The real wage bundle for a worker consists of b units of the consumption good. Thus, the augmented input coefficient matrix is

$$M = \begin{pmatrix} a_1 & a_2 \\ bl_1 & bl_2 \end{pmatrix}$$

and the equilibrium price equations are

$$p_1 = (1 + \pi)(p_1 a_1 + l_1) \tag{6.1}$$

$$p_2 = (1 + \pi)(p_1 a_2 + l_2) \tag{6.2}$$

$$1 = p_2 b \tag{6.3}$$

where we observe our previous convention that the wage is unity. Equations 6.1, 6.2, and 6.3 can be written as

$$\mathbf{p} = (1 + \pi)\mathbf{p}M \tag{6.4}$$

The innovation procedure is this: Capitalists introduce a viable, cost-reducing innovation when one appears. As before, a cost-reducing innovation, in sector 1, say, is a technical change (a_1^*, l_1^*) satisfying

$$p_1 a_1^* + l_1^* < p_1 a_1 + l_1 \tag{6.5}$$

where (p_1, p_2) are the current equilibrium prices. This eventually leads to a new equilibrium rate of profit, π^*, and new prices, $\mathbf{p}^*$, according to the theory of Chapter 4. Then, workers adjust their real wage bundle, to b^*, so as to achieve the same relative ratio as they enjoyed prior to the innovation.

Before being more precise, we must note that there is some indeterminancy as to what one means by "achieving the same relative share" as before. The ratio of profits to wages in the economy is

$$\nu = \frac{\pi \mathbf{p} M \mathbf{x}}{\mathbf{L}\mathbf{x}} \tag{6.6}$$

where $\mathbf{x}$ is the vector of output levels of the two sectors. After the technical change to $M^* = A^* + b\mathbf{L}^*$, the new profits–wages ratio is

$$\nu^* = \frac{\pi^* \mathbf{p}^* M^* \mathbf{x}}{\mathbf{L}^* \mathbf{x}}$$

assuming that the output mix remains the same at $\mathbf{x}$. Clearly, if workers were to adjust b so that the relative share is again made equal to ν, their behavior must depend on $\mathbf{x}$. That is, any theory that requires the *global* profits–wages share to be maintained constant must also develop a theory of how the output mix changes with technical change. Presumably, the output mix will change with technical change, and so we are immediately led to a rather complicated story. Furthermore, it is difficult to imagine a mechanism in the economy that would maintain *ex post* equality of the aggregate profits–wages share with its previous value.

A second approach is to posit that workers in each sector struggle, through their trade unions, to adjust their real wages so that the profit–wage ratio in their *sector* remains equal to what it had been prior to the innovation. The sectoral profit–wage ratios are

$$\nu_i = \frac{\pi(p_1 a_i + l_i)}{l_i} \tag{6.7}$$

The sector shares ν_i are independent of output mix, and hence the problem discussed above does not exist for this formulation. There is also a behavioral reason for favoring the sectoral-share adjustment story to the aggregate-share adjustment story: If we imagine trade union action as the mechanism that will achieve *ex post* equality of shares, then a particular sector, rather than the whole economy, is a more plausible jurisdiction within which the bargaining takes place.

There is, however, a cost to adopting the sectoral-share adjustment model: As we shall see below, if workers in each sector are to change their real wage b to achieve their *ex ante* relative share position, this will necessitate a divergence in real wages between the two sectors. Thus, we cannot maintain the following two assumptions simultaneously: (1) *ex post* equalization of sectoral relative shares following technical change; (2) an economy-wide competitive labor market. We shall, therefore, dispense with assumption 2. This is not inconsistent with the model, for if the mechanism for adjusting the real wage consists of labor unions specific to each sector, then it is also not unreasonable that sectoral wages would differ, due to differential bargaining strengths across sectors.

In summary, the assumption of a "constant relative share" is problematical. To discuss it on an economy-wide basis necessitates not only a theory relating technical change to the real wage, but also output levels to technical change. To discuss it on a sectoral basis requires dispensing with the assumption of an economy-wide competitive labor market. We do the latter, and posit different real wages in the two sectors.

6.3 A model of relative share constancy within sectors

The model is this. Initially, the economy is specified:

$$\text{Tableau 1} \quad \begin{cases} p_1 = (1 + \pi)(p_1 a_1 + l_1) \\ p_2 = (1 + \pi)(p_1 a_2 + w l_2) \\ p_2 b_1 = 1 \\ p_2 b_2 = w \end{cases} \tag{6.8}$$

or

$$\mathbf{p} = (1 + \pi)\mathbf{p}M$$

where

$$M = \begin{pmatrix} a_1 & a_2 \\ b_1 l_1 & b_2 l_2 \end{pmatrix}$$

The wage of the sector 1 workers is numeraire and w is the ratio of real wages between the two sectors. Cost-reducing, capital-using, labor-saving technical change (CU–LS) takes place (in sectors 1 or 2 or both), establishing a second tableau:

$$\text{Tableau 2} \quad \begin{cases} p_1^* = (1 + \pi^*)(p_1^* a_1^* + l_1^*) \\ p_2^* = (1 + \pi^*)(p_1^* a_2^* + w l_2^*) \\ p_2^* b_1 = 1 \\ p_2^* b_2 = w \end{cases} \tag{6.9}$$

or

$$\mathbf{p}^* = (1 + \pi^*)\mathbf{p}^* M^*$$

where

$$M^* = \begin{pmatrix} a_1^* & a_2^* \\ b_1 l_1^* & b_2 l_2^* \end{pmatrix}$$

Finally, real wages adjust so as to reestablish sectoral relative share constancy with Tableau 1, thus:

$$\text{Tableau 3} \quad \begin{cases} p_1^{**} = (1 + \pi^{**})(p_1^{**} a_1^* + l_1^*) \\ p_2^{**} = (1 + \pi^{**})(p_1^{**} a_2^* + w^{**} l_2^*) \\ p_2^{**} b_1^{**} = 1 \\ p_2^{**} b_2^{**} = w^{**} \end{cases} \tag{6.10}$$

and

$$\nu_1 = \nu_1^{**}, \ \nu_2 = \nu_2^{**} \quad \text{or} \quad \mathbf{p}^{**} = (1 + \pi^{**})\mathbf{p}^{**} M^{**}$$

where

$$M^{**} = \begin{pmatrix} a_1^* & a_2^* \\ b_1^{**} l_1^* & b_2^{**} l_2^* \end{pmatrix}$$

It is our task to show: (1) that for a given technical change, a final Tableau 3 reestablishing relative share constancy always exists; (2) the effect on the rate of profit and real wages.

Using Equations 6.8 and the definition of relative share (6.7), we can solve for p_1, π, b_1, b_2 as follows:

$$\pi = \frac{\nu_1(1 - a_1)}{1 + \nu_1 a_1} \tag{6.11}$$

$$p_1 = \frac{(\nu_1 + 1)l_1}{1 - a_1} = (\nu_1 + 1)\lambda_1 \tag{6.12}$$

(where λ_1 = embodied labor value of commodity 1);

$$b_1 = \frac{\nu_2(1 + \nu_1 a_1) - \nu_1(1 - a_1)}{\lambda_1(\nu_1 + 1)^2 \nu_2 a_2} \tag{6.13}$$

$$b_2 = \frac{\nu_1(1 - a_1)}{\nu_1 + 1} \cdot \frac{1}{\nu_2 l_2} \tag{6.14}$$

We can now demonstrate the following theorem.

THEOREM 6.1: Let technical change take place. Then there is a unique pair of real wages (b_1^{**}, b_2^{**}) that will render sectoral relative shares equal to their *ex ante* values. Furthermore, if the technical change is cost-reducing, CU–LS, then:

(*i*) The final equilibrium rate of profit at real wages (b_1^{**}, b_2^{**}) falls if technical change occurs in sector 1, and remains the same if change occurs only in sector 2.

(*ii*) If technical change occurs in sector 1 only (sector 2 only), then $b_1^{**} > b_1$ and $b_2^{**} < b_2$ ($b_1^{**} < b_1$, $b_2^{**} > b_2$).

(*iii*) If technical change occurs in both sectors, then at least one real wage must increase to maintain share constancy. Both, however, may increase.

Proof of Theorem 6.1: After technical change takes place and real wages have been adjusted to maintain constant shares, Equations 6.11–6.14 must hold for the variables π^{**}, b_1^{**}, b_2^{**}, a_1^*, l_1^*, l_2^*, λ_1^{**} with $\nu_i = \nu_i^{**}$. It follows immediately from (6.13) and (6.14) that a unique pair (b_1^{**}, b_2^{**}) exists.

Proof of (*i*). From (6.11), it is clear that π decreases if and only if a_1 increases, because $\nu_1 = \nu_1^{**}$; *if* a_1 is unchanged, so is π.

Proof of (*ii*). Let change occur only in sector 1. By the Theorem 4.9, a CU–LS change is progressive and so $\lambda_1^{**} < \lambda_1$. It follows immediately from (6.13) that $b_1^{**} > b_1$ and from (6.14) that $b_2^{**} < b_2$.

Let change occur only in sector 2. It follows immediately from (6.14) that $b_2^{**} > b_2$, and from (6.13) that $b_1^{**} < b_1$. (Observe that λ_1 is unchanged if there is no technical change in sector 1.)

Proof of (iii). If technical change occurs in both sectors, the profit rate falls [see (*i*)]. If neither real wage changed, then the profit rate would have risen under cost-reducing technical change, as discussed in Chapter 4. *A fortiori,* if neither real wage increases, the profit rate would have risen. But because the profit rate is known to have fallen, at least one real wage must have increased. By continuity it is clear from the proof of (*ii*) that examples may be constructed where either real wage rises and the other falls; it is furthermore possible to construct examples where both real wages rise, or one stays the same. Q.E.D.

Thus, under the assumption of constant relative sectoral shares, the rate of profit does fall as a consequence of cost-reducing technical change in sector 1.

What happens if there is a ratchet effect on absolute real wages? Suppose that technical change occurs only in sector 1 and workers in sector 2 will not permit an erosion of the absolute real wage to reestablish relative share to its *ex ante* value. Notice that π^{**} was determined solely by considerations of sector 1 relative share (Equation 6.11), so π^{**} remains the same. Our final tableau, in this case, will be characterized by a technology

$$M^{**} = \begin{pmatrix} a_1^* & a_2 \\ b_1^{**} l_1^* & b_2 l_2 \end{pmatrix}$$

It can easily be deduced by application of the Frobenius–Perron theorem that a unique equilibrium value b_1^{**} exists rendering the correct profit rate π^{**} to the matrix M^{**}, that $b_1^{**} > b_1$, and that the value b_1^{**} here is smaller than it would have been were there no ratchet effect. Furthermore, $\nu_2^{**} < \nu_2$ in this case.

The interesting conclusion in the ratchet-effect case is that the final equilibrium profit rate will be the same as in the no-ratchet-effect case. The difference between the two cases lies only in distribution of real wages between the two sectors. In particular, if sector 2 workers are strong enough to enforce the ratchet, it is not their bosses who are hurt, but the workers in the other sector! (Actually, this is an overstatement; the workers in the first sector still win a larger real wage than before technical change, but the increase is not so great as it would have been with no ratchet in sector 2.)

It should be noted what economic structure is responsible for this apparent anomaly. In this construction, sector 2 is "nonbasic." If each sector were an input into the other, then the final profit rate would be affected by a ratchet in sector 2. It should also be noted that the fall in the rate of profit that transpires according to the Theorem 6.1 is a consequence of the fact that the technical change is assumed to be capital-using and labor-saving. There may also be cost-reducing innovations that are capital-saving and labor-using, or that save on all inputs. It has been argued that capital-saving changes are not the kind envisioned by Marx. From Equation 6.11, it is clear that the rate of profit will rise in such cases, assuming that share constancy is maintained.

The qualitative conclusions are these. In general, the rate of profit falls if constant sectoral relative shares are maintained. The real wage rises, at least, in the sector with "most" technical change; if the technical change is very uneven in the two sectors, then the real wage may fall in the backward sector.

In a more complete Marxian model, we would have to consider the effect on these dynamics of the increased unemployment from the displaced workers created by technical change. (This, at least, is Marx's vision of the effect of technical change.) The larger industrial reserve army would make it more difficult for workers in the sector with technical change to reestablish the *ex ante* relative share; their bargaining power would be reduced. This effect tends to mollify the dynamics here.

6.4 Technical change and class struggle: efficient versus controlling technical changes

The writings of Braverman, Marglin, and Stone have raised the question: Do capitalists introduce technical change because it reduces costs or because it allows better control over workers? Gordon (1976) states the question in sharpest form when he asks if it is possible for capitalists to introduce technical changes that are not cost-minimizing because they allow more control.

There is more to the discussion of technical change by these writers than this encapsulation implies; they are concerned with the forms that such change takes under capitalism, its effect on the work process and workers. One aspect of the economic question of "controlling" versus "efficient" technologies can be cast in terms of the model used here.

We may decompose the effect on the profit rate from a technical change into two effects: the change in π that occurs from the change in technological coefficients $\{a_1, a_2, l_1, l_2\}$ while real wages $\{b_1, b_2\}$ are fixed, and the subsequent change in π when real wages change to $\{b_1^{**}, b_2^{**}\}$. That is, there is the change in moving, first, from Tableau 1 to Tableau 2, and second, in moving from Tableau 2 to Tableau 3. Thus, in the notation of the previous sections,

$$\pi^{**} - \pi = (\pi^* - \pi) + (\pi^{**} - \pi^*)$$

or

$$\Delta\pi = \Delta\pi_e + \Delta\pi_b$$

Now the essence of technical efficiency is the relation of output to units of input. To measure technical efficiency, we must therefore consider workers as mechanical inputs into the production process; as such, their labor is relevant only insofar as it commands a certain amount of replenishment, b_1 or b_2. Thus, improvements in technical efficiency are measured by assuming that the real wage – that is, the real input into the production process of the wage good – remains fixed per unit of labor. Hence the change $\Delta\pi_e = \pi^* - \pi$ is the *efficiency effect* of a technical change. However, if the real wages change as a consequence of the technical change, that is solely because labor is embodied in living workers who are conscious of their role in production, and are therefore able to command a larger input of the wage good when technical conditions make their labor more productive. This is captured in the second effect, $\Delta\pi_b = \pi^{**} - \pi^*$, which is the *real-wage effect* of a technical change. In particular, if the labor were supplied by horses, we would always have $\Delta\pi_b = 0$. The horse will not receive more hay per unit of labor expended even if a revolutionary advance is made in the design of the plough to which it is harnessed.[1]

The real-wage effect captures, in a limited way, the "controlling" aspects of new technology. New technology changes the social relations, it changes the bargaining position of capital and labor, and implies consequent changes in the real wage. There is, however, certainly more to the controlling effect of technology as described by the radical writers than is captured in the real-wage effect defined here. As a consequence of new technologies, capital does not reap the advantages only – or even, perhaps mainly – in the lower real wages it can pay, but in the hegemony it thereby establishes over the production process [see Braverman (1974) and Edwards (1979)]. These systematic aspects of control cannot be captured in the type of model presented here.

In the story told in Section 6.3, the mechanism of technical change and class struggle was such that

$$\Delta\pi_e > 0 \qquad \Delta\pi_b < 0 \qquad |\Delta\pi_b| > \Delta\pi_e$$

The real-wage effect was negative and dominated the efficiency effect. More generally, we should not suppose that relative shares will be reestablished at *ex ante* values following a technical change; the purpose, in fact, of the type of technical change introduced by capitalists, according to Marglin et al., is to establish a balance of class forces that prevents this from happening. Capitalists, it would be claimed, will not introduce a technical change unless the real-wage effect is positive, or small in absolute value if negative.

If capitalists do plan with this much foresight – which is the important question with which these theories must come to grips[2] – then their gaze will be focused on the net effect $\Delta\pi$, and not simply the efficiency effect $\Delta\pi_e$. (This is assuming that they can estimate the real-wage effect $\Delta\pi_b$ which, of course, is not the job of the plant engineer but rather that of the "industrial psychologist.") It is, in fact, certainly conceivable that a technical change will be introduced with $\Delta\pi_e < 0$ if $\Delta\pi_b > 0$ and $\Delta\pi_b > |\Delta\pi_e|$. Consider this example: A process operates under Tableau 1 with a small number of skilled workers who receive a high real wage. The capitalist introduces sophisticated machinery, so that the process can be performed with the same number of workers but with less skill. The efficiency effect in this case would be negative; however, because the capitalist can now bring to bear the pressure of the entire unskilled industrial reserve army in the bargaining process, the real wage will fall; the real-wage effect is positive and sufficient to nullify the efficiency effect. This story is not dissimilar to the one told by Stone about the deskilling of the labor process in the steel industry.

To make the same point with technical language, the model of Section 6.3 was a myopic, Cournot-type model. It was assumed that capitalists adopt technically efficient innovations when they appear, without consideration of what the workers' reactions shall be. A more sophisticated game-strategic approach is clearly called for in modeling the type of process under discussion.

There is an obvious taxonomy of technical change according to the real-wage and efficiency effects:

Type 1a: $\Delta\pi_e > 0,\ \Delta\pi_b < 0,\ \Delta\pi < 0$
Type 1b: $\Delta\pi_e > 0,\ \Delta\pi_b < 0,\ \Delta\pi > 0$
Type 2a: $\Delta\pi_e < 0,\ \Delta\pi_b > 0,\ \Delta\pi < 0$
Type 2b: $\Delta\pi_e < 0,\ \Delta\pi_b > 0,\ \Delta\pi > 0$
Type 3: $\Delta\pi_e > 0,\ \Delta\pi_b > 0$
Type 4: $\Delta\pi_e < 0,\ \Delta\pi_b < 0$

Clearly, type 4 changes will never appear.[3] Any of the others might appear. Type 3 changes are evidently the safest ones for the capitalist, but because they entail a drop in absolute real wages for the working class as a whole (because $\Delta\pi_b > 0$), it is unlikely that they appear. Type 1 technical change is the neoclassically conceived type: Technical change is cost-reducing ($\Delta\pi_e > 0$), but then some of the added fruits of increased productivity trickle down to the workers ($\Delta\pi_b < 0$). Type 2 technical change is the most extreme form of Marglin–Stone change: It is cost-increasing in the short run but allows greater control, as manifest in decreased real wages.

Using this taxonomy, one could in theory test the Marglin–Stone hypothesis by classifying technical changes that have occurred into various types. Most technical changes are probably of type 1, and so the judgment must be based more subtly on whether there exist feasible technical changes with large $\Delta\pi_e$ values that are not introduced because of even larger suspected negative values of $\Delta\pi_b$. The point of this discussion is not to formulate a model sufficiently well specified for empirical work, but to show how the two effects discussed in the literature can be dichotomized and identified.

A final comment is necessary to identify the description here with the way the controlling effect of technical change is pictured as operating in much of the radical literature. The introduction of new machinery may not be followed by a decrease in the real wage per unit of labor power (say, a day's work), but by increased intensity of work. For instance, the assembly line may not introduce any strictly technical advances over craft work, but it enables the capitalist to speed up the work process. This is a phenomenon considered important by Marglin in the advent of the factory system and the assembly line. In Marxist terminology, the technical change has the effect of extracting more labor from a given amount of labor power. A unit of labor power, however, may command the same wage – in which case the wage decreases per unit of labor, or work actually performed. Now we must ask: In the description of a technology as $\{a_1, a_2, l_1, l_2\}$, do the l_i represent amounts of labor or labor power? The implicit neoclassical assumption is that they stand for units of labor power. It is assumed that the intensity of work is fixed. Thus, suppose that there are two processes for making a pin, each requiring the same amount of capital-good input, but one requiring one worker-day and the other two worker-days. The neoclassical conclusion is that the first process is more technically efficient. The Marxist, however, asks: How hard are the workers laboring in the two processes? If the organization of work in the first process is such that the capitalist can force the worker to work twice as fast as workers labor in the second process, then it cannot be said that the first process is technically more efficient. From the radical–Marxist point of view, the coefficients l_i must measure some standard of *labor performed,* not the commodity labor power purchased, to render an accurate picture of technical efficiency in production.

Suppose that a technical change is described by $\{a_1, l_1\} \rightarrow \{a_1^*, l_1^*\}$, where $l_1^* < l_1$ and $a_1^* > a_1$, where the framework is neoclassical and l_1 and l_1^* stand for units of labor power (worker-days). Perhaps the real wage b_1 stays fixed in Tableau 3. Does this mean that the real-wage effect is zero? No. An accurate assessment would necessitate the following construction. If the workers under the new technology worked at the same intensity as they did under the old one (however that may be measured), how much labor time would be necessary to produce a unit of output now? If the answer is l_1^{**} and $l_1^{**} > l_1^*$, then we must consider the new technology to be properly characterized by $\{a_1^*, l_1^{**}\}$.

This, in turn, implies that the new real wage, instead of remaining fixed at b_1, will have fallen to a value b_1^{**} *per unit of labor expended,* defined by

$$b_1^{**} = \frac{b_1 l_1^*}{l_1^{**}} < b_1$$

Hence, it is clear the real-wage effect, $\Delta\pi_b$, is positive.

In summary, although a neoclassical description of the production process may appear to imply that the real-wage effect is zero, to gain an accurate assessment labor coefficients must be recalculated in terms of labor *expended,* using as a standard of measurement the intensity of labor that was performed in the former technology. (It is not obvious, however, how such intensity should be measured.) The real wage must then be amortized over units of labor actually performed. It is in this way that the hidden control effect arising from the more "efficient" extraction of labor from labor power due to the innovation may be isolated. Marxists consider this type of effect to be of utmost importance, and it is kept clearly in mind by recalling the distinction between labor and labor power. Neoclassical economists might attempt to describe the same phenomenon with the concept of x efficiency.

6.5 Summary

This discussion shows that Marx's classical concern with the tendency for the rate of profit to fall is resurrected in the current radical–Marxian concerns with the nature of technological change under capitalism, with the effect of technical change on the balance of class forces. Although Marx's original conjecture was incorrect – that the rate of profit could fall with cost-reducing technical changes and constant real wages – it has been shown that with cost-reducing, capital-using, labor-saving changes, the rate of profit will in general fall, if it is the sectoral relative shares of workers that remain fixed, not the absolute level of the wage. This formulation, however, is itself too narrow, and serves only as a standard to which actual history may be compared. More generally, the effect on the real wage resulting from technical change is not settled *a priori* and is considered to be a focus of the considerations of capitalists, in the modern radical literature. A full assessment of the changes in the rate of profit must evaluate both the strictly technically induced increment (decrement) and the increment (decrement) induced from the control effect that a technology enables capital to exercise over workers. An accurate measurement of these two effects can be made only by clearly separating the concept of labor from labor power. Thus, whether the rate of profit rises or falls as a result of capitalist technical innovations is a question that cannot be answered by purely technical considerations; it is a question that is, at heart, Marxian, as it involves consideration of the social consequences of the confrontation between living labor and dead labor in a new form. These social consequences, at a first approximation, are reflected in the effect of technical change on the real wage.

7 The law of value and the transformation problem

7.1 Marx's project: where do profits come from?

A main task of a theory of value for capitalist economy, for Marx, was to answer the question: Where do profits come from? Perhaps it is easier to comprehend why this question was of a somewhat paradoxical nature by comparing capitalism to the two major precapitalist, class-stratified modes of production: feudalism and slavery. Under slavery, the class of slave owners forcibly expropriated unpaid labor from slaves. Thus, slave owners lived off slaves in a most obvious way. Under the feudal organization of production, the expropriation of the surplus was almost as obvious. Serfs performed the *corvée* for several days a week and worked several days a week on their own plots. The product of their plots was theirs for consumption; the labor time spent on the *corvée* was transformed into goods expropriated directly by the lord. Again, there can be no confusion concerning the locus of surplus production, and the locus of its expropriation. In both slavery and feudalism, the key to the division of society into a rich, expropriating class and a poor, expropriated one was the existence of a coercive institution for the exchange of labor.

What was puzzling to Marx concerning capitalism was this: The institution of labor *exchange* was not coercive. Nevertheless, one class became incredibly rich, and the other remained impoverished. Marx insisted on modeling capitalism as a regime in which markets are fair, an idea he tried to capture in his value theory by requiring commodities of equal value to be exchanged for each other. In particular, the commodity labor power is exchanged for its value, the wage, on the labor market. The riddle was, how could expropriation of labor come about – for come about it must to explain the huge difference between class fortunes under capitalism – in the absence of a coercive institution for the exchange of labor? Marx constructed an answer to this question with his version of the labor theory of value, surplus value, and exploitation. What is important for our purposes is just this: The task of the theory was to show that the coerciveness of the institution of labor exchange was not a necessary condition for the existence of exploitation of one class by another.

Marx believed that the preconditions for the existence of the wage labor market were themselves coercive – that is, workers had no choice but to sell their labor power, as they had been separated from the means of production, and had no alternative for survival. In a precise sense, however, this simply sets certain initial conditions on the bargaining strength of the two parties in the market; it does not obviate the fact, juridically, that participation in the labor market is voluntary, at least in a model of pure capitalism. This is one example of Marx's "scientific," as opposed to "utopian," approach to capitalism. He wished to explain the existence of exploitation in a noncoercive model, in the sense described. This is obviously more difficult than appealing simply to the omnipotence of the capitalist class.

How did Marx approach the problem of showing profits can arise from fair exchanges? The solution, in Volume I of *Capital,* involved developing two tools:

1. A theory of exchange where the exchange value of every commodity is based on an objective property of the commodity
2. A way of measuring that objective property for the special commodity labor power, to arrive at its exchange value

The necessity for some objective property of commodities was to enable Marx to define exchanges as fair – fair in not being based on subjective considerations, but on a detached, objective property of commodities. The notion of fairness contains no moral or ethical connotations; on this Marx was clear.

Marx's solution was to take as the objective property of a commodity its socially embodied labor time; the way of attributing such a number to the commodity of a day's labor power was to posit a subsistence real wage or *subsistence bundle* for workers. The socially necessary labor time embodied in the commodity labor power is the labor value of the subsistence bundle. With these definitions, Marx was able to come up with a concept of surplus value as the difference between a day's labor time and the value of the day's labor power. The notion of exploitation followed.

From the necessity of answering questions 1 and 2 above, it is clear why Marx had to insist on a subsistence bundle for workers. If a subjective element were to be introduced in the determination of workers' consumption, then the value of the commodity labor power could not be said to be determined *objectively.* Consequently, the notion of "fair" or "competitive" exchange on the labor power market would dissolve. (We might better describe Marx's exchange concept as competitive; each commodity was supposed to exchange for its value, properly defined.) The subsistence concept, then, was not simply one that perhaps captured the conditions of nineteenth-century capitalism; it was logically necessary to accomplish Marx's purpose, given the methodological approach outlined by questions 1 and 2.

That Marx's theory logically mandated the concept of a subsistence real wage does not mean he adopted that concept in order to make this theory work. On the contrary, the evidence presented in the next section demonstrates that Marx saw capitalism as maintaining the real wage of workers at a subsistence level and that his theory developed around this fact. Furthermore, the subsistence wage was a classical premise. The argument here, then, is made *ex post* in an effort to expose the structure of Marx's problem and his solution. Our task will be to construct a Marxian theory without a subsistence wage.

It is worthwhile to summarize briefly how prices actually do relate to labor values in the Marxian system to see how the Marxian *numéraire* of an hour's embodied labor as the unit of exchange holds up. We shall assume the standard linear, Leontief technology (A, $\mathbf{L}$) that was studied in Chapters 1 and 4. First, let us assume that the organic compositions of capital are equal in all sectors. Let $\mathbf{\Lambda}$ be the vector of commodity labor values, $\mathbf{p}$ the vector of commodity prices relative to the wage, the wage being taken as 1, and $\mathbf{b}$ be the (constant) vector of subsistence commodities for workers. Let e be the rate of surplus value, defined by

$$e = \frac{1 - \mathbf{\Lambda b}}{\mathbf{\Lambda b}} \tag{7.1}$$

If the prices $\mathbf{p}$, which are competitively arrived at, equalize the profit rates in all sectors, then it is easily computed that in the case of equal organic compositions of capital, there is a unique such price vector, and it satisfies the relations

$$\mathbf{p} = (1 + e)\mathbf{\Lambda} \tag{7.2}$$

and

$$\mathbf{pb} = 1 \tag{7.3}$$

(Equation 7.3 says that subsistence bundle $\mathbf{b}$ can just be purchased with the wage.)

Let us rewrite (7.2) as

$$\frac{p_i}{\lambda_i} = 1 + e \qquad \text{for all } i \tag{7.4}$$

This says that the price per hour of embodied labor time of all *produced* commodities is constant, and equal to 1 + e. We must ask: Is the price per hour of embodied labor time of the one remaining commodity, labor power, also equal to 1 + e? By definition, the price per hour of embodied labor time of labor power is $w/\mathbf{\Lambda b} = 1/\mathbf{\Lambda b} = 1 + e$, by (7.1), and it is, therefore, true that *all* commodities, including labor power, exchange at prices that are proportional to embodied labor values. The labor theory of value as a quantitative theory of exchange is validated.

Let us now drop the assumption of equal organic compositions of capital. It is still true that the rate of exploitation or surplus value is defined by (7.1). Furthermore, if prices are assigned to commodities according to Equation 7.2, it remains true that all commodities, including labor power, will exchange at prices proportional to their embodied labor times. However, such prices will not, in this case, bring about equal rates of profit in all sectors. (In fact, such prices can be arrived at by a uniform markup on wages alone in all lines of production, rather than a uniform markup on total costs of production.) Thus, the competitive assumption of a uniform profit rate violates the quantitative-labor-value exchange theory: Competitive prices do not bring about an exchange of commodities according to amounts of embodied labor time.

The bourgeois critics of Marx's theory rest their case at this point. The exchange theory of *Capital,* Volume I, holds only in a very special case. Consequently, Marx's theories of value, surplus value, and exploitation must be discarded. This, however, is not the case, for the Marxian theory of exploitation can be constructed quite independently of the labor theory of value as a quantitative exchange theory. We have already shown this to be the case in the general Marxian model of Chapters 2 and 3. What, then, is the purpose of the present chapter? It is to argue, more explicitly, for a reinterpretation of Marxian value theory and the transformation problem. In particular, this will involve discarding the concept of a subsistence wage. We shall propose an interpretation of the so-called Marxian law of value, and discuss the implications of this interpretation for the transformation problem.

In brief, the effort will be to propose a value theory that preserves the two great Marxian ideas: (1) that the arena of social relations among men and women can be understood by studying relations of labor expropriation, although the observable manifestation of these relations becomes reified through prices, commodities, and money; (2) in particular, that exploitation, the expropriation of surplus value, produces profit. Yet the value theory must discard what we have argued are the two incidental concepts of Marx's analysis: (3) that workers are paid a subsistence wage, and (4) prices of commodities are such that equivalent exchanges for equivalent, and that, in some sense, price can be fruitfully conceived of as a distortion of embodied labor value.

7.2 Marx and the subsistence wage

This section is a historical excursus. Its purpose is to argue that, in at least one of his important writings, Marx argued quite explicitly that under capitalism workers would be paid a subsistence wage. I have argued that a subsistence wage is logically necessary for Marx's approach, because he requires an objective way of assigning a value (i.e., embodied labor time) to the commodity labor power, to preserve the notion that labor power exchanges for its proper equivalent on the labor market.

It is usually argued that Marx did not subscribe to a literal subsistence theory, but believed that subsistence is defined according to historical and social norms. Although Marx says the latter clearly, it must be pointed out that a surplus-value theory in which subsistence is a subjective concept loses its power as a theory of fair exchange. It is tautological to speak of workers' subsistence being whatever they consume; at that level, Marx's argument loses its persuasion as an objective economic argument demonstrating the origin of profits. Ronald Meek makes this point:

> If the value of labour-power at any given time is taken to be simply what the workers happen to have been getting for their labour-power during the previous few years, Marx's theory of wages becomes so general as to be virtually meaningless. Marx, I think, would have recognized quite frankly that the average worker in advanced capitalist countries today was getting a real wage substantially higher than the value of his labour-power, and would have tried to explain why [Meek, 1967, p. 119].

Our historical locus is Marx's pamphlet, *Wages, Price and Profit* (1973), which was written to counter the argument of an Owenite named Weston, who argued that workers should not bother to fight for higher wages, because the iron laws of economics condemned them to whatever the given wage was. One would expect that *if* Marx believed workers could win a higher-than-subsistence wage, this would have been the place to say it! (Marx is here thinking of the wage as a particular money wage or gold wage, which allows, in normal times, a given level of subsistence.) He argued, however, in Chapter

XIII, entitled "Main Cases of Attempts at Raising Wages or Resisting Their Fall," that wage raises take place for four reasons:

1. Due to changes in productivity, the value of labor power may rise, necessitating a higher wage. The example given is that the movement to less fertile farmland means that the subsistence food bundle will embody more social labor time.
2. Price inflation. The discovery of new gold mines will cheapen the value of gold and hence raise the money price of goods.
3. The struggle over the length of the working day may raise workers' real hourly wage, though leaving their daily subsistence bundle unchanged.
4. The business cycle. On the downswing, workers get paid less than the value of their labor power, and so on the upswing they must struggle for more than its value to break even.

In none of the four cases does the struggle for an increase in wages affect the real subsistence bundle the worker receives. Almost as an aside, not at a numbered point, Marx mentions that a rise in labor productivity can give rise to a real wage increase. Suppose that the real wage stays the same following a productivity increase:

> Then profits would rise . . . Although the labourer's absolute standard of life would have remained the same, his *relative* wages, and therewith his *relative social position,* as compared with the capitalist, would have been lowered. If the working man should resist that reduction of relative wages, he would only try to get some share in the increased productive powers of his own labour, and to maintain his former relative position in the social scale (Marx, 1973, p. 66).

This is the lone example of workers increasing their real wage, that is, improving upon the old subsistence bundle, and it is clear from the context that it is not a main point. Marx concludes the chapter by saying that the cases discussed account for ninety-nine wage increases out of a hundred.

> . . . despite all the ups and down, and do what he may, the working man will, on the average, only receive the value of his labour, which resolves into the value of his labouring power, which is determined by the value of the necessities required for maintenance and reproduction, which value of necessities finally is regulated by the quantity of labour wanted to produce them.

However, having driven home the literal nature of the subsistence concept, Marx qualifies it with the remark:

> But there are some peculiar features which distinguish the *value of the labouring power, or the value of labour,* from the val-

> ues of other commodities. The value of labouring power is formed by two elements – the one merely physical, the other historical or social. The *ultimate limit* is determined by the physical element . . . the value of labour is in every country determined by a *traditional standard of life.*

Then follows the resolution between the literal subsistence theory and the historical–social subsistence theory. In fact, class struggle is constantly occurring around the wage:

> The fixation of its actual degree (the rate of profit) is only settled by the continuous struggle between capital and labour, the capitalist constantly tending to reduce wages to their physical minimum, and to extend the working day to its physical maximum, while the working man constantly presses in the opposite direction. The question resolves itself into a question of the respective powers to the combatants.

Why cannot the wage, then, be raised above subsistence? Because, due to the nature of technological change, which makes workers relatively less scarce, the bargaining power of capital is such that it will, in fact, be able to force the wage to its physical minimum:

> In the progress of industry the demand for labour keeps, therefore, no pace with the accumulation of capital. It will still increase, but increase in a constantly diminishing ratio as compared with the increase of capital.
>
> These few hints will suffice to show that the very development of modern industry must progressively turn the scale in favour of the capitalist against the working man, and that consequently the general tendency of capitalistic production is not to raise, but to sink the average standard of wages, or to push the *value of labour* more or less to its *minimum limit.*

The wage theory of *Wages, Price and Profit* may now be synthesized. *Ex ante,* real wages are determined by class struggle, by the "respective powers of the combatants." However, because of the peculiar nature of another law of capitalist development (labor-saving technical innovation), the class power of workers is not sufficient to win them more than the physical subsistence level.

Although it might be claimed that *Wages, Price and Profit* was not Marx's mature work, and that it is unfair to claim that the wage theory presented there was Marx's final theory, these arguments of Marx have been reproduced because they show how important the subsistence concept was in the *genesis* of Marx's thought on the theory of exploitation. In *Capital,* Volume I, Chapter 25 ("The General Law of Capitalist Accumulation"), Marx presents a wage theory somewhat modified from the subsistence theory outlined earlier. The possibility that the real wage rises with accumulation is given more weight in that chapter of *Capital.* There is, however, a natural upper bound on the level of the real wage, and that is the wage above which capitalists will cease investing because of a profit squeeze. If the real wage rises to too high a level, then:

> The rate of accumulation lessens; but with its lessening the primary cause of that lessening vanishes, i.e., the disproportion between capital and exploitable labour-power. The mechanism of the process of capitalist production removes the very obstacles that it temporarily creates. The price of labour falls again to a level corresponding with the needs of the self-expansion of capital, whether the level be below, the same as, or above the one which was normal before the rise of wages took place (Marx, 1947, p. 633).

Here the subsistence wage is not so sharp a concept as in *Wages, Price and Profit;* it is, rather, a subsistence band that is determined by the requirements of capital's expansion. This position is more consonant with the theory of the real wage presented in the following section. Yet what Marx fails to do in the chapter on accumulation, and in *Capital,* is to discuss what objective meaning can be assigned to the value of labor power when the real wage is to some degree indeterminate. Even in *Capital,* it must be said, Marx maintained the position that there is not much leeway in the real wage. This is seen in the quotation above, and also, later in the same paragraph, when he states: "To put it mathematically: the rate of accumulation is the independent, not the dependent, variable; the rate of wages, the dependent, not the independent variable."

A modern Marxian theory, then, should maintain the general concept that class struggle determines real wages. Class struggle may determine a real wage that is greater than "subsistence." We need not debate whether "subsistence" is a biological or historical concept. With wages no longer held at subsistence, the value of labor power loses its well-definedness. Not only, then, is the reformulation of Marxian value theory without a subsistence wage a *possible* way of developing a theory of exploitation not based on the labor theory of value as exchange theory, it becomes a *necessary* reformulation if an effort is made to construct a Marxian theory in which class struggle is thought of as determining the real wage.

7.3 The law of value

For Marx, economic categories (price, commodity) were reflections of social categories (work, labor, exploitation). If we posit social relations at a given point in time as being embodied in the relations of labor expropriation and the intensity of that expropriation, the *economic* question becomes: How do the economic categories – price, profit rate, money wage – emerge so as to allow the system to reproduce itself at the given constellation of social relations? This is often stated in terms of Marx's two worlds – a world of social relations among people, and a world of relations among things (as reflected in prices). How, precisely, do the categories in the phenomenal world of things arrange themselves so as to reify consistently the underlying relations in the social world? How can a given constellation of prices and commodity exchanges reproduce social relations? The *law of value* is the name we shall give to the principle which says that the world of social relations regulates relations in the world of prices and commodities. I think this is the most fruitful interpretation of what Marx meant by the law of value.

This question can be discussed at many levels. At the deepest level, it must include discussion of the way in which market relations reenforce institutions and beliefs that reproduce capitalism. Our task is only to propose an economic interpretation of the law of value.

For present purposes, it is convenient to distinguish between the goods that workers consume, which will be produced by department II, and the capital-goods sector, department I. Because we wish to dispense with the subsistence-wage premise, we shall allow workers to choose among goods by evaluating a "utility" function u_i. This should not be taken to imply that a subjective theory of demand is the preferred theory: The purpose of this construction is to show that a Marxian theory of exploitation can be consistent even while allowing workers to choose goods. Recall that in Chapter 2, another theory was put forth of the social determination of workers' consumption.

Let:

A_{I} be the $n \times n$ indecomposable, productive matrix of physical input–output coefficients in department I, capital-goods industries

A_{II} be the $n \times r$ input–output matrix for department II, consumption-goods industries

$\mathbf{p}_{\mathrm{I}}$, $\mathbf{p}_{\mathrm{II}}$ be the row price vectors for the two departments

$\mathbf{b}_i$ be the r column vector of consumption goods for the ith worker

$u_i(\mathbf{b})$ be the utility function for worker i

$\mathbf{L}_{\mathrm{I}}$, $\mathbf{L}_{\mathrm{II}}$ be the row vectors of direct labor inputs in the two departments

π be the rate of profit

The labor-value vectors, $\mathbf{\Lambda}_{II}$ and $\mathbf{\Lambda}_{I}$, for the two departments can be defined in the usual Leontief way:

$$\mathbf{\Lambda}_I = \mathbf{\Lambda}_I A_I + \mathbf{L}_I$$

$$\mathbf{\Lambda}_{II} = \mathbf{\Lambda}_I A_{II} + \mathbf{L}_{II}$$

and the social rate of exploitation is

$$e\left(\sum_1^N \mathbf{b}_i\right) = \frac{N - \mathbf{\Lambda}_{II}(\Sigma\, \mathbf{b}_i)}{\mathbf{\Lambda}_{II}(\Sigma\, \mathbf{b}_i)}$$

where N is the number of workers in the economy. (The unit for denominating working time and the consumption bundle is one working day, of constant magnitude.)

If the social rate of exploitation is at some level e^*, then

$$e(\Sigma\, \mathbf{b}_i) = e^* \tag{7.5}$$

The money wage is taken as numeraire, and the equal profit-rate price equations are

$$\mathbf{p}_I = (1 + \pi)(\mathbf{p}_I A_I + \mathbf{L}_I) \tag{7.6}$$

$$\mathbf{p}_{II} = (1 + \pi)(\mathbf{p}_I A_{II} + \mathbf{L}_{II}) \tag{7.7}$$

Workers choose $\mathbf{b}_i$ as follows:

$$\forall i \quad \mathbf{b}_i \text{ maximizes } u_i(\mathbf{b}_i) \text{ subject to } \mathbf{p}_{II}\mathbf{b}_i = 1 \tag{7.8}$$

We can now state the theorem that embodies the law of value.

THEOREM 7.1 (Law of value): Given any nonnegative number e^*:
(*i*) There exists an equilibrium $\{\pi, \mathbf{p}_I, \mathbf{p}_{II}, \mathbf{b}_1, \ldots, \mathbf{b}_N\}$ satisfying Equations 7.5–7.8.
If the utility functions satisfy Assumption A below, then:
(*ii*) For any e^*, the equilibrium is unique.
(*iii*) The function $\pi(e^*)$ that is therefore defined is strictly monotone increasing, with $\pi(0) = 0$.

Assumption A. Let $\mathbf{D}_i(\mathbf{p}_{II})$ be the demand function generated by u_i, when workers maximize u_i subject to the budget constraint $\mathbf{p}_{II}\mathbf{b} = 1$. It is assumed that $\mathbf{D}_i(\mathbf{p}_{II})$ is a function and that

$$\hat{\mathbf{p}}_{II} > \mathbf{p}_{II} \Rightarrow \mathbf{D}_i(\hat{\mathbf{p}}_{II}) < \mathbf{D}_i(\mathbf{p}_{II})$$

That is, if the wage–price of every consumption good increases, then consumption of all goods decreases.[1]

Proof of Theorem 7.1

Proof of part (*i*). Let e^* be given. Let $\mathcal{B}$ be any nonnegative vector such that $e(\mathcal{B}) = e^*$ (see Equation 7.5). $\mathcal{B}$ is to be thought of as a candidate for aggregate workers' consumption. Consider the set of equations (7.6), (7.7), and (7.9), where

$$N = \mathbf{p}_{\mathrm{II}}\mathcal{B} \tag{7.9}$$

By the indecomposability of A_{I} and the Frobenius theorem, there exists a unique solution set $\{\boldsymbol{\pi}, \mathbf{p}_{\mathrm{I}}, \mathbf{p}_{\mathrm{II}}\}$ to these three equations. Because $\mathbf{p}_{\mathrm{II}}$ is determined by (7.8), a set $\{\mathbf{b}_i\}$ is determined. Define $\mathcal{B}' = \Sigma\, \mathbf{b}_i$. Let $\mathcal{B}''$ be that multiple of $\mathcal{B}'$ such that $e(\mathcal{B}'') = e^*$ (such a multiple always exists).

What has been defined is a continuous function $\phi : \mathcal{B} \rightarrow \mathcal{B}''$, which maps the compact convex set $\{\mathcal{B} \,|\, e(\mathcal{B}) = e^*\}$ into itself. By Brouwer's fixed-point theorem, there is a fixed point $\mathcal{B}^*$ such that $\mathcal{B}^* = \mathcal{B}^{*''}$.

Now $\mathcal{B}^{*'} = \Sigma\, \mathbf{b}_i^*$ and $\mathbf{p}_{\mathrm{II}}^*\mathbf{b}_i^* = 1$ implies that $\mathbf{p}_{\mathrm{II}}^*\mathcal{B}^{*'} = N$. Because $\mathcal{B}^{*''} = \alpha\mathcal{B}^{*'}$, we have $\mathbf{p}_{\mathrm{II}}^* \cdot \mathcal{B}^{*''} = \alpha N$ and therefore $\mathbf{p}_{\mathrm{II}}^*\, \mathcal{B}^* = \alpha N$. By (7.9), it follows that $\alpha = 1$, and hence

$$\Sigma\, \mathbf{b}_i^* = \mathcal{B}^{*'} = \mathcal{B}^* \tag{7.10}$$

Hence, the bundles $\mathbf{b}_i^*$ maximize $u_i(\mathbf{b}_i)$ with respect to budget constraints $\mathbf{p}_{\mathrm{II}}^* \cdot \mathbf{b}_i^* = 1$ and give rise to a social rate of exploitation e^*; that is, the set $\{\pi^*, \mathbf{p}_{\mathrm{I}}^*, \mathbf{p}_{\mathrm{II}}^*, \mathbf{b}_i^*\}$ is a solution to (7.5)–(7.8).

To prove parts (*ii*) and (*iii*), we require the following lemma.

Lemma 7.2: Under Assumption A, if $\mathcal{B}_1^*$ and $\mathcal{B}_2^*$ are two fixed points of the function ϕ defined above, then $\pi(\mathcal{B}_1^*) = \pi_1^* = \pi(\mathcal{B}_2^*)$.

Proof: Suppose that $\pi(\mathcal{B}_2^*) = \pi_2^* > \pi_1^* = \pi(\mathcal{B}_1^*)$. It can be shown by differentiating Equation 7.6 with respect to $\boldsymbol{\pi}$ that in this case $\mathbf{p}_{\mathrm{I},2}^* > \mathbf{p}_{\mathrm{I},1}^*$ and from equation 7.7,

$$\mathbf{p}_{\mathrm{II},2}^* > \mathbf{p}_{\mathrm{II},1}^* \tag{7.11}$$

(That is, equilibrium wage–prices rise with the profit rate.) From (7.11) and Assumption A, we have $\mathcal{B}_2^* < \mathcal{B}_1^*$, which contradicts the supposition that $e(\mathcal{B}_1^*) = e^* = e(\mathcal{B}_2^*)$. Q.E.D.

Proof of part (*ii*). By the lemma, all fixed points $\mathcal{B}^*$ for e^* generate the same profit rate $\boldsymbol{\pi}^*$, and hence the same price vectors $\mathbf{p}_{\mathrm{I}}^*$, $\mathbf{p}_{\mathrm{II}}^*$ by (7.6) and (7.7), and hence the same $\{\mathbf{b}_i^*\}$ by (7.8). But $\mathcal{B}^* = \Sigma\, \mathbf{b}_i^*$; hence the fixed point is unique.

Proof of part (iii). $\pi(e^*)$ is a function by the lemma. Suppose that $e^{**} > e^*$ but $\pi(e^{**}) < \pi(e^*)$. It follows that $\mathbf{p}_{\mathrm{II}}^{**} < \mathbf{p}_{\mathrm{II}}^*$ by consideration of (7.6) and (7.7). By Assumption A, $\mathscr{B}^{**} > \mathscr{B}^*$, which contradicts the supposition. It is easily seen that if $\pi(e^{**}) = \pi(e^*)$, then $\mathscr{B}^{**} = \mathscr{B}^*$, which contradicts the supposition. Hence, $\pi(e^*)$ is strictly monotone increasing.

Furthermore, if $e^* = 0$, then $\mathbf{\Lambda}_{\mathrm{II}}\mathscr{B}^* = N = \mathbf{p}_{\mathrm{II}}\mathscr{B}^*$. But it is well known that $\mathbf{p}_{\mathrm{II}} > \mathbf{\Lambda}_{\mathrm{II}}$ if $\pi > 0$. It follows that $\pi = 0$. Q.E.D.

In what sense does Theorem 7.1 capture the Marxian "law of value?" It says that, corresponding to any given constellation of social relations, as captured in the social variable e^*, which measures the intensity of exploitation, there exists a set of prices, profit rate, and commodity consumptions for workers that realize or reify the social conditions e^* as an equilibrium in the world of profits and commodities – in the sense that profit-maximizing production by capitalists can take place and reproduce the economy at those prices (because the rate of profit is equalized in all sectors), while every worker maximizes utility subject to his wage constraint. If, moreover, we wish to admit Assumption A or some similar sufficient condition, then it is true that the correspondence between the social variable e^* and its phenomenal realization $\{\pi_{\mathrm{I}}, \mathbf{p}_{\mathrm{II}}, \mathbf{b}_1, \ldots, \mathbf{b}_N\}$ is unique, and that the struggle over the social rate of exploitation is reflected in the movements of the rate of the profit, because $\pi(e^*)$ is a monotonic function. In any case, the important part of Theorem 7.1 is part (*i*): that uniqueness and monotonicity are not assured without some stringent assumption on utility functions is a consequence of the weak relationship between prices and values. This aspect of the transformation problem is studied further in the next chapter.

Some further points must be mentioned. Notice that labor values enter only into the definition of the social rate of exploitation, and exchanges are described only in terms of prices. In general, the individual rates of exploitation of workers will differ when workers choose different consumption bundles: $e_i = (1 - \mathbf{\Lambda}_{\mathrm{II}}\mathbf{b}_i)/\mathbf{\Lambda}_{\mathrm{II}}\mathbf{b}_i$. e^* is an appropriate average of the individual e_i. The notion of labor value is thus useful in this formulation to discuss the social distribution of labor time but not the individual renumeration of workers. This is a consequence of discarding the subsistence bundle. Notice that the insight that profits are possible only because social labor time exceeds socially necessary labor time is clearly brought out, because $\pi > 0$ if and only if $e^* > 0$. (This is true even in the absence of Assumption A, as can easily be shown.)

It is important to point out that Theorem 7.1 does not imply that the level of exploitation is set *first* at e^*, and *then* prices, a profit rate, and workers' consumption bundles are determined. The statement is rather one of the existence of a well-defined correspondence or a relationship between the "two worlds." If e^* is thought of as a proxy for the relative strengths of the two classes, then the theorem says: There is a consistent reification of any relative class position into prices, profits, and so on. The reason this remark must be insisted upon is that it cannot be claimed that in actual class struggle the rate of exploitation is the bone of contention at the bargaining table between workers and capitalists. (That value magnitudes cannot be properly established logically prior to prices is discussed further in Chapter 10.) Nor is it claimed that the rate of exploitation is the best index of income distribution. What is demonstrated is simply this: that a Marxian theory of exploitation (that profits arise from surplus value) is valid independently of the labor theory of value as exchange theory. It is valid independently of the subsistence-wage concept. For this purpose, it suffices to take the social rate of exploitation, e^*, as a datum of the problem, and to show how profits, prices, and consumptions are necessarily realized according to the laws of capitalist reproduction (competition).

Theorem 7.1 presents, then, an algorithm for what Marx referred to as the law of value: that specific way in which a given distribution of society's labor time (as captured in the entity e) corresponds to a particular equilibrium of production and distribution of physical goods through the market. This seems the most fruitful and consistent interpretation of the Marxian law of value, the claim that (labor) value "regulates" the market process. By contrast, it is not particularly fruitful to view the law of value as a mechanism which sees to it that commodities exchange at their labor values modified by various deviations.

It is finally possible to reiterate why the model used in this chapter is of the simple circulating capital, no-joint-production type. If this simple model is replaced with the most general production model of Chapter 2, then the use of labor values as exchange magnitudes necessarily evaporates, because there is no consistent way of defining individual labor values in that case. (These problems are summarized in Steedman (1977) for the von Neumann joint-production model.) The point of this chapter, however, has been to argue for a reformulation of Marxian value theory independently of the technical problems that arise in more complex models.

Briefly, the argument has been this: the cleftswitch of Marxian value theory has been the necessity of maintaining that exchange on the labor market is an exchange of equivalents, in terms of labor values. Workers get a wage that commands, in commodity form, the labor time embodied in their labor power. That is, labor value exchanges for equivalent labor value on the labor-power market. As long as one insists on this interpretation, one is insisting on the labor theory of value as an exchange theory, at least on the labor-power market. This done, one can, of course, show that profits arise from exploitation. The problem is that the principle, which was insisted on to regulate exchange on the labor-power market, does not seem to regulate exchange on other commodity markets: namely, labor value does not exchange for its equivalent labor value on the automobile market (unless organic compositions of capital are all equal). Thus, even when Marxists defend Marxian value theory by saying that labor values are not *intended* to be exchange values, the defense rings false, because of the implicit use of labor equivalents exchange on at least one market, the very important labor-power market. The reformulation that has been proposed here to solve the problem has been this: We discard the notion that labor equivalents exchange for each other on *any* market. We do not define the value of labor power. We lose the notion, therefore, of "fair" exchange on the labor-power market. The laws of exchange are not fair in some sense of the exchange of some abstract equivalent: They are governed by competition and class struggle. Class struggle sets the distributional variable – whether this is to be thought of as the wage, the real wage bundle, the profit rate, labor's share, or the rate of exploitation can vary in different models – and competition regulates prices to allow capitalist reproduction consistent with the distributional boundary condition of class struggle. (Or, more generally, competition and class struggle co-determine prices and wages.) The labor theory of value is discarded entirely as an exchange theory but is preserved as a measure of exploitation.

7.4 The transformation problem

For Marx, relationships observed in the phenomenal world of prices and commodities had to be explained by social relations between people. The transformation problem in its more general form is the exhibition of the correspondence between these two worlds; as such, it is the subject of investigation of all volumes of *Capital.* Moreover, the transformation problem can be cast in as many different molds as there are disciplines in social science: There is a sociological transformation problem (the doctrine of commodity fetishism), a historical transformation problem (How does the correspondence in question evolve as the mode of production changes?), a philosophical transformation problem (Which is real, the price world or the social world? In what sense is there a causal relationship between the two worlds?), and an economic transformation problem. Most writing on the subject views the problem only in its economic dimension.

Specifically, the economic transformation problem seeks to relate the concepts of value and exploitation that describe the social world to the commodity-based concepts of price and profit. This has given rise to two exercises: the exhibition of (1) the functional relationship between labor values and prices, and (2) the functional relationship between exploitation–surplus value and profit-making–profits. It has been argued in this chapter that problem (2) is the appropriate economic translation of the transformation problem, and that problem (1) is a nonproblem, a misconceived project, whose origin lies in an effort to think of labor values as regulating exchange in some important way.

A simple conclusion follows from the approach of this chapter: Any comparison of microdenominated value magnitudes to microdenominated price magnitudes is misconceived. Only if our theory implies some meaningful relationship of individual prices to individual labor values would such comparison be interesting. The demystification of the expropriation of surplus value is accomplished without any ambiguity concerning the relation of labor values to the exchange process. The labor theory of value is used directly as an exploitation theory, without going through the conduit of a labor theory of exchange to get there. It is by understanding that workers' power as a class is only sufficient to command a fraction of society's labor time that the locus of expropriation is exposed. *Why* labor gets only a part of the product is not addressed here, nor is it specified precisely through what economic mechanisms class power becomes manifest.

7.5 Summary

It may be useful to summarize the points of this chapter, because the theory put forth differs in some important ways from received Marxian value theory:

The fundamental aspects of the Marxian value theory presented are these:

1. The real level of consumption of workers as a class is determined by their power as a class relative to capital and is not necessarily limited to subsistence.

2. Exchange of labor power for the wage is not characterized as fair in the sense of an exchange of equivalents, but as determined by class struggle.
3. The labor theory of value is preserved to define exploitation and is discarded as a theory of microexchanges.
4. The commodity-price veil placed over social relations is removed by seeing that class struggle and competition determine wages and profits and that the latter can exist only with social exploitation.
5. There is no social insight gained from making comparisons of microvalue-defined magnitudes to microprice-defined magnitudes: values to prices, sectoral surplus values to sectoral profits, etc..
6. The Marxian "law of value" states not that labor values determine prices, but that a given set of social relations is reified into a particular set of economic variables (prices, outputs, profits) in such a way as to reproduce the system. This reification or realization process of social relations into commodity relations is the process by which value "regulates" price, or the law of value.
7. The rate of exploitation describes the social distribution of the product but does not describe precisely the allocation of any individual worker's labor time between him and the capitalist.
8. The compatability of a choice mechanism of demand for workers and a Marxian theory of social exploitation is shown explicitly.

These conclusions all follow from replacing the *special* subsistence theory of wages by the *general* class struggle theory of wages. Once this replacement is made, Marx's implicit motivation for using the labor theory as an exchange theory, at *some* level of abstraction, dissolves.

8 The transformation correspondence

8.1 Introduction

In the last chapter we proposed an interpretation of Marxian value theory that views the transformation problem as being meaningful only at an aggregate level. In this chapter we shall study more carefully a correspondence between the rate of exploitation and prices, in a simple linear model. From studying this correspondence, we can see accentuated some of the pitfalls of a misconceived microdenominated value approach; we can also remark on the relationship between "marginal utilities" and "class struggle" in the determination of relative prices, in a fairly quantitative way. As was exhibited in Theorem 7.1, we show that both subjective utilities and class struggle can be thought of as having a role in determining prices. There is no logical contradiction in admitting a place for both approaches, although one might wish to choose between them on other grounds.

In Chapter 7, the utility functions of workers were fixed at some specific set $\{u^i\}$; now, we think of the utility function(s) as varying and ask: For a given rate of exploitation, what relative prices can be achieved as the utility function, or consumption basket, of the worker varies?

8.2 The transformation correspondence

As in Chapter 1, we shall work in the environment of an $n \times n$ indecomposable input–output matrix A. The n vector of direct labor coefficients, $\mathbf{L}$, is assumed to be semipositive. We denote a worker's consumption basket as $\mathbf{b}$, in which case equilibrium prices satisfy:

$$\mathbf{p} = (1 + \pi)(\mathbf{p}A + \mathbf{L}) \tag{8.1}$$

$$1 = \mathbf{pb} \tag{8.2}$$

The vector of labor values is

$$\Lambda = \mathbf{L}(I - A)^{-1} \tag{8.3}$$

If we allow the consumption bundle to vary, the rate of profit varies.

THEOREM 8.1: There is a continuous nonnegative function $\pi(\mathbf{b})$, defined on set $\mathscr{B} = \{\mathbf{b} \mid \Lambda\mathbf{b} \leqq 1\}$, which assigns to a particular $\mathbf{b} \in \mathscr{B}$ the equilibrium profit rate satisfying Equations 8.1 and 8.2. $\pi(\mathbf{b})$ is strictly monotone decreasing in each component.

Proof: This is a direct consequence of Theorem 1.1; monotonicity of $\pi(\mathbf{b})$ follows from that part of the Frobenius theorem which asserts that the maximum eigenvalue of an indecomposable matrix is a strictly increasing function of the entries of the matrix. Q.E.D.

Although the profit rate is a well-defined function of the consumption bundle, it is not a well-defined function of the rate of exploitation. That is, the rate of exploitation is

$$e(\mathbf{b}) = \frac{1 - \Lambda\mathbf{b}}{\Lambda\mathbf{b}}$$

and we have the following theorem:

THEOREM 8.2: If the organic compositions of capital of technology $\{A, \mathbf{L}\}$ are not all equal, then, for any $e > 0$, there always exist $\mathbf{b}_1, \mathbf{b}_2 \in \mathscr{B}$ such that $e = e(\mathbf{b}_1) = e(\mathbf{b}_2)$ but $\pi(\mathbf{b}_1) \neq \pi(\mathbf{b}_2)$.

Note. Theorem 8.2 says that we cannot conceive of $\boldsymbol{\pi}$ as a single-valued function of e, as $\mathbf{b}$ varies.

Proof: Choose $\mathbf{b}_1 \in \mathscr{B}$ and let $\pi(\mathbf{b}_1) = \pi_1$. The set of consumption bundles $\mathbf{b}$ giving rise to profit rate π_1 is

$$D = \{\mathbf{b} \mid \pi(\mathbf{b}) = \pi_1\} = \{\mathbf{b} \mid \mathbf{p}(\pi_1)(\mathbf{b} - \mathbf{b}_1) = 0\} \tag{8.4}$$

The set of consumption vectors that give rise to the same rate of exploitation as $\mathbf{b}_1$ is

$$Eq(\mathbf{b}_1) = \{\mathbf{b} \mid \Lambda(\mathbf{b} - \mathbf{b}_1) = 0\} \tag{8.5}$$

From (8.4) and (8.5), $Eq(\mathbf{b}_1) \subseteq D$ if and only if $\Lambda = \alpha\mathbf{p}(\pi_1)$, for some scalar $\alpha > 0$. But it is well known that values are not proportional to prices unless (1) the profit rate is zero, or (2) there are equal organic composition of capital in all sectors. Thus, we may conclude that $Eq(\mathbf{b}_1) \not\subset D$, and the theorem is verified. Q.E.D.

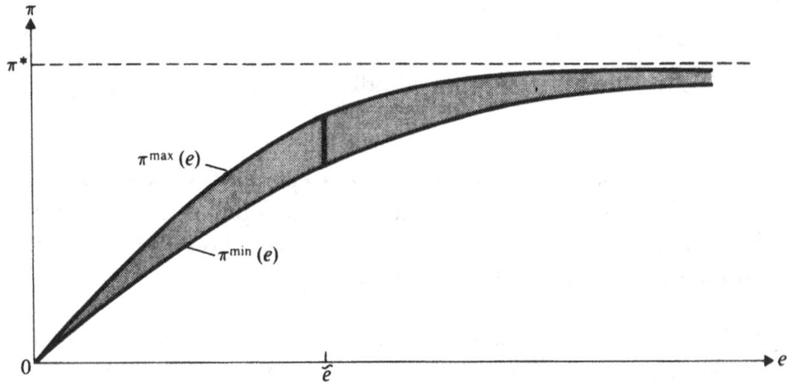

Figure 4

What is the array of profit rates to which one rate of exploitation can give rise? According to Theorem 8.2, we define the *correspondence* (multivalued function):

$$\Pi(e) = \{\pi \mid \exists \mathbf{b} \in \mathcal{B} \text{ s.t. } e(\mathbf{b}) = e \text{ and } \pi(\mathbf{b}) = \pi\}$$

We proceed to show that $\Pi(e)$ has a graph as depicted in Figure 4. This is summarized in Theorem 8.3.

Theorem 8.3
(*i*) $\pi^{\max}(e)$ and $\pi^{\min}(e)$ are continuous functions.
(*ii*) $\pi^{\max}(e)$ and $\pi^{\min}(e)$ are strictly monotone increasing.
(*iii*) $\pi^{\max}(0) = \pi^{\min}(0) = 0$.
(*iv*) $\Pi(e)$ is a positive closed interval for all $e > 0$, if the organic composition of capital are not all equal.
(*v*) $\lim_{e\to\infty} \pi^{\min}(e) = \lim_{e\to\infty} \pi^{\max}(e) = \pi^*$
where $\pi^{\max}(e)$ and $\pi^{\min}(e)$ are the functions defined by $\pi^{\max}(e) = \max \Pi(e)$, $\pi^{\min}(e) = \min \Pi(e)$, and π^* is the maximal profit rate associated with A. [That is, $\pi^{\max}(e)$ is the largest profit rate that can correspond to the rate of exploitation e.]

We first require a lemma:

Lemma 8.4: $\Pi(e)$ is a continuous correspondence.

Proof

(*a*) *Upper hemicontinuity.* Choose a sequence of exploitation rates $e_n \to e_0$, with $\pi_n \in \Pi(e_n)$ and $\pi_n \to \pi_0$. It must be shown $\pi_0 \in \Pi(e_0)$.

We have been given a sequence $\mathbf{b}_n$ s.t.: $\pi(\mathbf{b}_n) = \pi_n$ and $e(\mathbf{b}_n) = e_n$ for each n, and $\mathbf{b}_n \in \mathcal{B}$. Because $\{\mathbf{b}_n\}$ lie in the compact set $\mathcal{B}$, $\mathbf{b}_n \rightarrow \mathbf{b}_0$. By continuity of the function $e(\mathbf{b})$, we have $e(\mathbf{b}_0) = e_0$. Because $\mathbf{b}_0 \in \mathcal{B}$, $\pi(\mathbf{b}_0)$ is defined. By continuity of $\pi(\mathbf{b})$, $\pi(\mathbf{b}_n) = \pi_n \rightarrow \pi(\mathbf{b}_0)$ and so $\pi(\mathbf{b}_0) = \pi_0$. Hence $\pi_0 \in \Pi(e_0)$.

(*b*) *Lower hemicontinuity.* Given a sequence $e_n \rightarrow e_0$, $\pi_0 \in \Pi(e_0)$. To show

$$\exists\{\pi_n\} \text{ s.t. } \pi_n \rightarrow \pi_0 \text{ and } \pi_n \in \Pi(e_n)$$

We are given $\mathbf{b}_0$ s.t. $e(\mathbf{b}_0) = e_0$ and $\pi(\mathbf{b}_0) = \pi_0$. Define

$$\alpha_n = \frac{1}{(e_n + 1)\Lambda\mathbf{b}_0}$$

Notice that

$$\Lambda(\alpha_n\mathbf{b}_0) = \frac{1}{e_n + 1} \leqq 1$$

and so $\mathbf{b}_n \equiv \alpha\mathbf{b}_0$ are all feasible (i.e., are in $\mathcal{B}$). Furthermore, $e(\mathbf{b}_n) = e_n$ and $\alpha_n \rightarrow 1$. Thus $\mathbf{b}_n \rightarrow \mathbf{b}_0$ and because $\boldsymbol{\pi}$ is defined on $\mathbf{b}_n$, by continuity $\pi(\mathbf{b}_n) \rightarrow \pi(\mathbf{b}_0)$. Let $\pi_n \equiv \pi(\mathbf{b}_n)$, and the required sequence is provided.

From (a) and (b), Π is continuous.

Proof of Theorem 8.3: First, observe that the functions $\pi^{\max}$ and $\pi^{\min}$, the upper and lower boundaries of the graph, are defined. Because

$$\pi^{\max}(e) = \max_{\substack{\mathbf{b} \text{ s.t.} \\ e(\mathbf{b}) = e}} \pi(\mathbf{b}) \qquad \pi^{\min}(e) = \min_{\substack{\mathbf{b} \text{ s.t.} \\ e(\mathbf{b}) = e}} \pi(\mathbf{b})$$

the functions $\pi^{\max}(e)$ and $\pi^{\min}(e)$ are defined for all nonnegative e, because the set $\{\mathbf{b} \mid e(\mathbf{b}) = e\}$ is compact.

Proof of

(*i*) This follows from the maximum theorem of Berge, by Lemma 8.4, because Π is a continuous correspondence. (See Debreu, 1973, p. 19.)

(*ii*) Choose $e_1 > e_2$, and $\mathbf{b}_2^*$ s.t. $\pi^{\max}(e_2) = \pi(\mathbf{b}_2^*)$. Let

$$\alpha = \frac{e_2 + 1}{e_1 + 1} < 1$$

Let $\mathbf{b}_1^* \equiv \alpha\mathbf{b}_2^*$. Check that $e(\mathbf{b}_1^*) = e_1$. By definition, $\pi^{\max}(e_1) \geq$

$\pi(\mathbf{b}_1^*)$. Furthermore, by the monotone decreasing property of $\pi(\mathbf{b})$ shown in Theorem 8.1, $\pi(\mathbf{b}_1^*) > \pi(\mathbf{b}_2^*)$. Hence $\pi^{\max}(e_1) \geq \pi(\mathbf{b}_1^*) > \pi(\mathbf{b}_2^*) = \pi^{\max}(e_2)$, as required. A similar argument demonstrates $\pi^{\min}(e)$ is also strictly monotone increasing.

(*iii*) It follows from Theorem 1.1 that $\pi(0) = 0$.

(*iv*) $\Pi(e)$ is the image under the continuous function π of the connected set $\{\mathbf{b} \mid e(\mathbf{b}) = e\}$, and so $\Pi(e)$ is connected. $\Pi(e)$ is thus a bounded interval because $\pi^{\min}(e)$ and $\pi^{\max}(e)$ are always defined. $\Pi(e)$ has positive measure for $e > 0$ by Theorem 8.2, because it has more than one element for $e > 0$, if the technology is not of the equal-organic-composition type.

(*v*) It is sufficient to show that $\lim_{e\to\infty} \pi^{\min}(e) = \pi^*$ because $\pi^{\max}(e) \geqq \pi^{\min}(e)$ and $\pi^{\max}(e) \leqq \pi^*$ for all e, by definition of π^*. (π^* is the least upper bound of feasible values of π, which exists by the Frobenius theorem. $\pi^* = 1/\rho - 1$, where ρ is the dominant eigenvalue of A.) Choose a sequence $e_n \to \infty$. Let $\mathbf{b}_n^*$ be such that

$$\pi(\mathbf{b}_n^*) = \pi^{\min}(e_n)$$

Because $e_n \to \infty$, $\mathbf{\Lambda b}_n^* \to 0$, and because $\mathbf{\Lambda} > 0$ we must have $b_n^* \to 0$. Define $\pi_n \equiv \pi(\mathbf{b}_n^*)$. We have $\mathbf{p}_n(\pi_n)\mathbf{b}_n^* = 1$ for all n, and so the sequence $\{\mathbf{p}_n(\pi_n)\}$ has at least one unbounded component.

Now suppose that $\pi_n \to \pi^{**} < \pi^*$. By continuity of the function $\mathbf{p}(\pi)$, we have $\mathbf{p}(\pi_n) \to \mathbf{p}(\pi^{**})$. But this is impossible because $\{\mathbf{p}(\pi_n)\}$ has an unbounded component and $\mathbf{p}(\pi^{**})$ is a finite vector. Hence $\lim \pi_n = \pi^*$. Thus, by the monotonicity of $\pi^{\min}(e)$, $\lim_{e\to\infty} \pi^{\min}(e)$ exists and equals π^*. Q.E.D.

As an immediate result of Theorem 8.3, it is clear that the correspondence achieves a maximum thickness at some value $\tilde{e}$. That is, the continuous function $\mu(e) \equiv \pi^{\max}(e) - \pi^{\min}(e)$ becomes arbitrarily small for sufficiently large e; so on a suitably large (compact) interval $[0, N]$, μ achieves a maximum (at $\tilde{e}$) that must therefore be a global maximum for μ. Let us call the maximum thickness $\tilde{\mu}$.

What determines the maximum thickness $\tilde{\mu}$? Clearly, some measure of the dispersion in the organic compositions of capital. In particular, if the organic compositions are equal to each other, then the correspondence $\Pi(e)$ becomes a *function*, and the maximum thickness is zero.

Because it is not easy to calculate $\tilde{\mu}$, we introduce a related correspondence, which associates to each value of labor power $\mathbf{\Lambda b}$, the range of profit rates that can result:

$$\hat{\Pi}(v) = \{\pi \mid \exists \mathbf{b} \in \mathcal{B} \text{ s.t. } \mathbf{\Lambda b} = v \text{ and } \pi(\mathbf{b}) = \pi\}$$

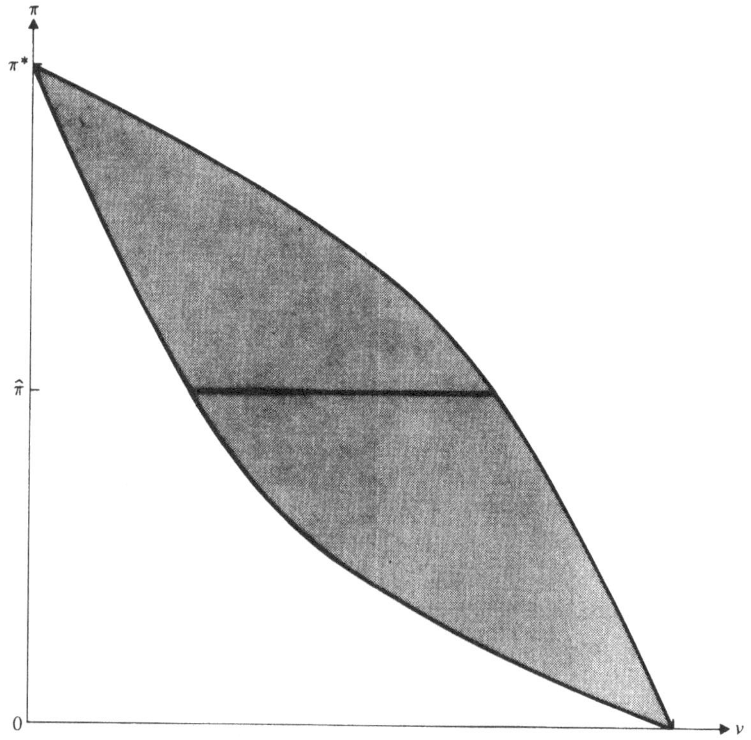

Figure 5

$\hat{\Pi}$ is simply the correspondence Π defined on the transformed variable $v = 1/(e + 1)$; that is,

$$\hat{\Pi}\left(\frac{1}{e+1}\right) \equiv \Pi(e)$$

The graph of $\hat{\Pi}(v)$ is depicted in Figure 5. (This follows immediately from Theorem 8.3.) As before, the degree of thickness of $\hat{\Pi}$ is a reflection of the dispersion in the organic compositions of capital. This time, we consider the maximal horizontal thickness, achieved at $\hat{\pi}$ in Figure 2:

$$\hat{v} \equiv \max_{\pi} \{v^{\max}(\pi) - v^{\min}(\pi)\}$$

where $v^{\max}(\pi)$ is the function that assigns to a given profit rate π the maximal value of labor power, $\mathbf{\Lambda b}$, consistent with it as $\mathbf{b}$ varies over $\mathcal{B}$.

We can now prove the following theorem.

Theorem 8.5: The maximal thickness $\hat{v}$,

$$\hat{v} = \max_{\pi} \{v^{\max}(\pi) - v^{\min}(\pi)\}$$

is equal to

$$\hat{v} = \max_{i,j,\pi} \left[\frac{\lambda_i}{p_i(\pi)} - \frac{\lambda_j}{p_j(\pi)}\right]$$

where $\mathbf{p}(\pi) = (1 + \pi)\mathbf{L}[I - (1 + \pi)A]^{-1}$ and λ_i and $p_i(\pi)$ indicate the ith components of $\mathbf{\Lambda}$ and $\mathbf{p}(\pi)$.

Note that $\mathbf{p}(\pi)$ is simply the price vector that corresponds to a profit rate π, according to Equations 8.1 and 8.2.

Theorem 8.5 asserts that the maximum horizontal thickness of $\hat{\Pi}(v)$ is precisely the maximal possible dispersion in the value–price ratios among sectors. Because the value–price ratio dispersion is a consequence of the inequality in organic composition, we see the relationship between the thickness of the correspondence $\hat{\Pi}(v)$ and organic compositions. Put another way, the thickness of the correspondence is a precise measure of the degree of "failure" of the micro "transformation problem," rigidly interpreted as the proportionality of prices and values.

Proof of Theorem 8.5: To find $v^{\max}(\pi)$, for π fixed, we solve the linear programming problem:

choose $\mathbf{b}$ to

$$\max \mathbf{\Lambda b}$$

$$\text{s.t. } \mathbf{p}(\pi)\mathbf{b} = 1$$

or

$$\max \mathbf{\Lambda b}$$

$$\text{s.t. } \mathbf{p}(\pi)\mathbf{b} \leqq 1$$

$$-\mathbf{p}(\pi)\mathbf{b} \leqq -1$$

whose dual problem is

$$\min(y_1 - y_2)$$

$$\text{s.t. } (y_1 - y_2)\mathbf{p}(\pi) \geqq \mathbf{\Lambda}$$

The dual solution is clearly

$$y_1^* - y_2^* = \max_i \frac{\lambda_i}{p_i(\pi)} \quad \text{and so} \quad v^{\max}(\pi) = \max_i \frac{\lambda_i}{p_i(\pi)}$$

by the fundamental theorem of linear programming. In like manner, it is shown that

$$v^{\min}(\pi) = \min_i \frac{\lambda_i}{p_i(\pi)} \quad \text{and so} \quad \hat{v} = \max\left\{\max_i \frac{\lambda_i}{p_i(\pi)} - \min_j \frac{\lambda_j}{p_j(\pi)}\right\}$$

from which the theorem follows.

Because the study of the correspondence $\hat{\Pi}$ (or Π) is of use in the classical question of value–price ratios, it may be convenient to state the content of Theorem 8.5 in a slightly different form.

Corollary 8.6: Let π be a rate of profit and $\mathbf{p}(\pi)$ be the associated price vector. Then the maximum and minimum value–price ratios over the n sectors are

$$\max_i \frac{\lambda_i}{p_i(\pi)} = \frac{1}{e_{\min} + 1}$$

$$\min_i \frac{\lambda_i}{p_i(\pi)} = \frac{1}{e_{\max} + 1}$$

whose $e_{\max}$ and $e_{\min}$ are the maximum and minimum rates of exploitation consistent with a profit rate of π. That is,

$$e_{\max} \equiv \max_{\mathbf{b} \text{ s.t. } \mathbf{p}(\pi)\mathbf{b} = 1} \{e(\mathbf{b})\}$$

Proof: This is a restatement of part of the proof of Theorem 8.5. It was shown there that

$$v^{\max}(\pi) = \max \frac{\lambda_i}{p_i(\pi)}$$

but

$$v^{\max}(\pi) = \frac{1}{e_{\min} + 1}$$

One way of viewing Corollary 8.6 is as a generalization of the easily computed fact that, if the organic compositions of capital are equal, then

$$\frac{\mathbf{\Lambda}}{\mathbf{p}} = \frac{1}{e + 1}$$

(That is, the vectors $\mathbf{\Lambda}$ and $\mathbf{p}$ are proportional.) Corollary 8.6 asserts that in general there is a double inequality that holds for any e that can correspond to a given equilibrium price vector:

$$\max_i \frac{\lambda_i}{p_i} \geqq \frac{1}{e+1} \geqq \min_i \frac{\lambda_i}{p_i}$$

and that, furthermore, this double inequality is as sharp as possible, for there exists a value of e for which either of the inequalities becomes an equality.

8.3 Some applications of the transformation correspondence

Quantitative questions concerning the "transformation of values into prices" can be answered by examining the transformation correspondence. In particular, the severity of the violation of the rigid notion that values are proportional to prices is given by the maximum thickness of the correspondence Π or $\hat{\Pi}$ that has been studied. Because the perspective put forth in the previous chapter directs our attention away from examination of price–value ratios, we shall not concern outselves further with this here. There are, however, two important applications of the transformation correspondence that we shall discuss.

Marginal utilities versus class struggle

Let us think of the rate of exploitation as fixed at a value e. We ask: What vectors of relative prices can correspond to rate of exploitation e? This is equivalent to asking what profit rates can correspond to e, because prices are uniquely determined from the profit rate according to

$$\mathbf{p}(\pi) = (1 + \pi)\mathbf{L}[I - (1 + \pi)A]^{-1}$$

Given the rate of exploitation, variations in π take place because workers could consume a variety of consumption vectors **b,** each giving rise to a rate of exploitation e. We might think of different utility functions giving rise to different fixed demands **b.** By looking at Figure 4, we see that for very large or very small rates of exploitation, marginal utilities have very little influence on relative prices – in the precise sense that the range of π's, and hence prices $\mathbf{p}(\pi)$, is very limited for large and small e. Also, the effect of subjective demand on relative prices is greater if the dispersion of the organic compositions is greater: If the organic compositions are all equal, then $\Pi(e)$ is a function, and marginal utilities have no effect on prices, once the rate of exploitation is fixed.

It should be pointed out that workers do not actually optimize (if they have utility functions) by maximizing $u(\mathbf{b})$ with respect to a constraint that requires them to consume at a certain rate of exploitation. They optimize constrained by the wage. Hence the point in the above paragraph is not a behavioral one; it is, rather, an aggregate observation. If we wish to view the Marxian law of value as asserting that the rate of exploitation "determines" prices à la Theorem 7.1, and we wish to conceive of the marginal utility approach as saying that demand has an influence on prices, then the thickness of the correspondence $\Pi(e)$ enables us to evaluate the relative importance of the two causations. We see that marginal utilities are important only insofar as the rate of exploitation is not too high or too low, and the organic compositions of capital are dispersed.

There are other ways that demand can influence price, of course. Notably, if there are scarce resources such as land in the system, or, more generally, techniques for operating sectors that can be operated only at finite activity levels, then the level of demand determines the array of techniques that will be used, and hence influences relative prices through differential rent. (That is, if the demand for corn is high, inferior land is drawn into production, thus changing the relative price structure from what it would have been with a lower level of demand.)

Differential exploitation and unequal exchange

Suppose that there are two groups of workers: workers of the first type receive a consumption bundle $\mathbf{b}_1$, and workers of the second type receive a consumption bundle $\mathbf{b}_2$. The wage each worker type receives is just sufficient to purchase the required bundle. We may suppose that the workers are distributed in different proportions throughout the different sectors:

n^i_j = the fraction of workers in sector i who are type j, for $i = 1, n$; $j = 1, 2$

Define

$$w^i = n^i_1 + wn^i_2 \qquad i = 1, n \tag{8.6}$$

as the average (daily) wage paid in sector i. Let W be an $n \times n$ diagonal matrix whose diagonal elements are w^i, $i = 1, n$. Then $\mathbf{L}W$ is the row vector of wages paid for production of one unit of each sector's output. The price equations become

$$\mathbf{p} = (1 + \pi)(\mathbf{p}A + \mathbf{L}W) \tag{8.7}$$

$$1 = \mathbf{p}\mathbf{b}_1 \tag{8.8}$$

$$w = \mathbf{p}\mathbf{b}_2 \tag{8.9}$$

(*Note:* We have normalized by setting the wage of the first worker type equal to unity.)

What we show below is that it is possible for the second worker to receive the *higher* wage, $w > 1$, but to be simultaneously *more exploited* than the first worker – $e(\mathbf{b}_2) > e(\mathbf{b}_1)$. This pathology results precisely because of the nonzero thickness of the transformation correspondence.

First, we must show that equilibrium prices exist in this model:

THEOREM 8.7: Given a distribution of workers $\{n_j^i\}$ and the technology $\{A, \mathbf{L}\}$, there exist continuous functions $\pi(\mathbf{b}_1, \mathbf{b}_2)$, $\mathbf{p}(\mathbf{b}_1, \mathbf{b}_2)$, $w(\mathbf{b}_1, \mathbf{b}_2)$ defined on the domain $\mathscr{B} \times \mathscr{B}$, where $\mathscr{B} = \{\mathbf{b} \mid \Lambda\mathbf{b} \leqq 1\}$, satisfying Equations 8.7–8.9. Furthermore, $\pi(\mathbf{b}_1, \mathbf{b}_2) \geqq 0$ and $\pi(\mathbf{b}_1, \mathbf{b}_2) = 0$ if and only if $\Lambda\mathbf{b}_1 = \Lambda\mathbf{b}_2 = 1$.

Proof: Define N_j for $j = 1, 2$ to be the $n \times n$ diagonal matrix with elements n_j^i along its diagonal. Then, from (8.6),

$$W = N_1 + wN_2 \tag{8.10}$$

defines the wage matrix where w is the wage of the second type of worker.

Given $\langle \mathbf{b}_1, \mathbf{b}_2 \rangle \in \mathscr{B} \times \mathscr{B}$, we seek a vector $\mathbf{p}$ and profit rate π such that

$$\mathbf{p} = (1 + \pi)\mathbf{p}(A + \mathbf{b}_1\mathbf{L}N_1 + \mathbf{b}_2\mathbf{L}N_2) \tag{8.11}$$

[Equation 8.11 follows from substituting (8.8), (8.9), and (8.10) into (8.7).] Because A is indecomposable, so is $M = A + \mathbf{b}_1\mathbf{L}N_1 + \mathbf{b}_2\mathbf{L}N_2$; by the Frobenius–Perron theorem, it follows that $\mathbf{p}$ is the unique positive eigenvector associated with the dominant eigenvalue, ρ, of the matrix M and $\pi = 1/\rho - 1$. The scale of $\mathbf{p}$ is chosen by (8.8), and the value of w follows from (8.9). Hence functions $\mathbf{p}(\mathbf{b}_1, \mathbf{b}_2)$, $w(\mathbf{b}_1, \mathbf{b}_2)$, and $\pi(\mathbf{b}_1, \mathbf{b}_2)$ have been shown to exist; they are continuous, because it is known that the eigenvector and dominant eigenvalue of a nonnegative matrix are continuous functions of its elements.

It remains to show $\pi(\mathbf{b}_1, \mathbf{b}_2) \geqq 0$. By definition of M,

$$\Lambda M \leqq \Lambda A + \mathbf{L} = \Lambda \tag{8.12}$$

If $\pi(\mathbf{b}_1, \mathbf{b}_2) < 0$ then, because $\mathbf{p} = (1 + \pi)\mathbf{p}M$,

$$\mathbf{p} < \mathbf{p}M \tag{8.13}$$

From (8.13) it follows that M possesses a right eigenvector, $\mathbf{x} > 0$, such that

$$\mathbf{x} < M\mathbf{x} \tag{8.14}$$

From (8.14) it follows that $\Lambda\mathbf{x} < \Lambda M\mathbf{x}$; however, from (8.12) it follows that $M\mathbf{x} \leqq \mathbf{x}$, a contradiction. Hence $\pi(\mathbf{b}_1, \mathbf{b}_2) \geqq 0$.

Finally, if $\Lambda\mathbf{b}_1 = \Lambda\mathbf{b}_2 = 1$, then (8.12) becomes an equality and $\Lambda = \Lambda M$; hence the dominant eigenvalue of M is unity and $\pi = 0$ follows. Conversely, if $\pi = 0$, then $\mathbf{p} = \mathbf{p}M$ and there exists $\mathbf{x} > 0$ such that $\mathbf{x} = M\mathbf{x}$. Thus $\Lambda\mathbf{x} = \Lambda M\mathbf{x}$. If, however, $\Lambda\mathbf{b}_1 < 1$, say, then $\Lambda M \leqq \Lambda$, which would imply that $\Lambda M\mathbf{x} < \Lambda\mathbf{x}$. Thus, $\pi = 0$ implies that $\Lambda\mathbf{b}_j = 1$. Q.E.D.

We next demonstrate that if any component of $\mathbf{b}_2$ increases, then the relative wage of the second worker increases.

LEMMA 8.8: $w(\mathbf{b}_1, \mathbf{b}_2)$ is a strictly increasing function in any component of $\mathbf{b}_2$.

Proof: From (8.7),

$$\mathbf{p} = \mathbf{L}W\left(\frac{1}{1+\pi}I - A\right)^{-1} \tag{8.15}$$

Let b_2^i be a component of $\mathbf{b}_2$. The functions $\mathbf{p}(\mathbf{b}_1, \mathbf{b}_2)$, $w(\mathbf{b}_1, \mathbf{b}_2)$, and $\pi(\mathbf{b}_1, \mathbf{b}_2)$ are in fact differentiable, and from (8.15),

$$\frac{\partial \mathbf{p}}{\partial b_2^i} = \frac{\partial(\mathbf{L}W)}{\partial b_2^i}\left(\frac{1}{1+\pi}I - A\right)^{-1} + \mathbf{L}W\left(\frac{1}{1+\pi}I - A\right)^{-2}(1+\pi)^{-2}\frac{\partial \pi}{\partial b_2^i} \tag{8.16}$$

We know that $\partial\pi/\partial b_2^i < 0$; because the matrix M is indecomposable, any increase in its elements increases its dominant eigenvalue and decreases π. Suppose, now, that $\partial w(\mathbf{b}_1, \mathbf{b}_2)/\partial b_2^i \leqq 0$ at some point $(\mathbf{b}_1, \mathbf{b}_2) \in \mathcal{B} \times \mathcal{B}$. Then $\partial(\mathbf{L}W)/\partial b_2^i \leqq 0$. It follows from (8.16) that $\partial\mathbf{p}/\partial b_2^i < 0$ at that point. This, however, is impossible, because $\mathbf{p}(\mathbf{b}_1, \mathbf{b}_2) \cdot \mathbf{b}_1 = 1$. It follows that $\partial w(\mathbf{b}_1, \mathbf{b}_2)/\partial b_2^i > 0$ as required. Q.E.D.

It can now be established that the wage pathology referred to occurs:

THEOREM 8.9: There exist pairs of bundles $(\mathbf{b}_1, \mathbf{b}_2)$ such that $e(\mathbf{b}_2) > e(\mathbf{b}_1)$ and $w(\mathbf{b}_1, \mathbf{b}_2) > 1$.

Proof: We know that there exist bundles $\mathbf{b}_1$ and $\mathbf{b}_2$ of different (labor) values, both satisfying Equations 8.17–8.18 for the same π:

$$\mathbf{p} = (1 + \pi)(\mathbf{p}A + \mathbf{L}) \tag{8.17}$$

$$1 = \mathbf{p}\mathbf{b}_j \qquad j = 1, 2 \tag{8.18}$$

(Say, $\Lambda\mathbf{b}_2 < \Lambda\mathbf{b}_1$.) Note that this is equivalent to saying that $\exists(\mathbf{b}_1, \mathbf{b}_2)$ s.t. $w(\mathbf{b}_1, \mathbf{b}_2) = 1$ and $\Lambda\mathbf{b}_2 < \Lambda\mathbf{b}_1$. By Lemma 8.8, a small increase in any component of $\mathbf{b}_2$ (call the new vector $\mathbf{b}_2'$) will render $w(\mathbf{b}_1, \mathbf{b}_2') > 1$; the adjustment can be sufficiently small that $\Lambda\mathbf{b}_2' < \Lambda\mathbf{b}_1$. Q.E.D.

We might say that Theorem 8.9 shows a naive transformation intuition is incorrect – that workers who are paid higher wages are exploited less. Clearly this pathology can exist because of the thickness of the transformation correspondence. We now show this precisely, in this sense: that for the pathological situation to occur, the values of labor power of the two worker types must differ by less than $\hat{v}$, the maximum thickness $\hat{\Pi}(v)$ studied in Section 8.2.

THEOREM 8.10: Let $v_2 \equiv \Lambda\mathbf{b}_2 < \Lambda\mathbf{b}_1 \equiv v_1$ and $w(\mathbf{b}_1, \mathbf{b}_2) > 1$. Then $v_2 - v_1 < \hat{v}$.

Proof: Recall the definition of the function $v(\mathbf{b}) = \Lambda\mathbf{b}$.

Let $\hat{\mathbf{b}}_2$ be chosen s.t.

$$\hat{\mathbf{b}}_2 \leqq \mathbf{b}_2 \qquad \hat{\mathbf{b}}_2 \leqq \mathbf{b}_1$$

Then

$$w(\mathbf{b}_1, \hat{\mathbf{b}}_2) = \mathbf{p}(\mathbf{b}_1, \hat{\mathbf{b}}_2) \cdot \hat{\mathbf{b}}_2 < \mathbf{p}(\mathbf{b}_1, \hat{\mathbf{b}}_2) \cdot \mathbf{b}_1 = 1$$

It is given that $w(\mathbf{b}_1, \mathbf{b}_2) > 1$. Hence, by continuity of the function w, there exists $\bar{\mathbf{b}}_2$ s.t.:

$$\hat{\mathbf{b}}_2 \leqq \bar{\mathbf{b}}_2 \leqq \mathbf{b}_2 \quad \text{and} \quad w(\mathbf{b}_1, \bar{\mathbf{b}}_2) = 1$$

Notice that by choice of $\bar{\mathbf{b}}_2$ and the given pair $(\mathbf{b}_1, \mathbf{b}_2)$:

$$v(\bar{\mathbf{b}}_2) < v(\mathbf{b}_2) < v(\mathbf{b}_1) \tag{8.19}$$

Because $w(\mathbf{b}_1, \bar{\mathbf{b}}_2) = 1$, $\mathbf{b}_1$ and $\bar{\mathbf{b}}_2$ each satisfy equations of the form (8.17)–(8.18), for some constant π. In terms of correspondence $\hat{\Pi}$, we have $\pi \in \hat{\Pi}[v(\mathbf{b}_1)] \cap \hat{\Pi}[v(\bar{\mathbf{b}}_2)]$. Hence, by definition of $\hat{v}$, $v(\mathbf{b}_1) - v(\bar{\mathbf{b}}_2) \leqq \hat{v}$. By (8.19), it follows that $v(\mathbf{b}_1) - v(\mathbf{b}_2) < \hat{v}$. Q.E.D.

Thus, the thickness of the correspondence $\hat{\Pi}(v)$ gives a precise measure of the possibilities of differential exploitation pathology: that the more exploited worker is paid the higher wage.

What is the significance of this phenomenon? It can be taken as an example indicating the misconception of treating labor values as instruments for evaluating micro phenomena, following the discussion of the previous chapter. In this case, even disaggregating into two groups of workers can lead to a nonsensical result if microvalue analysis is used. But there is another reason for working out this particular example in such detail: It illustrates a fallacy of the international trade model known as unequal exchange (see, for instance, Immanuel, 1972). The general claim of the unequal exchange model is that (labor) value is expropriated from countries in the periphery through exchange with countries in the core because the workers in the core are paid higher wages than workers in the periphery, from which it is thought to follow that workers in the periphery are more highly exploited. (The assumptions of a uniform profit rate and prices in core and periphery are maintained, as in the model here.) The pathology demonstrated above shows the incorrectness of the logic of the unequal exchange argument, for we have exhibited an example of a wage profile that is associated with an exploitation profile of the "wrong" order. More basically, the unequal exchange argument is based on a comparison of microdenominated price magnitudes and microdenominated value magnitudes; as such, it should come as no surprise that it must be logically fallacious, following the discussion of Chapter 7.

This is not to say that unequal exchange cannot be a meaningful description of trade relations between core and periphery. But the understanding of such a phenomenon will not be furthered by a comparison of microdenominated value and price magnitudes.

8.4 Summary

The transformation correspondence is a device that permits an analysis of the relationship between prices of production and labor values when workers have utility functions that can vary over time or across workers, or different workers have different subsistence bundles, if that terminology is preferred. Two applications of the device have been examined here. Pitfalls arise if too literal an interpretation of the classical transformation problem is adhered to – wages may not be inversely related to the degree of exploitation as one might expect. If one accepts the treatment of the transformation problem of Chapter 7, this is not bothersome, for it was maintained that one should not try to make microeconomic comparisons of value-denominated and price-denominated concepts. This chapter has shown, in the same vein, that the comparative statics of the rate of exploitation may be pathological. These pathologies all arise from the same source: the nonproportionality of labor values and prices.

The resolution that has been proposed to these pathologies is to use the value concept of exploitation only to assert the existence of the aggregate phenomenon of exploitation. One can be led astray by trying to use the rate of exploitation, and labor values, for finer observations, whether they be about particular sectors of the economy, or the comparative statics of different economies. Alternatively, one might wish to construct a theory of exploitation that is independent of the particular subjective preferences workers hold. This can be done, but it is beyond our scope here.

9 Simple reproduction, extended reproduction, and crisis

9.1 Introduction

In the general equilibrium model of Chapters 1–3, some of the critical features of a capitalist economy that are responsible for crises are absent. The purpose of those chapters was to study Marxian value theory; the questions of crisis can be studied somewhat independently of that theory. In this chapter, a model is proposed that permits an exposition of various Marxian and neo-Marxian crises: in particular, the profit-squeeze crisis, the realization or underconsumptionist crisis, and the fiscal crisis. To do this, we need to introduce a distinction between *ex ante* and *ex post* investment and savings, a government sector, and a reserve army of the employed.

The chapter begins with an exposition of a model of Marxian simple reproduction, and then proceeds to study extended reproduction. We do not propose that the models studied in this chapter are definitive, or that the ideas lying behind them are original. In fact, more than the other chapters, this chapter represents only a "foundation" to a study of an aspect of Marxian economics, rather than an extension or elaboration of a body of Marxian theory. Some of the most important attributes of capitalism, which contribute to crises, are not modeled here, such as the role of money. Thus, the chapter should be taken simply as an exposition of some of the classical Marxian ideas. Even this, however, can contribute to our ability to develop a cogent crisis theory, as the classical Marxian crises have nowhere been systematically presented as the possible outcomes of one macroeconomic model, to my knowledge.

Finally, no attempt is made to include a falling-rate-of-profit crisis in the model of this chapter. Readers of Chapters 4–6 are aware of the reasons for this apparent omission.

9.2 Simple reproduction

In this section, we present a model of simple reproduction that builds upon Theorem 7.1 of Chapter 7. In that theorem, it was shown that for a given level of social exploitation e^*, there is a price system that equilibrates the economy, allowing each worker to consume his or her choice of goods subject to the wage constraint. We now introduce capitalists, and endow them with utility functions. Capitalists, naturally, get the surplus product. Question: Does there exist a price system, for a given social level of exploitation e^*, that equilibrates the system in the sense that every worker gets his or her choice of consumption goods, subject to the wage constraint, and every capitalist gets his or her choice of goods, subject to the profits constraint? In simple reproduction – that is, reproduction without growth – this is the natural question to ask. The theorem of this section answers this question in the affirmative.

We now set up the apparatus for this theorem. Reviewing the model of Chapter 7, let:

- A_{I} be the $n \times n$ productive, indecomposable matrix of physical input–output coefficients in department I, capital-goods industries
- A_{II} be the $n \times r$ input–output matrix for department II, consumption-goods industries
- $\mathbf{p}_{\text{I}}$, $\mathbf{p}_{\text{II}}$ be the row price vectors for the two departments
- $\mathbf{b}_i$ be the r column vector of consumption goods for the ith worker
- $u_i(\mathbf{b})$ be the utility function for consumption goods for worker i
- $\mathbf{L}_{\text{I}}$, $\mathbf{L}_{\text{II}}$ be the row vectors of direct labor inputs for the two departments
- π be the rate of profit on circulating capital and wages (there is no fixed capital: All capital circulates in the period of production)
- $\mathbf{\Lambda}_{\text{I}}$, $\mathbf{\Lambda}_{\text{II}}$ be the vectors of labor values for the two departments
- N be the number of workers in the economy

The labor value vectors are defined by:

$$\mathbf{\Lambda}_{\text{I}} = \mathbf{L}_{\text{I}}(I - A)^{-1} \tag{9.1}$$

$$\mathbf{\Lambda}_{\text{II}} = \mathbf{\Lambda}_{\text{I}}A_{\text{II}} + \mathbf{L}_{\text{II}} \tag{9.2}$$

The social rate of exploitation is

$$e\left(\sum_{i=1}^{N} \mathbf{b}_i\right) = \frac{N - \mathbf{\Lambda}_{\text{II}}(\Sigma\ \mathbf{b}_i)}{\mathbf{\Lambda}_{\text{II}}(\Sigma\ \mathbf{b}_i)} \tag{9.3}$$

(The unit for denominating working time and the consumption bundle is one working day, of constant magnitude.) The money wage is taken as numeraire, and the price–profit rate equations are

$$\mathbf{p}_{\mathrm{I}} = (1 + \pi)(\mathbf{p}_{\mathrm{I}}A_{\mathrm{I}} + \mathbf{L}_{\mathrm{I}}) \tag{9.4}$$

$$\mathbf{p}_{\mathrm{II}} = (1 + \pi)(\mathbf{p}_{\mathrm{I}}A_{\mathrm{II}} + \mathbf{L}_{\mathrm{II}}) \tag{9.5}$$

The social rate of exploitation will be taken as given at some level, e^*:

$$e(\Sigma\, \mathbf{b}_i) = e^* \tag{9.6}$$

Workers choose goods to satisfy their needs according to

$$\forall i,\ \mathbf{b}_i \text{ maximizes } u_i(\mathbf{b}_i) \text{ subject to } \mathbf{p}_{\mathrm{II}}\mathbf{b}_i = 1 \tag{9.7}$$

($\mathbf{p}_{\mathrm{II}}\mathbf{b}_i = 1$ is the budget constraint, because the wage is unity.)

As in Chapter 7, e^* is taken as the exogenously specified social rate of exploitation. However, capitalists will now demand goods as well as workers, and there will be no accumulation: Profits are consumed entirely by the capitalist class. Capitalists choose goods by using utility functions v_i. For simplicity, it is assumed that there is one capitalist in each sector. It is also assumed, for simplicity, that full employment prevails. Unemployment and the reserve army are introduced in the model of extended reproduction.

If $\mathbf{x}_{\mathrm{I}}$ and $\mathbf{x}_{\mathrm{II}}$ are the column vectors of outputs in the two departments, then the labor demand equation is

$$\mathbf{L}_{\mathrm{I}}\mathbf{x}_{\mathrm{I}} + \mathbf{L}_{\mathrm{II}}\mathbf{x}_{\mathrm{II}} = N \tag{9.8}$$

Let the ith capitalist consume a bundle of consumption goods $\mathbf{f}_i$. Then total demand for consumption goods is

$$\mathbf{x}_{\mathrm{II}} = \sum_{1}^{N} \mathbf{b}_i + \sum_{1}^{N} \mathbf{f}_i \tag{9.9}$$

Capital goods are needed only to produce consumption goods, because there is no accumulation. The demand for capital goods is thus composed of a final demand for production of consumption goods and an intermediate demand for production of capital goods:

$$\mathbf{x}_{\mathrm{I}} = A_{\mathrm{I}}\mathbf{x}_{\mathrm{I}} + A_{\mathrm{II}}(\Sigma\, \mathbf{b}_i + \Sigma\, \mathbf{f}_i) \tag{9.10}$$

Profits in sector i are defined as

$$\Pi^i = \pi(\mathbf{p}_{\mathrm{I}}\mathbf{a}^i x^i + L^i x^i) \tag{9.11}$$

where L^i and x^i are the ith components of the vectors $\mathbf{L}$ and $\mathbf{x}$, and $\mathbf{a}^i$ is the ith column of the appropriate A matrix.

Capitalists choose goods according to

$$\forall i,\ \mathbf{f}_i \text{ maximizes } v_i(\mathbf{f}_i) \text{ subject to } \mathbf{p}_{\mathrm{II}}\mathbf{f}_i = \Pi^i \tag{9.12}$$

The system of equations 9.1–9.12 specifies a Marxian system of simple reproduction at the social rate of exploitation e^*. The next theorem asserts that a complete equilibrium in fact exists.

THEOREM 9.1 (Simple reproduction): For any nonnegative number e^*, an equilibrium $\{\pi, \mathbf{p}_I, \mathbf{p}_{II}, \mathbf{b}_1, \ldots, \mathbf{b}_N, \mathbf{f}_1, \ldots, \mathbf{f}_N, \mathbf{x}_I, \mathbf{x}_{II}\}$ exists fulfilling Equations 9.1–9.12. We assume, in addition, Assumption A of Chapter 7.

Before proving Theorem 9.1, let us review its meaning. Theorem 9.1 may be viewed as an extension of the "law of value" (of Theorem 7.1) to include the problem of how the surplus product is disposed of by capitalists. For any given level of the rate of exploitation e^*, there is a system of equal-profit-rate prices that allows the system to reproduce (simply) in the following sense: The outputs produced will be such that the prices are market-clearing, where demands expressed on the market are for workers' consumption goods, capitalists' consumption goods, and intermediate capital goods.

We can put the present model into the context of the other models studied in this book thus far, as follows: the Sraffian model (Sraffa, 1960) studies only the conditions for price equilibrium, ignoring the output side of the economy; the model of Chapters 1–3 and of Chapter 7 requires outputs (and demands) to be considered insofar as workers' demands are concerned – that is, the market for workers' consumption goods clears in these models; the model stated here accounts, as well, for the demand of capitalists. Thus, the model of simple reproduction is the simplest model in which account is taken of the disposition of all outputs. Marx's approach was to study first this simple case, when all net output is consumed, and then to introduce the problem of accumulation. We follow the same procedure.

Proof of Theorem 9.1: As a first step, notice that once e^* is given, then $\mathbf{p}_I$, $\mathbf{p}_{II}$, π, and $\mathbf{b}_1, \ldots, \mathbf{b}_N$ are determined according to Theorem 7.1. This follows from (9.1)–(9.7), which are identical to the specifications of Theorem 7.1. Assumption A enables us to determine $\mathbf{b}_1, \ldots, \mathbf{b}_N$ uniquely.

As a next step, it is useful to show that total capitalists' consumption is equal in labor value to total surplus value. Let total capitalists' consumption be called $\mathbf{F} = \Sigma\, \mathbf{f}_i$. Equation 9.10 can be inverted to solve for $\mathbf{x}_I$; substituting this expression for $\mathbf{x}_I$ and Equation 9.9 into Equation 9.8 yields

$$[\mathbf{L}_I(I - A_I)^{-1}A_{II} + \mathbf{L}_{II}](\Sigma\, \mathbf{b}_i + \mathbf{F}) = N$$

From the value equations (9.1), (9.2), it is seen that the expression in the first set of parentheses is simply $\mathbf{\Lambda}_{\mathrm{II}}$, and so

$$\mathbf{\Lambda}_{\mathrm{II}}\mathbf{F} = N - \mathbf{\Lambda}_{\mathrm{II}}\mathbf{B} \qquad (9.13)$$

where $\mathbf{B} = \Sigma\, \mathbf{b}_i$, which says that the value of capitalists' consumption is total surplus value.

Now $\mathbf{B}$ is already determined, because e^* is given. Hence $\mathbf{F}$ must lie in the compact convex set, H, defined by (9.13):[1]

$$H = \{\mathbf{F} \geqq 0 \mid \mathbf{\Lambda}_{\mathrm{II}}\mathbf{F} = N - \mathbf{\Lambda}_{\mathrm{II}}\mathbf{B}\}$$

The proof proceeds by constructing a function Ψ: $H \rightarrow H$ and producing a fixed point that equilibrates the system.

Choose any $\mathbf{F} \in H$. Recall that $\{\pi, \mathbf{p}_{\mathrm{I}}, \mathbf{p}_{\mathrm{II}}, \mathbf{b}_1, \ldots, \mathbf{b}_N\}$ are already determined. From (9.10), a vector $\mathbf{x}_{\mathrm{I}}(\mathbf{F})$ is generated consistent with $\mathbf{F}$ [i.e., substitute $\mathbf{F}$ for $\Sigma\, \mathbf{f}_i$ in (9.10)]. From (9.9), a vector $\mathbf{x}_{\mathrm{II}}(\mathbf{F})$ exists. Substituting these output vectors in (9.11) generates sectoral profits $\Pi^i(\mathbf{F})$, for each i. According to (9.12), there is a choice $\mathbf{f}_i$ such that $\mathbf{p}_{\mathrm{II}}\mathbf{f}_i = \Pi^i(\mathbf{F})$, for each i. Define $\mathbf{F}' = \Sigma\, \mathbf{f}_i$. Now shrink or stretch $\mathbf{F}'$ into H by defining

$$\mathbf{F}'' = \alpha \mathbf{F}'$$

where $\alpha > 0$, $\mathbf{F}'' \in H$. (Such an α clearly exists.) A function Ψ: $\mathbf{F} \rightarrow \mathbf{F}''$ has been defined on the compact, convex set H, and hence by Brouwer's theorem a fixed point, $\mathbf{F}^*$, exists.

As in the proof of Theorem 7.1, to show that $\mathbf{F}^*$ equilibrates the system it is necessary to show that the scale factor α associated with $\mathbf{F}^*$ is unity. We know that $\mathbf{F}^*$ determines individual $\mathbf{f}_i^*$ for all i and by definition $\mathbf{F}^{*\prime} = \Sigma\, \mathbf{f}_i^*$ and so $\mathbf{p}_{\mathrm{II}}\mathbf{F}^{*\prime} = \Sigma\, \mathbf{p}_{\mathrm{II}}\mathbf{f}_i^* = \Pi(\mathbf{F}^*)$, total profits. If it can be shown that $\mathbf{p}_{\mathrm{II}}\mathbf{F}^* = \Pi(\mathbf{F}^*)$, then it will follow that $\alpha = 1$, because $\mathbf{p}_{\mathrm{II}}\mathbf{F}^* = \mathbf{p}_{\mathrm{II}}\mathbf{F}^{*\prime\prime}$. The proof of the theorem is therefore completed by use of the following lemma.

Lemma 9.2: $\mathbf{p}_{\mathrm{II}}\mathbf{F}^* = \Pi(\mathbf{F}^*)$

Proof: (*Note:* The notation $\Pi(\mathbf{F}^*)$ is meant to convey that the value of total profits $[\Pi(\mathbf{F}^*)]$ is that value which results from plugging $\mathbf{F}^*$ into (9.10) and proceeding along the sequence of steps used to define the mapping Ψ, until Π is defined. $\mathbf{x}_{\mathrm{I}}(\mathbf{F}^*)$ and $\mathbf{x}_{\mathrm{II}}(\mathbf{F}^*)$ have similar meaning.)

Post-multiplying Equations 9.4 and 9.5, by $\mathbf{x}_{\mathrm{I}}(F^*)$ and $\mathbf{x}_{\mathrm{II}}(F^*)$, respectively, and adding gives, after substitution from (9.10) and (9.8),

$$\mathbf{p}_{\mathrm{I}}\mathbf{x}_{\mathrm{I}}(\mathbf{F}^*) + \mathbf{p}_{\mathrm{II}}\mathbf{x}_{\mathrm{II}}(\mathbf{F}^*) = (1 + \pi)[\mathbf{p}_{\mathrm{I}}\mathbf{x}_{\mathrm{I}}(\mathbf{F}^*) + \mathbf{L}_{\mathrm{I}}\mathbf{x}_{\mathrm{I}}(\mathbf{F}^*) + \mathbf{L}_{\mathrm{II}}\mathbf{x}_{\mathrm{II}}(\mathbf{F}^*)] \qquad (9.14)$$

From (9.13) and (9.8), it can be shown that

$$\mathbf{L}_{\mathrm{I}}\mathbf{x}_{\mathrm{I}}(\mathbf{F}^*) + \mathbf{L}_{\mathrm{II}}\mathbf{x}_{\mathrm{II}}(\mathbf{F}^*) = N = \mathbf{p}_{\mathrm{II}}\mathbf{B}$$

and hence

$$\mathbf{p}_{\mathrm{I}}\mathbf{x}_{\mathrm{I}}(\mathbf{F}^*) + \mathbf{p}_{\mathrm{II}}\mathbf{x}_{\mathrm{II}}(\mathbf{F}^*) = (1 + \pi)[\mathbf{p}_{\mathrm{I}}\mathbf{x}_{\mathrm{I}}(\mathbf{F}^*) + \mathbf{p}_{\mathrm{II}}\mathbf{B}] \tag{9.15}$$

Subtracting $\mathbf{p}_{\mathrm{I}}\mathbf{x}_{\mathrm{I}}(\mathbf{F}^*) + \mathbf{p}_{\mathrm{II}}\mathbf{B}$ from both sides of (9.15) yields

$$\mathbf{p}_{\mathrm{II}}[\mathbf{x}_{\mathrm{II}}(\mathbf{F}^*) - \mathbf{B}] = \pi[\mathbf{p}_{\mathrm{I}}\mathbf{x}_{\mathrm{I}}(\mathbf{F}^*) + \mathbf{p}_{\mathrm{II}}\mathbf{B}]$$

However, $\mathbf{x}_{\mathrm{II}}(\mathbf{F}^*) - \mathbf{B} = \mathbf{F}^*$ by definition, and so

$$\mathbf{p}_{\mathrm{II}}\mathbf{F}^* = \pi[\mathbf{p}_{\mathrm{I}}\mathbf{x}_{\mathrm{I}}(\mathbf{F}^*) + \mathbf{p}_{\mathrm{II}}\mathbf{B}] \tag{9.16}$$

But the right-hand side of (9.16) is seen to be $\Pi(F^*)$.[2] The lemma follows.

Hence, the scale factor α is unity for $\mathbf{F}^*$; thus, the individual capitalist's consumption vectors $\{\mathbf{f}_i^*\}$ equilibrate the entire system. Q.E.D.

This model of simple reproduction tells us, simply, that its specification is consistent in the sense that it is possible for the system to reproduce itself in a stationary state at "any" level of exploitation. ("Any," because above a certain rate of exploitation, workers will not get sufficient goods to survive; and below a certain level, capitalists starve.) Note that regardless how the determination of prices is resolved (as between the causal importance of workers' utilities or the social rate of exploitation – see the discussion of Chapter 8), capitalists' marginal utilities play no role in price and profit-rate determination. A different specification of the utility functions v_i can only shift the composition of output. Of course, in equilibrium, capitalists equate their marginal rates of substitution to price ratios, through (9.12).

9.3 Extended reproduction

It is in extended reproduction that the essence of capitalism, from Marx's point of view, is seen: the drive to accumulate. Out of profits a certain portion is set aside for new investment. In the model presented now, three modifications of Marx's schematic models are added: (1) Full employment is not assumed, and the unemployed act as an industrial reserve army to exert upward pressure on the social rate of exploitation; (2) unemployed workers do not starve or disappear, but are provided a minimal subsistence bundle by the state, which is financed through a tax on profits; (3) capitalists do not automatically reinvest their profits net of consumption.

Before writing down the formal model, a verbal synopsis of its workings will be given. Suppose that there are N^* workers, and N are employed at a given moment. This gives rise to an industrial reserve army of the unemployed, $N^* - N$, which affects the bargaining strength of workers. Thus, the rate of exploitation will be postulated to be inversely related to the rate of employment. A given level of employment N thus gives rise to a rate of exploitation which in turn gives rise to a system of prices and a before-tax profit rate, through the mechanism of Theorem 7.1. However, the government now sets a tax rate on profits that is just sufficient to provide goods in some subsistence amount to the unemployed. This gives rise to an after-tax profit rate. Clearly, then, unemployment is a double-edged sword for the capitalist class: On the one hand, a high level of unemployment *increases* the before-tax profit rate; on the other hand, it increases the tax rate and therefore *decreases* the after-tax profit rate.

We shall suppose that capitalists save a certain fraction s of their profits. They always consume fraction $(1 - s)$ of their profits, but they do not automatically invest what is saved. Savings may take the form of planned investments, or they may accumulate as unwanted inventories. An acceptable simplifying assumption would be to set $s = 1$, and we do that in the simplified model of Section 9.4.

A given level of employment gives rise to a certain after-tax rate of profit. It can be shown that this after-tax rate of profit is also the *achievable growth rate* g of the economy divided by the capitalists' savings propensity s; that is, in balanced growth, a surplus of goods over current consumption and replacement requirements accumulates at rate $s\pi$. (This is the so-called Cambridge equation.) However, capitalists also desire or *plan* to accumulate at a certain rate, g^D, and in the model we postulate that rate to be a function of the after-tax profit rate. This *planned accumulation function* of capitalists will be discussed more later. In general, the achievable growth rate and the planned growth rate of the economy will differ. This gives rise to a dynamic. If $g > g^D$, then growth is occurring faster than capitalists are willing to sustain, and unwanted inventories begin accumulating; capitalists lay off workers. If $g^D > g$, then capitalists wish to grow faster than they are achieving, and they hire on more workers. An equilibrium for the system is a level of employment N at which planned and achievable growth rates coincide. This is the form that the equalization of *ex ante* investment decisions with *ex post* investment takes in this model. When the economy is not in equilibrium, it is either increasing its employment (a boom), or decreasing it (a crisis), according as $g^D > g$ or $g > g^D$. Thus, a study of this model should enable an exposition of several of the Marxian crises.

We proceed to formalize the model now, as a model of balanced growth. It is possible to present this as a many-sector model, as in the previous section; however, it is felt that the simplicity of an aggregate model is desirable at this point, because the additional complications of a reserve army, a tax rate, and a planning function have been added. Hence, we shall develop the model as a two-sector model, where sector 1 (or department 1) is the capital good and sector 2 is the consumption good. This will allow us to dispense with workers' utility functions, as a given wage will permit workers only the leeway to decide on a level of the consumption good to be consumed. In the fourth section of the chapter, an even simpler one-good macro version of the model is presented, which allows more explicit computation.

The technology for sector 1 is specified by a pair (a_{11}, L_1), where a_{11} is the input of good 1 needed to operate sector 1 at unit level, and L_1 is the amount of direct labor required. The technology for sector 2 is (a_{12}, L_2), where a_{12} is the input of the capital good of sector 1 into the operation of sector 2. Prices are p_1 and p_2. Let t be the tax rate on profits, which will be necessary to support the unemployed. Then the after-tax profit rate in sector 1 is

$$\pi = \frac{(1 - t)[p_1 - (p_1 a_{11} + L_1)]}{p_1 a_{11} + L_1}$$

which in equilibrium must be the same as the after-tax profit rate in sector 2. This leads to the price equations:

$$p_1 = \left(1 + \frac{\pi}{1 - t}\right)(p_1 a_{11} + L_1) \tag{9.17}$$

$$p_2 = \left(1 + \frac{\pi}{1 - t}\right)(p_1 a_{12} + L_2) \tag{9.18}$$

where $\pi/(1 - t)$ is the before-tax profit rate.

The workers' budget constraint is

$$p_2 b = 1 \tag{9.19}$$

where b is the level of consumption of the consumption good.

In this two-sector model, there is no need to introduce workers' utility functions, because there is no choice possible among consumption goods. The level of b shall be set by the balance of class forces (the industrial reserve army–rate of unemployment), which will be brought into the picture later.

The output vector (x_1, x_2) satisfies

$$x_1 = a_{11}(1 + g)x_1 + a_{12}(1 + g)x_2 \tag{9.20}$$

$$x_2 = bL_1(1 + g)x_1 + bL_2(1 + g)x_2 + b_0(1 + g)(N^* - N) + (1 + g)F \tag{9.21}$$

where g is the balanced rate of expansion of the economy, b_0 is the level of consumption of the unemployed worker, and $N^* - N$ is the number of unemployed. Equation 9.20 says that, if the output of the economy is to grow at rate g, then the production of good 1 today must be precisely at a level that will provide capital goods at a factor $(1 + g)$ times what is required for today's production. Equation 9.21 says that the production of the consumption good must be at a factor of $(1 + g)$ times today's demand, which consists of four parts: the consumption requirements of workers employed in sector 1, which are in amount bL_1x_1; the consumption requirements of workers employed in sector 2, which are bL_2x_2; the consumption requirement of unemployed workers, $b_0(N^* - N)$; and capitalists' consumption. Each unemployed worker is provided with a subsistence level b_0 of the consumption good by the government.

The labor demand condition is

$$L_1x_1 + L_2x_2 = N \tag{9.22}$$

Before-tax profits are

$$\Pi = \sum_1^2 [p_i - (a_{1i}p_1 + L_i)]\, x_i \tag{9.23}$$

Time in this model works in the following way: Goods are produced in this period and used in the next period. This applies to both consumption goods and capital goods, as can be seen from (9.20) and (9.21). Similarly, income and expenditure must be arranged so that income from this period is used to buy goods next period.

In particular, the tax rate t on total profits must be set so as to enable the unemployed next period to buy their subsistence; that is,

$$t\Pi = (1 + g)(N^* - N)p_2b_0 \tag{9.24}$$

where it is assumed that the rate of growth of the unemployed is also g. (More on this later.) Similarly, because capitalists are assumed to have a uniform savings propensity, s, out of after-tax profits, their budget constraint for consumption, as a class, is[3]

$$(1 - s)(1 - t)\Pi = p_2(1 + g)F \tag{9.25}$$

Finally, the class-struggle equation is

$$f\left(\frac{N}{N^*}\right) = e \qquad f' < 0 \tag{9.26}$$

The employment rate is inversely related to the social rate of exploitation – that is, the rate of exploitation of the employed workers, as previously defined. It is (9.26) that incorporates the effect of the industrial reserve army. Notice that in this two-sector model, once N/N^* is specified, b is completely determined through (9.26) and the definition of e.

All equations of the model have now been supplied except the capitalists' planning function, which relates the planned rate of accumulation to the after-tax profit rate. For the moment, we shall not introduce that function, but shall solve the system represented by (9.17)–(9.26). This is equivalent to assuming that capitalists will automatically invest what is left over of the surplus after their consumption needs.

Before stating the theorem, we must explain the necessary and sufficient condition for the solution of the system. Let a rate of employment, $r = N/N^*$, be given. According to (9.26), this determines a rate of exploitation, e, of employed workers. This, in turn, determines a consumption level $b(r)$ for employed workers, which we therefore write as a function of r. Clearly a necessary condition for the system to possess a solution is that the number of workers employed be capable of producing sufficient goods to feed themselves plus the unemployed. In labor value terms this may be stated as

$$N \geqq \Lambda_{\text{II}}[Nb(r) + (N^* - N)b_0]$$

or

$$r \geqq \Lambda_{\text{II}}[rb(r) + (1 - r)b_0] \tag{9.27}$$

This condition is also sufficient for the existence of an equilibrium.

We shall now state the theorem asserting the existence of a solution to this system, recalling that at this point we are still working under the confines of Say's law, as we assume any surplus is automatically invested by capitalists.

Theorem 9.3 (Extended reproduction with Say's law): Let $N/N^* = r$ be any rate of employment such that:

$$r \geqq \Lambda_{\text{II}}[rb(r) + (1 - r)b_0] \tag{9.27}$$

Then there exists a unique equilibrium $\{p_1, p_2, \pi, t, b, F, x_1, x_2\}$ to the economic system (9.17)–(9.26). Conversely, if there exists such an equilibrium, (9.27) must hold.

Before proving this theorem, let us review its interpretation. It asserts that, within a certain range of employment rates, any employment rate is consistent with extended reproduction of the economy – where unemployed workers must be fed by a tax on profits, and capitalists consume and accumulate out of the surplus. If the employment rate r gets too close to 1, perhaps the demands of workers, $b(r)$, will become so high that the economy can no longer reproduce; and if r becomes too small, there will be so many unemployed that the few employed workers will not be able to produce enough for themselves and the unemployed, let alone any surplus for capitalists. These are the two causes of failure of inequality (9.27).

Before proceeding to the proof, it is convenient to show that a well-known relationship among g, s, and π is embedded in the model, although there is no explicit formulation of the relationship between the rate of accumulation (g) and the after-tax rate of profit (π) in the equations. It is not surprising that the familiar Cambridge equation emerges, which is the content of Lemma 9.4:

LEMMA 9.4: From (9.17)–(9.25), it follows that $g = s\pi$.

Remark. Because this equation is a very general property of growth models, its veracity here may be taken as a check that the dating of incomes and expenditures has been consistently done.

Proof: Let the present period be period 0 and next period 1. Then $\Pi(1) = (1 + g)\Pi(0)$ in balanced growth and hence

$$\begin{aligned}\Pi(1) &= \sum_1^2 [p_i - (a_{1i}p_1 + L_1)](1 + g)x_i \\ &= (1 + g)\left[p_1x_1 + p_2x_2 - p_1\left(\frac{1}{1 + g}x_1\right) - N\right] \text{ [using (9.20) and (9.22)]} \\ &= g\mathbf{p}\cdot\mathbf{x} + p_2[x_2 - (1 + g)Nb] \quad \text{[using (9.19)]}\end{aligned}$$

From (9.21), it is seen that $x_2 - (1 + g)Nb = (1 + g)[F + b_0(N^* - N)]$ and so

$$\begin{aligned}\Pi(1) &= g\mathbf{p}\cdot\mathbf{x} + p_2(1 + g)F + p_2(1 + g)b_0(N^* - N) \\ &= g\mathbf{px} + (1 - s)(1 - t)\Pi(0) + t\Pi(0)\end{aligned}$$

from which it follows that

$$\{(1 + g) - [(1 - s)(1 - t)] + t\}\Pi(0) = g\mathbf{p}\cdot\mathbf{x}$$

This can be manipulated to

$$g = s(1 - t)\left(\frac{\Pi}{\mathbf{p}\cdot\mathbf{x} - \Pi}\right)$$

But the expression in the second set of parentheses is simply the before-tax profit rate, which is $\pi/(1 - t)$, and hence this last equation becomes $g = s\pi$.

Proof of Theorem 9.3: By hypothesis, we begin with a level of employment N, whose associated employment rate $r = N/N^*$ satisfies (9.27). Because N is given, e is known by (9.26), and b is known by

$$e = \frac{1 - \Lambda_{II} b}{\Lambda_{II} b}$$

Consequently, the triplet of prices and before-tax profit rate $\{p_1, p_2, \pi/(1 - t)\}$ can be solved for from Equations 9.17–9.19. It is left to determine $\{\pi, t, g, F\}$. It is convenient to define the matrix of augmented input coefficients, which is now a function of r, through the dependence of b on r:

$$M(r) = \begin{pmatrix} a_{11} & a_{12} \\ bL_1 & bL_2 \end{pmatrix}$$

Then Equations 9.20 and 9.21 can then be rewritten as

$$\mathbf{x} = \left[\frac{1}{1 + g} I - M(r)\right]^{-1} \begin{pmatrix} 0 \\ F + (N^* - N)b_0 \end{pmatrix} \tag{9.28}$$

By substituting from (9.24) into (9.25), we can eliminate π and p_2 and write

$$F = \left(\frac{1 - t}{t}\right) (1 - s)(N^* - N)b_0 \tag{9.29}$$

Note that the condition 9.27 is what guarantees that there exists a number t less than or equal to one which makes this possible. If (9.27) fails, it may be computed from (9.20), (9.21), and (9.22) that "material balance" of consumption goods is impossible for the system. The details of this computation are omitted, as the intuitive idea is sufficiently clear – that an equilibrium can be arranged if and only if the system produces value surplus to the consumption requirements of the working class.

Pre-multiplying (9.28) by $\mathbf{L}$ and using (9.22), we have

$$N = \mathbf{L} \left[\frac{1}{1 + g} I - M(r)\right]^{-1} \begin{pmatrix} 0 \\ F + (N^* - N)b_0 \end{pmatrix} \tag{9.30}$$

and substituting from (9.29) into (9.30),

$$N = \mathbf{L} \left[\frac{1}{1 + g} I - M(r)\right]^{-1} \begin{pmatrix} 0 \\ b_0(N^* - N)\left(s + \frac{1 - s}{t}\right) \end{pmatrix} \tag{9.31}$$

Equation 9.31 expresses a relationship between t and g, for given N. As t increases, the second component in the column vector in (9.31) decreases. Hence, to maintain equality in (9.31), g must increase, because the components of the matrix

$$\left[\frac{1}{1+g}I - M(r)\right]^{-1}$$

are seen to be increasing functions of g. Hence (9.31) gives an implicit monotonic increasing relation $g(t)$. From the Cambridge equation ($\pi = g/s$), it follows that there is a monotonic relation $\pi(t) = g(t)/s$. Hence the function $\hat{\pi}(t) \equiv \pi(t)/(1 - t)$ is monotonic increasing. But the before-tax profit rate $\hat{\pi}$ is already known, from (9.17)–(9.19) and (9.26), as was remarked in the beginning of this proof. By monotonicity of $\hat{\pi}(t)$, there is a unique t fulfilling $\hat{\pi}(t) = \hat{\pi}$.

This completes the proof. For now that t is known, π is known [because $\pi = \hat{\pi} \cdot (1 - t)$] and g is known from the Cambridge equation. The value of F follows from (9.29), and the vector $\mathbf{x}$ from (9.28). Q.E.D.

Theorem 9.3 asserts that any rate of employment which is consistent with the production of value surplus to needs of the entire working class, employed and unemployed, can be an equilibrium for the economy in extended reproduction, *if* the capitalists obligingly invest all their profits above consumption needs. This model bears some resemblance to Marx's two- and three-department schemes, where the problem of the disparity between available investment funds and desired investment was not addressed, at least in the algebraic models. The model of Theorem 9.3 assumes Say's law. We next relax Say's law, by adding another determination to the system: the capitalists' planning function. According to Theorem 9.3, there is a whole range of employment levels consistent with a solution to the system (9.17)–(9.26). When, however, we also endow capitalists with a plan to accumulate at a certain rate, which is a function of the after-tax profit rate, there will in general be only one or two equilibria. That is, for only a small number of employment rates will *ex post* and *ex ante* investment coincide.

We postulate that the planned growth rate of capitalists is a function:

$$g^D = \rho(\pi) \qquad \rho' > 0 \tag{9.32}$$

Capitalists desire to grow at an increasing rate as the rate of (after-tax) profit increases. If the rate of profit is zero or small, our capitalists will not desire to grow at all: They will not wish to produce. For some pos-

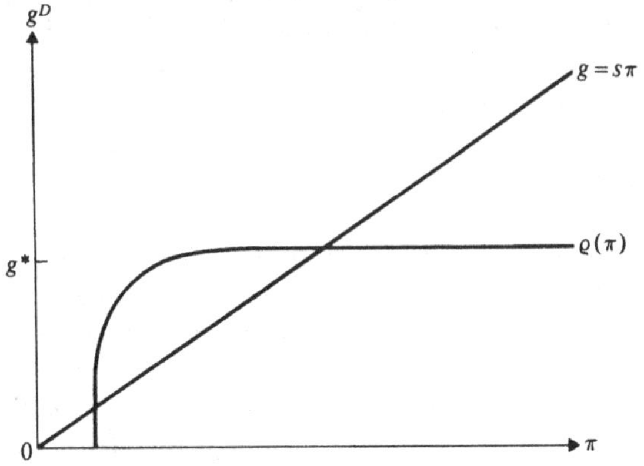

Figure 6. Capitalists' planned accumulation.

itive profit rate, they do desire to accumulate. Beyond this, the motivation for (9.32) will remain somewhat vague. It is clearly a formulation that is different from the simple "profit-maximizing" one of Chapters 1–3. We may think of g^D as the rate of inventory accumulation that capitalists are willing to sustain, because growth, in this model, takes the form of inventories that capitalists must hold until next period. With a higher rate of (after-tax) profit π, the costs of holding inventories, including risk, become relatively more worth bearing, and this gives rise to the increasing functional relation (9.32).

For our purposes, it is sufficient if the function $\rho(\pi)$ looks something like that depicted in Figure 6: Below a certain after-tax rate of return, there is no desire to grow. After that there is a fixed desire to grow. This picture is consistent with what J. Steindl claims as Marx's position on this question. Steindl (1952, p. 231) writes that Marx thought there was some long-run planned rate of accumulation, like g^* of Figure 6, that capitalists planned for independent of the rate of profit. We shall, however, as well be able to conceive of $\rho(\pi)$ as having more of a positive slope; for our interpretation of Marxian crises, it will only be necessary to maintain at least the concave shape of the function $\rho(\pi)$ (see Figure 7 and Section 9.4). We may also think of (9.32) as embodying the Keynesian "animal spirits" that prompt capitalists to invest at a certain rate.

If we combine the planned accumulation schedule (9.32) with Theorem 9.3, we arrive at a full solution of the model. As is illustrated in Figure 6, the Cambridge equation $g = s\pi$, which gives *achievable* growth rates as a function of π, intersects the schedule $g^D = \rho(\pi)$ in

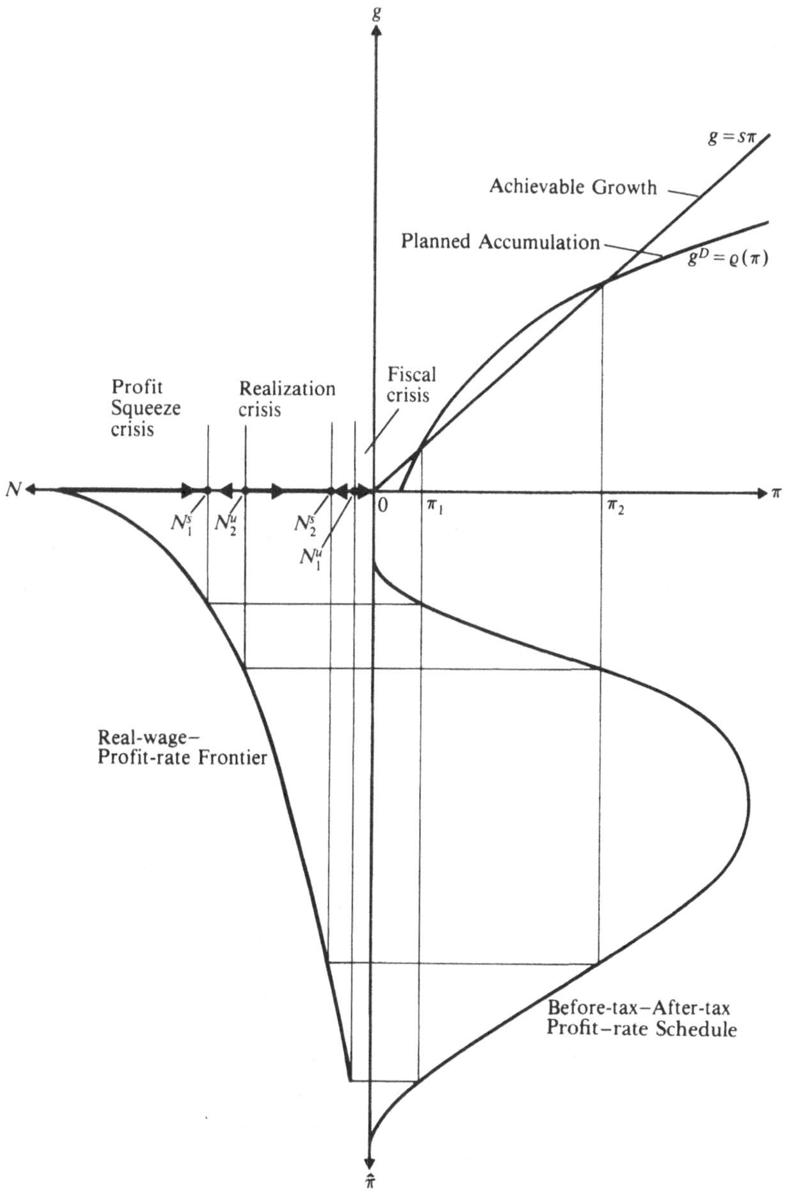

Figure 7. Regions of Marxian crises.

several places. At each of the (in this case, two) values of π that equate planned and achieved rates of accumulation, the system is at rest. In turn, each of these two after-tax profit rates are produced by certain rates of employment. These rates of employment constitute the *equilibrium employment rates of the economy.*

9.4 Three Marxian crises

We proceed to analyze the various types of equilibria that can exist, and the types of crisis that are associated with deviations from these equilibria. A graphical treatment is most transparent for this analysis; we represent the model of the previous section in the three-panel Figure 7. Quadrant III of the figure graphs the level of employment, N, against the before-tax profit rate, $\hat{\pi} = \pi/1 - t$. Because a higher N leads to a higher real wage, through the industrial reserve army mechanism (9.26), the curve of N against $\hat{\pi}$ is negatively sloped, as indicated. This is simply the *real-wage–profit-rate frontier,* familiar from Sraffian analysis. It embodies the price equations 9.17–9.19 and the bargaining equation 9.26. In quadrant IV, we graph the before-tax profit rate $\hat{\pi}$ against the after-tax profit rate π. If $\hat{\pi}$ is very low, then clearly π is low, because $\pi \leqq \hat{\pi}$. This happens for high levels of employment. However, for very high $\hat{\pi}$, which come about from low levels of employment, taxes will be high to feed the large reserve army, and here π will again be low. This leads to the curve depicted in quadrant IV. In quadrant I are graphed the *achievable accumulation schedule,* $g = s\pi$, and the *capitalists' planned accumulation schedule,* familiar from Figure 6.

The equilibrium for the system can exist only at after-tax profit rates π_1 and π_2, where planned accumulation equals achieved accumulation. If $\pi > \pi_2$, then achieved growth exceeds planned growth: Unwanted inventories build up, and capitalists cut back on production, laying off workers. If π is such that $\pi_1 < \pi < \pi_2$, capitalists will hire on additional workers; if $\pi < \pi_1$, capitalists lay off workers because the achievable growth is not sufficiently large to induce investment.

The profit rate π_1 can be achieved at two levels of employment, N_1^s and N_1^u on the employment axis. (This is seen by starting at N_1^s, for instance, and tracing through the three quadrants to arrive at the equilibrium profit rate π_1.) Similarly, associated with the equilibrium profit rate π_2 are the two equilibrium employment levels N_2^u and N_2^s.

The reader can verify, by tracing through the three quadrants, that the two employment equilibria N_1^s and N_2^s are stable, and N_1^u and N_2^u

are unstable. This is seen as follows. If $N > N_1^s$, tracing through the quadrants produces a profit rate $\pi < \pi_1$, which causes N to decrease. Thus, a displacement of N away from N_1^s to some higher level sets in motion an equilibrating mechanism to again reduce employment to N_1^s. Similarly, a displacement of N below N_1^s sets in motion an increase in employment. The arrows drawn on the N axis indicate the motion of system in each of five regions on the N axis, defined by the four equilibria.

Regions of crisis and expansion

Region 1	$N > N_1^s$	(profit-squeeze crisis)
Region 2	$N_1^s > N > N_2^u$	(low-wage stimulus)
Region 3	$N_2^u > N > N_2^s$	(realization crisis)
Region 4	$N_2^s > N > N_1^u$	(fiscal stimulus)
Region 5	$N < N_1^u$	(fiscal crisis)

There are, therefore, three regions of crisis – that is, regions where employment is decreasing – and two regions of expansion. We now indicate why the three regions 1, 3, and 5 deserve to be called the regions of profit-squeeze, realization, and fiscal crisis, respectively. When $N > N_1^s$, the employment level is so high that the bargaining power of workers keeps the real wage high and the before-tax profit rate low. The tax rate is not important, because so few workers are unemployed. The ensuing low achievable growth is not sufficient to encourage capitalists to accumulate. Capitalists lay off workers because the latters' bargaining strength makes accumulation not worthwhile. This is the scenario of what Marxists have called the *profit-squeeze crisis,* and it takes place precisely in region 1.

Consider, next, what happens in region 2, when $N \in (N_2^u, N_1^s)$. In this region, real wages have become sufficiently low, due to the industrial reserve army, to create an expansionary desire by capitalists, because $g^D > g$. Although the employment rate is sufficiently low to soften wage demands, it is not so low as to necessitate a large tax rate, which would destroy after-tax profits. Hence, the tax rate is unimportant in this region: The mechanism that creates the expansionary stimulus is due to relatively low wages – hence we call this the region of *low-wage stimulus.*

Let us consider next what occurs in region 3, for N such that $N \in (N_2^s, N_2^u)$. For this region, it is seen from Figure 7 that achievable growth rates have now become greater than planned growth rates. Capitalists consequently lay off workers because they are forced to accumulate unwanted inventories. Note that the genesis of the unwanted inventories is very different for this region than for region 1.

In region 1, unwanted inventories accumulated because the profit rate was negligible, and investment was not worthwhile. In region 3, however, the profit rate is reasonably high. Hence region 3 is properly called the region of *realization crisis;* if final demand were greater in region 3 than it is, the excess inventories would be absorbed, and no crisis would come about. It is, however, the lack of an effective demand consonant with the high productivity (i.e., high g) of the economy in this region that produces the crisis. In region 3, the low wages have produced a growth rate that is too far out of line with final demand. We see, therefore, why this region also deserves to be called the region of *underconsumptionist crisis.*

Notice that a mollifying influence on the realization crisis begins to assert itself as N approaches N_2^s: the after-tax profit rate π begins to fall, thus bringing achievable growth g more into line with planned growth. This occurs because the industrial reserve army is growing, and hence the tax rate t must grow, which cuts into before-tax profits. When this mollifying influence becomes sufficiently strong, we reach the next equilibrium, N_2^s. Hence, the existence of the equilibrium N_2^s is due to the *fiscal stimulus* of taxes. It may appear to be somewhat inverted to view a profit *tax* as a stimulus, but in this model it is. The profit tax has the effect of clearing off the excess inventories from the capitalists' shelves, thus increasing effective demand, and bringing the achievable growth rate into line with the smaller planned rate.

Continuing the descent of N into the region $N \in (N_1^u, N_2^s)$, it is seen this is the region of *fiscal stimulus.* The after-tax profit rate in this region is rendered low enough so that planned growth is greater than achievable growth, and hence capitalists wish to expand, and hire on workers. This region is the closest analog to Keynesian fiscal stimulus in this model.

As N passes the final equilibrium, we reach the doldrums of fiscal crisis. For $N < N_1^u$, employment is so low, and the industrial reserve army is so high, that the employed labor force can barely support the consumption requirements of the working class as a whole. What is left over for capitalists, as measured by the after-tax profit rate π, is extremely small. Capitalists have no incentive to invest. They lay off workers. This is clearly the *fiscal crisis:* State expenditures, financed by a tax or profits, are so great as to render investment a useless activity from the capitalists' point of view.

This completes the analysis of crises in the model. Some other observations can be made about the three types of crisis. Profit-squeeze crisis is associated with a low profit rate, realization crisis with a high profit rate, and fiscal crisis with a low (after-tax) profit rate. The crisis regions are separated from each other by regions of expansion. Thus, one crisis cannot lead directly into another, as the employment level adjusts through the dynamic mechanism. The two stable equilibria are associated with (1) the boundary of the profit-squeeze region and the low-wage-stimulus region, and (2) the boundary of the realization-crisis region and the fiscal-stimulus region. Thus, if we think of different capitalist economies as being at various *stable* equilibria, we would expect some of them to be plagued by intermittent profit-squeeze crises, and some by intermittent realization crises, depending on whether their respective long-term equilibria positions are at N_1^s or N_2^s. For those economies suffering from profit-squeeze crisis, we would expect the expansionary periods to be characterized by low-wage stimulus; we would expect the expansionary periods of the realization-crisis economies to be characterized by fiscal stimulus. Economies in fiscal crisis will tend to be in stagnation, according to Figure 7, as there is no mechanism so far postulated that will bring them out of the crisis.

9.5 A one-sector model

As a final exercise with the macro model of this chapter, we simplify even further to a one-sector model. To render the model even simpler, we assume at this point that $s = 1$: capitalists are simply accumulating machines, who do not consume.

There is one good, whose technology is (a, L). The model of Section 9.3 becomes:

$$f\left(\frac{N}{N^*}\right) = b; f' > 0 \qquad \text{(industrial reserve army)} \qquad (9.33)$$

(b is the real wage in units of the good.)

$$p = \left(1 + \frac{\pi}{1-t}\right)(pa + L) \qquad \text{(price equation)} \qquad (9.34)$$

$$pb = 1 \qquad \text{(worker's budget constraint)} \qquad (9.35)$$

$$x = a(1 + g)x + (1 + g)[Nb + (N^* - N)b_0] \qquad \text{(material balance)} \qquad (9.36)$$

$$\Pi = \left(\frac{\pi}{1-t}\right)(pa + L)x \qquad \text{(definition of before-tax profits)} \qquad (9.37)$$

$$t\Pi = (1 + g)(N^* - N)pb_0 \qquad \text{(taxes feed unemployed)} \qquad (9.38)$$

$$Lx = N \qquad \text{(labor market demand)} \qquad (9.39)$$

$$g^D = \rho(\pi) \qquad \text{(capitalists' planned accumulation)} \qquad (9.40)$$

From (9.35), $p = 1/b$. From (9.33), b is a function of the employment rate $r = N/N^*$, $b(r)$. From (9.34), we solve for the before-tax profit rate:

$$\frac{\pi}{1-t} \equiv \hat{\pi} = \frac{1}{a + b(r)L} - 1 \tag{9.41}$$

Equation 9.41 gives the wage–profit frontier of quadrant III, Figure 7. Note $a + bL$ is the augmented input coefficient. Let us call:

$$m(r) \equiv a + b(r)L \tag{9.42}$$

Solving (9.36) for x:

$$x = \frac{(1+g)(N^* - N)b_0}{1 - (1+g)m} \tag{9.43}$$

Multiplying Equation 9.43 by L, and using Equation 9.39, we can solve for $(1 + g)$:

$$\frac{1}{1+g} = m(r) + b_0L\left(\frac{N^* - N}{N}\right) \tag{9.44}$$

Equation 9.44 says the achievable growth factor $(1 + g)$ is influenced by two things: the productivity of the economy, which is measured by $m(r)$, and the unemployment drag, measured by $b_0L[(N^*/N) - 1]$.

Because $g = s\pi$ and $s = 1$, we have $g = \pi$ and so (9.44) implies that

$$\frac{1}{1+\pi} = m(r) + b_0L\left(\frac{N^*}{N} - 1\right) \tag{9.45}$$

Using (9.45), if we know the functions f and ρ, we can solve for the equilibrium employment levels of the economy.

We compute the condition that characterizes the turning point of the before-tax–after-tax schedule of Figure 7, quadrant IV. The employment rate r^*, which is associated with this turning point, has this economic interpretation: It is that employment rate at which the marginally unemployed worker has decreased the real payments to the employed working class, due to its marginally inferior bargaining position, by just an amount that balances the increase in unemployment benefits the marginally augmented unemployed army must receive – so that the net change in the after-tax profit rate is zero.

From (9.45) and (9.41), using definition (9.42), we can write:

$$(\hat{\pi} + 1)^{-1} + b_0L\left(\frac{N^*}{N} - 1\right) = (\pi + 1)^{-1} \tag{9.46}$$

Equation 9.46 is the equation of the curve in Figure 7, quadrant IV. To simplify notation, let

$$q \equiv \pi + 1 = \text{the after-tax profit gactor}$$

$$\hat{q} \equiv \hat{\pi} + 1 = \text{the before-tax profit factor}$$

$$r \equiv \frac{N}{N^*} = \text{the employment rate}$$

Differentiating (9.46) with respect to $\hat{q}$ gives

$$\frac{dq}{d\hat{q}} = \frac{\hat{q}^{-2} + b_0 L r^{-2}(dr/d\hat{q})}{q^{-2}} \tag{9.47}$$

Notice that $dr/d\hat{q} < 0$; this is simply the statement that the wage-profit frontier is negatively sloped. For small values of $\hat{q}$, the numerator of (9.47) is positive; for large values of $\hat{q}$, because r will then be small, the numerator of (9.47) becomes negative. The turning point of the curve is that value $\hat{q}$ at which the derivative in (9.47) vanishes. Writing the vanishing-derivative condition in elasticity form, we have

$$-\left(\frac{d\hat{q}/\hat{q}}{dr/r}\right) = (b_0 L)\frac{\hat{q}}{r} \tag{9.48}$$

Using (9.41), we can independently compute the elasticity on the left-hand side of (9.48) as

$$-\left(\frac{d\hat{q}/\hat{q}}{dr/r}\right) = r\hat{q}\frac{db}{dr}L \tag{9.49}$$

Substitution of (9.49) into (9.48) yields

$$r\frac{db}{dr} = \frac{1}{r}b_0 \tag{9.50}$$

or, writing (9.50) in elasticity form,

$$\left(\frac{db/b}{dr/r}\right)_{r=r^*} = \frac{1}{r^*}\frac{b_0}{b(r^*)} \tag{9.51}$$

To summarize this computation, the employment rate r^* for which the elasticity condition (9.51) is met is that employment rate at which the fiscal effect of an increasing tax rate begins to force the after-tax profit to move in the opposite direction from the before-tax profit rate, as r decreases.

The computations in this section have been intended as an example to show how the one-sector model of this chapter can be solved explicitly. We could, as well, compute various "multipliers," which would describe the effect on the equilibrium of the system from changes in b_0, s, the schedule $b(r)$, the schedule $\rho(\pi)$, and the technology (a, L). We could study how the size of the various crisis regions changes as a function of the parameters of the economy.

9.6 Summary

The intent of this chapter has been to model three important Marxian crises: profit squeeze, realization, and fiscal. To produce a profit-squeeze crisis, an industrial-reserve army–bargaining mechanism was needed, which was specified in Equation 9.26, or Equation 9.33; to produce a realization crisis, a discrepancy between achievable growth and planned growth was necessary, which was specified by Equation 9.32, or Equation 9.40; to produce a fiscal crisis, it was necessary for government expenditures to reduce profits, which were captured by the tax mechanism of Equation 9.24 or Equation 9.38.

Crises associated with the monetary and credit aspects of capitalist economy are not touched on by the model of this chapter. This is perhaps the most important omission. In addition, no account has been taken of technical change, or the growth of the labor force. The implicit assumption of the present model is that the labor force grows at the equilibrium growth rate g; this assumption is embodied in Equation 9.21 or Equation 9.36, in which it is assumed that the growth of the consumption requirements of the workers, employed and unemployed, (and also of capitalists) is at rate g. Thus, even if we are at an equilibrium in this model, it is of the knife-edge type, for it can only be an equilibrium if the labor force, too, is growing at the equilibrium rate. Clearly a more complete model would rectify this deficiency, and perhaps the most natural way to start would be to postulate an exogenous rate of growth for the labor force. Steindl (1952, Chapter 14) has discussed what a Marxian theory of accumulation including population growth might be. Nevertheless, from the model presented in this chapter, we can conclude that even without the problems of "overdetermination" introduced by an exogenously growing labor force, the three crises types discussed can occur.

10 Summing up and new directions

Because issues discussed in the introductory chapter were primarily methodological, it is appropriate for these final words to summarize some main points of content of the book. In addition, because the line that defines where a book of this type stops must be drawn somewhat arbitrarily, the reader's indulgence is asked if some mention is made of current work not reported upon in previous chapters, but that bears upon the issues.

The task of Chapters 1 through 3 is to place the Marxian notions of economic reproduction and exploitation into a general equilibrium context. In most mathematical treatments of Marxian economics, only the production side of the economy is studied, and it is simply asserted that a certain price vector (the vector that equalizes profit rates across sectors) is the "equilibrium" vector. This formulation is inadequate, because no specific behavior of capitalists and workers is stipulated, with respect to which equilibrium has been defined. An equilibrium of an economy is a situation where the optimizing behavior of all individuals aggregates to social behavior that is consistent; clearly, then, the definition of equilibrium requires a prior specification of what the behavior of individuals *is*. This may seem a small point; it is not, as can be seen from common disagreements or confusions that have emerged between Marxists and neoclassicists concerning Marxian equilibrium. For instance, a neoclassicist asks how there can be an "equilibrium" with a positive rate of profit in an economy with constant returns to scale. This question, and others, is resolved, it is hoped, with the embedding of the Marxian production framework in a general equilibrium setting. Specifically, capitalists maximize *profits* in our model, given their initial stock of wealth. (In Marxian terms, they seek to expand M into the largest possible M' via the production circuit M–C–M'.) In the case of a linear production model, where production takes time and capitalists must finance inputs used this week out of current wealth, this behavior gives rise to an equilibrium price vector that equalizes profit rates across sectors, and in general exhibits a positive rate of profit. We can think of the positivity of the rate of profit as a consequence of the fact that the economy is *capital-limited:* Even if all the capital stock is used, there will be unemployed workers, and hence the wage is driven down to some subsistence level, giving rise to a positive profit rate. Were the economy *labor-limited,* the rate of profit would be zero, as capitalists would bid for scarce workers until profits were eliminated, in trying to employ their entire capital stock. Hence, the time-consuming nature of production plus the capital-limited nature of the economy (or the ubiquitous industrial reserve army) explain the emergence of a positive profit rate as an equilibrium in a constant-returns-to-scale economy.

That capitalists cannot borrow, in the model of Chapters 1 and 2, may appear to be a restriction; and so it is shown in Chapter 3 that this restriction is only a simplifying one, not an essential one. When a credit market exists, then the interest rate is equal to the profit rate in equilibrium. Capitalists are willing to operate at some finite scale of activities, because borrowing a lot of capital to finance "infinite" production would produce no extra profit, as the revenues would be dissipated in interest payments. From a neoclassical point of view, there are zero profits in these models, as what we have called profits could be called interest costs, or opportunity costs of capital. However, the neoclassical connection of the interest (or profit) rate with intertemporal preferences of agents is not made in our model. Rather, the profit rate is determined by the subsistence real wage, which in turn is determined by "class struggle," or in a variety of other possible ways. (In Chapter 2, a model is provided showing how we can conceive of the real wage as determined through technology; this treatment simply removes the role of class struggle one more stage.) For all practical purposes, the real wage is taken as exogenous to the economically specifiable phenomena of the models.

Labor values in these models are used only in defining the concept of surplus value and exploitation; they play no role whatsoever in the discussion of exchange and prices. This point is reinforced in Chapters 7 and 8. Labor value played a dual role for Marx – in a theory of exchange and a theory of exploitation. In fact, this dual role was necessary for Marx, as he derived the theory of exploitation using the theory of exchange as a conduit. We have recast the theory of exploitation to be independent of the labor-value theory of exchange, and hence have no need to argue any relationship between prices and labor values. In our recasting of the theory of exploitation we lose the notion that labor value in some way regulates the exchange of equivalents; we do not conceive of the exchange of labor power for the wage, in particular, as an exchange of equivalents, but as determined by bargaining and competition. The *law of value* is reformulated as follows: Corresponding to any prior specification of the distribution of aggregate social labor time between production for workers' consumption and capitalists' profits (investment or consumption goods), there is a set of prices and individual demands (by workers) that will realize that distribution of labor time. Nevertheless, there is no causal direction implied – that, for instance, workers and capitalists bargain over the distribution of labor time and *then* prices emerge to realize the agreed claims on labor. In fact, workers and capitalists bargain over the money wage. The *law of value,* as stated, is nevertheless the closest we can get to a formal statement that indicates the way in which the distribution of labor value "regulates" capitalist production. As will be mentioned later, in more general models of production than the linear one, it is not even possible to conceive of labor values before the market equilibrium has been arrived at, and so any *causal* inference one might wish to show of the emergence of prices from labor value is completely misconceived.

This liberation of the theory of exploitation from the labor-value exchange theory enables one to show that the Marxian theory of exploitation is robust; it remains valid when the production sets that capitalists face are much more general than Leontief linear production. Capitalists can face different production sets; these sets can be general convex sets. The "fundamental Marxian theorem" of Chapter 2 shows that in this general production environment, positive profits at equilibrium are equivalent to the existence of exploitation, or surplus value, given the technical and the social (i.e., the real wage) conditions of production. The generality of this production environment enables us to say that the Marxian notion of exploitation is viable even when: (1) there are scarce factors, such as land; (2) capitalists have different information or differential access to production; (3) there is substitution possible between inputs in production; (4) there is fixed capital, joint production, differential turnover times of actual production processes and so on. Thus, the association of Marxian exploitation theory with the linear, Leontief or Sraffian model is not necessary. What is lost in these general environments are individual labor values of commodities, and hence the possibility of a labor-value exchange theory. But we have argued that is no real loss, but a clarification.

The position that labor values are irrelevant in discussing exchange is not new with this book, but has been elaborated in different ways by others in the past decade, most notably Steedman (1977) and Morishima (1973). There is, in fact, an even more startling piece of evidence than has been provided in these works for the position that labor value cannot be conceived of as existing "logically prior" to the operations of the market. This evidence, unfortunately, is one of those exhibits that falls on the other side of the line demarcating what can be included in this book. A sketch, however, will be indicated.

In the models of this book, the demarcation of individuals into *classes* of workers and capitalists occurs prior to the specification of the model. Alternatively, we might wish to define individuals solely by their property ownership, and then conclude that certain people become capitalists and others become workers; we would thereby provide a theory of class formation. In fact, this project has been carried out (Roemer, 1979b and 1980c). We then are able to classify agents in the economy according to three separate dimensions, or criteria: (1) their wealth or property ownership; (2) their class membership; (3) their status as exploiter or exploited. A fundamental theorem of this analysis is dubbed the *class exploitation correspondence principle:* those who optimize by selling their labor power become exploited, and those who optimize by hiring labor power become exploiters. This is, of course, a classical Marxian idea, but it is usually a definition. It is something else to show the truth of the formal proposition when both class membership and exploitation status emerge endogenously in a model of rational economic behavior. Capitalists are exploiters, proletarians are exploited.

What has this to do with the labor theory of value? It turns out there are no problems in proving the class exploitation correspondence principle in economies with the linear Leontief technology; however, if one tries to generalize the theorem to an economy with a production set that is a general cone, and uses the definition of surplus value provided in Chapter 2, the principle is false! What can this mean? Is the correspondence between class and exploitation so ephemeral, depending for its validity on a simplistic model of production – one, for instance, in which there is no fixed capital?

The answer is no; the resolution is that we require another definition of exploitation in the model with general production for the validity of the theorem. There is another candidate for a definition of labor value embodied in goods for the cone technology (which includes the von Neumann technology). This definition stipulates that socially necessary labor time embodied in a commodity package be defined as labor expended to produce that package, minimized over *only* processes that are in fact maximally profitable at the going equilibrium prices. (Note that our definition of labor embodied in Definition

2.1 required us to minimize labor over *all* processes available, not just the profitable ones.) If one adopts this alternate definition of labor-embodied, then the class exploitation correspondence principle holds in the general model. Note that both of these definitions are generalizations of the labor-embodied in the Leontief model, because *all* processes are (maximally) profitable in the linear system, at equilibrium.

What is the significance of this rather complicated and technical set of ideas? *A priori*, we do not know which definition of labor-embodied (and hence surplus value and exploitation) is the appropriate one, of the two offered, when the technology is no longer linear. The definition that was adopted by Morishima for the von Neumann technology, and that has been here generalized to apply to general convex technology (Chapter 2) is adequate for preserving the "fundamental Marxian theorem," and in that definition labor-embodied is in fact *independent* of market phenomena, as it depends only on knowledge of the technology and real wage bundle. (Of course, one could argue that neither technology nor the real wage are independent of the market; but at the level of these models, their determination is exogenous. Hence, these models do not provide a theory of the market relatedness of technology, the real wage, and hence labor value.) However, to preserve the correspondence between exploitation and class, which should be viewed as a fundamental Marxian insight, one is required to adopt a different definition of labor-embodied, in which labor value depends on the market: One must know which processes are profitable to define labor value, and that can be known only after the market has chosen these processes from among the many in the technology. There are, in general, multiple equilibria associated with given data specifying an economy, and the different equilibria will in general pick out different processes as the profitable ones; hence, labor-embodied using the alternate definition cannot be specified prior to knowledge of the equilibrium prices. (It should be added that the market-oriented definition of labor-embodied also preserves the fundamental Marxian theorem.) Thus, value cannot be defined prior to the operation of market; it is a notion that derives from the commodity nature of capitalist production, rather than simply the engineering nature of production possibility sets. This classical Marxian idea emerges formally from the investigation. Any conception of prices as being determined by values, or at a later logical stage than values, is impossible to hold in the face of this evidence. If one rejects the evidence, one is simultaneously committed to rejecting the class exploitation correspondence principle. (Readers interested in pursuing the details of this argument are referred to Roemer, 1980c.)

In particular, it should also be mentioned, the "law of value" discussed in Chapter 7 must be seriously modified in the context of more general production sets, using the new definition of labor-embodied. Even if a version of that theorem is true in a general production environment, it is not so interesting as in the linear case, because the rate of exploitation will have no status as a notion that can be specified prior to the operation of the market, as has been mentioned earlier.

It is appropriate to reinforce a methodological point at this juncture, concerning the value of mathematical modeling. We have claimed a forceful philosophical position, that value cannot be conceived of independently of the market, as a consequence of rather intricate mathematical reasoning. I would assert that one could not possibly arrive at this theorem without mathematical apparatus. One might have an opinion on the matter of which of the two definitions of labor-embodied is more reasonable. But only with mathematical argument can one show that one of the definitions is actually incorrect – that is, it does not provide a model that captures our theory of reality (see the Introduction) – and we are therefore directed to adopting the other definition. Here, our theory of reality is of the correspondence between class and exploitation, and the model is the set of mathematical postulates and definitions that enable us to prove the class exploitation correspondence principle. Hence theory directs our choice of model, which then in turn informs us about an open question in the theory, the market relatedness of the labor value concept.

Another philosophical issue, which has not been dealt with in the book, concerns the choice to privilege labor power as the commodity that is exploited in capitalist production. It is well known that one can define corn values or energy values of commodities instead of labor values, and show that corn is exploited or energy is exploited if there are positive profits. Indeed, profits are positive if and only if any input into production is exploited, if we choose to define value embodied in terms of it. The validity of the fundamental Marxian theorem holds if we take as the numéraire for denominating value any other commodity than labor power. Why, then, do we choose labor power? Certain brief observations may be made. It is commonly asserted that labor is properly viewed as the exploited factor because it is the factor that is nonproduced and hence, in principal, scarce. It is highly problematic whether one should conceive of labor as nonproduced (in fact, the essence of the notion of labor power is to treat the factor as produced). But more significantly, it is essential in the Marxian model that labor power, whether produced or not, be plentiful, not scarce. It is the industrial reserve army that generates a positive rate of profit. It is obvious that labor is not scarce in Marx's own vision: It is the peculiar law of population of capitalism that guarantees a ubiquitous industrial reserve army. Thus, we cannot simultaneously hold that labor is the appropriate numéraire for value because it is scarce, and also the industrial reserve army is a key feature of capitalism. Moreover, at any given time there are truly scarce, nonproduced factors in our economy, but we do not choose to denominate exploitation in terms of them.

There are, certainly, various key differences between labor and corn or energy. One reply to the challenge is that we are interested in studying the history of people and not of corn – or, at least, the history of corn is interesting only so long as it has something to say about the history of people. Although this is certainly correct, the observation does not immediately tell us why we cannot get an informative history of the economic relations among people by studying their relations to each other using corn values instead of labor values. A second reason to privilege labor power is that it is the one inalienable commodity: For labor to be forthcoming from labor power, its owner must participate in production. This is not, of course, true of corn: The services of corn can be extracted from corn power while its owner is asleep a thousand miles away. Moreover, under capitalist property relations, everyone is guaranteed ownership of only one commodity, his or her labor power.

This issue is even more fundamental than those in this book, for on it rests the usefulness of our definition of exploitation. Nevertheless, an analytically convincing answer (as opposed to the plausible, intuitive answers of the previous paragraph) is subtle and not completely worked out at this writing. With the usual *caveat* concerning work in process, I shall indicate the general nature of the answer that I think pertains. To explain the ability of a capitalist economy to expand, and to make profits, it is sufficient to observe that the technology is productive, and that productivity can be characterized by one unit of *any* commodity embodying less than one unit of its own value. Although the productiveness of the capitalist system must be explained, at some level, by how much of the net product (after replacement for depreciation) workers receive as wage goods, the objective fact of positive profits need not be accounted for by choosing labor power as the value numéraire. The labor value numéraire, however, allows us to focus on class struggle, on the relations among people, as the most dynamic and important aspect of the economic process. We could characterize the struggle to increase productivity (and hence profits) as the struggle between people and corn, a struggle to transform productive technique to get more output of goods per unit of corn employed. Does this approach tell us as much about the evolution of economic institutions as viewing the struggle to increase productivity as the effort to extract more labor from one unit of labor power employed? If the answer is yes, then a corn theory of value would be appropriate. But the historical materialist who holds that all history is the history of class struggle is clearly mandated to view the struggle for productivity using the labor value numéraire. This does not mean that a labor-value theory of exploitation is at every instant the one with most explicative power; a case might be made that during the period 1970–90, an energy theory of value would be more informative of the forces that are molding economy and society. Over the long haul, however, a historical–materialist interpretation of history implies the labor theory of exploitation.

Another reason that the relations between capitalist and proletarian are best captured through the labor theory of exploitation is that proletarians own nothing but their labor power, and so if we wish to describe the terms of their exchange with capitalists with a commodity numéraire, labor power is the natural one to choose. Here, it is the inalienability of labor power that comes into play. This leads to a second reason to focus on the labor theory of exploitation, as follows.

If we wish to make a normative statement about the distribution of final net product among all economic agents, we require some uniform basis for comparing their contributions and receipts to and from production. We take as the model, now, that all agents have one unit of labor power in their endowment, but tangible property is distributed in some uneven way, so that some agents have nothing but their labor power, others have a lot of corn and no steel, and so on. Let us suppose, for simplicity of exposition, that everyone is maximizing his or her revenues, by employing all of his or her assets in production. In particular, everyone uses his or her one unit of labor power, and whatever else he or she has. (If one wishes to have nonlaboring rich people, then one can endow people with a desire for leisure, so that if they have sufficient nonlabor endowments, they do not have to work to satisfy their need for revenues.) In a linear model, the total labor value of the net product will be equal to total labor employed. How is the net product distributed? Some agents receive goods embodying less labor value than they used (i.e., one unit), and some receive goods embodying more labor value than they used. We refer to the former group as exploited and the latter as exploiters. But the normative usefulness of this classification depends on each agent's possessing the same amount of the numéraire commodity. If we assume homogeneous and identical labor endowment, then labor power is that unique commodity which is distributed in egalitarian fashion. In fact, one's ranking in the ordering of exploitation corresponds exactly to one's ranking in wealth, if labor is chosen as numéraire.

If corn is chosen as the value numéraire, we can define exploitation of people (evaluated in terms of corn) in the same way. A person who received as his or her share of the final net product goods embodying less corn value than the corn he or she employed in production would be "corn-exploited," and inversely for corn exploiters. The total value of corn embodied in the net product is equal to total corn employed, in a linear model, so there will in general be corn-exploited agents and corn exploiters; *but there is absolutely no distributional significance to this characterization.* There is no relationship of people's corn-exploitation status to their wealths or their welfares. In particular, proletarians who have no corn to sell, but receive some wage goods out of net product, will be corn exploiters.

The essence of this distinction between labor power and corn is that the endowment of the former is a natural numéraire for evaluating distribution, because of its unique egalitarian occurrence in the population. Moreover, many people (the proletarians) have *nothing* but their labor power, which forces us to choose that commodity as value numéraire to have a meaningful measure of the distribution of net product.

Hence, there are at least two reasons for choosing the labor value numéraire: a historical–materialist hypothesis, which views history as most convincingly presented as class struggle, is mandated to choose labor value as focusing on the main arena; and the inalienability of labor power privileges its choice not only for describing class struggle, but also as numéraire for the distributional consequences of capitalism.

A third reason for privileging labor as the numéraire in defining exploitation is also normative: It is the position that living labor is entitled to the product but that ownership of alienable factors of production (i.e., capital) does not entitle one to a share of the product. The ethical implication of the labor exploitation theory is that a nonexploitative allocation of the product is one that distributes it according to labor performed.

It should be reiterated that these last paragraphs are tentative. One might note that these proposals raise several questions. How compelling is a labor-exploitation theory when people own different amounts (or kinds) of labor power? Or when everyone owns some nonlabor endowments as well? It should be reiterated that the particular reason for choosing the labor theory of exploitation is not because it is the sole way to explain the emergence of profits and accumulation; labor is not the sole common attribute of all commodities, and hence the only means by which they may be compared. In this, the present suggestions depart from classical Marxism.

It is doubtless annoying to the reader who has struggled through a sometimes tedious, sometimes difficult text to be reminded that, in the author's opinion, these studies contribute only the foundations of the theory in question. (Witness the number of advanced treatises titled *An Introduction to* . . . or *Elements of*. . . .) In fact, the remarks above on the labor theory of value indicate that our analysis has not reached even some fundamental parts of the foundation. It is therefore incumbent upon the author to indicate the sense in which this work contributes only a foundation for Marxian economic theory.

It is clear that the problems discussed are virtually all classical ones in the Marxian literature: the theory of exploitation in a competitive, capitalist economy; the falling rate of profit; the transformation problem; and only the rudiments of theories of crisis. These problems arose out of Marx's concern with the laws of motion of nineteenth-century capitalism. For Marxian economic theory to break new ground, it must study the laws of motion of late twentieth-century society – in particular, advanced capitalist society and developing socialist society. (Without engaging in polemics concerning the existence of socialism, let us adopt the semantic convention that socialist society refers to the U.S.S.R., China, Eastern Europe, Cuba, etc.) Marxian economic discussions of late twentieth-century society often erroneously attempt to apply categories that were developed to analyze nineteenth-century capitalism to modern societies. It is frequently impossible to do so fruitfully – for instance, how can one discuss exploitation or the expropriation of surplus value when the means of production are not privately owned? – and consequently, no materialist theory of the laws of motion of socialist societies is produced. The proper procedure, instead, follows from understanding that Marxism is the application of historical materialism to nineteenth-century society; and that what is required today is not the application of Marxism as such but of the historical–materialist method to late twentieth-century society.

To make this point more precisely, observe two common errors that are made in Marxian discussions of socialist society. Some claim that because inequality, strata or classes, perhaps imperialism, continue to exist in these societies, they are therefore still capitalist, or have reverted to capitalism. This is a nonmaterialist approach: Capitalism emerges in a certain historical epoch and has certain special institutional and property forms, which are absent in socialist societies. This diagnosis is akin to saying that because the bourgeois revolutions from feudalism did not eliminate inequality, war, classes, and so on, society was still feudal. The polar claim is that because socialist society has eliminated private property in the means of production, it is impossible to speak of exploitation in these societies. Here, the error is in treating Marxian categories as universal: Even if capitalist exploitation does not exist in socialist society, perhaps there is a more general theory of exploitation than Marxian capitalist exploitation, which will indicate a phenomenon of socialist exploitation. The historical task of bourgeois revolution was to eliminate feudal exploitation; but other forms of inequality and exploitation persisted and came into being. Similarly, the historical task of socialist revolution is to eliminate capitalist exploitation; there is no presumption, however, that inequality in general is eliminated, or that it may not be meaningful to speak of new forms of exploitation. As was pointed out in the introductory chapter, the ingenuity of Marx's economic theory was in showing how one could conceive of exploitation in a meaningful way under capitalism despite its abolition of coercive institutions of labor exchange; similarly, a historical–materialist approach to socialism might produce a theory of exploitation under socialism that applies despite the absence of private property in the means of production. Such a theory would not necessarily imply that socialist society is not a progressive development over capitalist society, just as Marx's theory did not imply that capitalism was not progressive over feudalism. (A proposal for this theory is in my forthcoming book *A General Theory of Exploitation and Class.*)

It is perhaps possible to criticize Marxian attempts to study late twentieth-century capitalism in a similar way, but not having engaged in such work, it is not appropriate for me to comment on that.

To sum up in an aggressive way, it appears that Marxian theory is in a Ptolemaic crisis. At present Marxism does not provide a compelling theory for explaining the developments of late twentieth-century society. I think this is due, in large part, to the epicycle approach its practitioners often take: the hope that a small perturbation of the categories of a century-old theory can explain developments today. Of all methodologies, Marxism should be the last to fall into this trap, with its insistence on the nonuniversality and transiency of appropriate historical categories. The genesis of this dogmatism in the West is, perhaps, related to the efforts of Marxists to defend their barricades against a dominant, hostile ideology; a house beseiged is not one in which experimentation and questioning are welcome. The development of Marxism in the East is explained by its role as the official ideology of state apparatuses that have their own positions to defend, and are not necessarily interested in the most penetrating inquiry into the logic of their societies' development.

It is by separating the historical–materialist kernel from its specific application as Marxism, the theory of nineteenth-century capitalism, that progress will be made.

Notes

Introduction

1. My ideas on methodology have been influenced by many conversations with Duncan Foley, and by the approach of Lakatos (1976) to the development of mathematical ideas. Indeed, I can claim no great originality for whatever seems novel or useful in this introduction, as I am not sure where the ideas of Foley and Lakatos end and mine begin.

2. Smolinski gives a third reason, with which I do not completely agree, for the lack of mathematics in Marx: that the type of discrete and discontinuous phenomena with which Marx was concerned were not best modeled with calculus and algebra, but rather with linear algebra and finite mathematics, and he had little or no knowledge of these fields.

3. Since writing this I have encountered a more complete discussion of functionalism in Elster (1978).

1. Equilibrium and reproducibility: the linear model

1. A more lengthy discussion of the material in this section is Morishima (1973), Parts I and II. Other useful introductory sources are Pasinetti (1977) and Steedman (1977).

2. The following convention on vector orderings will be observed throughout the book. For two vectors **x** and **y**, $\mathbf{x} \geqq \mathbf{y}$ means that $x_i \geqq y_i$ for all components of the two vectors; $\mathbf{x} \geq \mathbf{y}$ means $\mathbf{x} \geqq \mathbf{y}$ but $\mathbf{x} \neq \mathbf{y}$; $\mathbf{x} > \mathbf{y}$ means that $x_i > y_i$; for components i.

3. A picayune point concerning Theorem 1.2 could arise. Are there trivial reproducible solutions ($\mathbf{x} = \mathbf{0}$) associated, perhaps, with price vectors other than $\mathbf{p}^*$? To exclude this possibility, we need to guarantee that at the RS, some capitalist has a positive amount of capital $\mathbf{p}\boldsymbol{\omega}^\nu > 0$. (This can be guaranteed, for example, by insisting that social capital is a positive vector: $\boldsymbol{\omega} > 0$.) Otherwise, there may exist trivial reproducible solutions associated with price vectors other than $\mathbf{p}^*$.

4. When a credit market is introduced, in Chapter 3, there is another genesis of the equalization of profit rates. This discussion is resumed at the end of that chapter.

5. This lemma is a form of the fixed-point theorem that is used to prove the existence of economic equilibria. Statement of the lemma is on page 42. A proof can be found in Debreu (1973, p. 82).

6. The temporary equilibrium model is treated again in Chapter 2, but not fully dealt with in this book. A more detailed treatment is available in Roemer (1980a).

2. Reproducibility and exploitation: a general model

1. For a proof of this Lemma, which is based on the Kakutani fixed-point theorem, see Debreu (1973, p. 82).

2. It is certainly true as well that production sets are socially determined. Nevertheless, the relaxation of the exogenous subsistence wage premise seems more important than relaxing the exogeneity of production sets.

3. The equalization of profit rates in Marxian general equilibrium

1. I am grateful to Xavier Calsamiglia for a discussion in which some of these ideas first took shape.

2. Another option for such a producer would be to borrow capital and finance production on loans; it can be shown that the disenfranchised producer is exploited just the same, this time through the operation of the credit market and not the labor market. His surplus labor, in this case, is transferred to the creditor in the form of interest. A full discussion of the equivalence of labor and credit markets in generating Marxian exploitation is contained in my forthcoming book, *A General Theory of Exploitation and Class.*

3. When conservatives argue that corporation profit taxes must be lowered to generate more investment activity, liberal opponents are limited to disagreeing with that statement of fact, as they respect the constraint of capitalist property relations. A Marxist reply is that the "necessity" of lowering profit taxes to stimulate investment (if true) proves not that taxes should be lowered but that capital should be socialized.

4. Viable and progressive technical change and the rising rate of profit

1. I cannot resist mentioning a slogan appearing on a poster that summarizes nicely a Marxist approach to the population "problem": "Take care of the people, and the population will take care of itself."

2. As follows: if we choose any capital good and ask what other goods enter into its production as intermediate inputs at any previous stage, we eventually generate all of department I, by the indecomposability of A_{I}. Because some capital good uses direct labor, we also require all department II sectors in the production of that capital good, because $\mathbf{b} > 0$. Hence, starting with any capital good eventually "generates" the whole economy as intermediate inputs. If we start with any consumption good, it requires either direct labor input or some capital input. It is easy to see that in either case, the whole economy is eventually generated as intermediate inputs, as long as $A_{\text{II}} \neq 0$.

3. To see this: by (4.19), $\mathbf{L}_{\text{II}}^{*}$ is constrained only so that $(\mathbf{L}_{\text{II}} - \mathbf{L}_{\text{II}}^{*})$ lies in the hyperplane $\mathbf{b}^{\perp}$. So long as $\mathbf{x}_{\text{II}}$ is not chosen as a multiple of $\mathbf{b}$, it is possible to choose $\mathbf{L}_{\text{II}}^{*}$ and $\mathbf{x}_{\text{II}}$ so that $\mathbf{L}_{\text{II}}\mathbf{x}_{\text{II}} \neq \mathbf{L}_{\text{II}}^{*}\mathbf{x}_{\text{II}}$. I have said that $\mathbf{L}_{\text{II}}^{*}\mathbf{x}_{\text{II}} < \mathbf{L}_{\text{II}}\mathbf{x}_{\text{II}}$, for the sake of being explicit.

4. An anonymous referee who read this theorem when it was published in a journal article has provided an intuitive economic argument for Theorem 4.7. He or she writes: "When the technical change is neutral, then production needs the same amounts of indirect labor if we disregard dating of labor. However, when the change is CU–LS, then there is a reshuffling so that one uses more labor earlier and less later. Obviously this must make the rate of profit fall."

5. It may appear restrictive not to consider a category of technical changes where some labor values increase and some decrease. This, however, is not so. It is reasonable to postulate technical change as taking place in one sector at a time; and it can easily be shown that such technical change will not produce value changes in opposite directions in different sectors. Furthermore, by the nonsubstitution theorem, from among known techniques there always exists one that simultaneously minimizes the labor values of all commodities.

6. Although Table 1 refers to the two-dimensional case depicted in Figure 3, the classification generalizes to the multidimensional case in this simple way: The four combinations of movement in the variables (π, e) are given by

1. $\bar{\mathbf{\Lambda}} \cdot \boldsymbol{\delta} < 0, \bar{\mathbf{p}} \cdot \boldsymbol{\delta} < 0$
2. $\bar{\mathbf{\Lambda}} \cdot \boldsymbol{\delta} < 0, \bar{\mathbf{p}} \cdot \boldsymbol{\delta} > 0$
3. $\bar{\mathbf{\Lambda}} \cdot \boldsymbol{\delta} > 0, \bar{\mathbf{p}} \cdot \boldsymbol{\delta} < 0$
4. $\bar{\mathbf{\Lambda}} \cdot \boldsymbol{\delta} > 0, \bar{\mathbf{p}} \cdot \boldsymbol{\delta} > 0$

6. Changes in the real wage and the rate of profit

1. The point made here is a simplification. It ignores changes in the workers' consumption that become necessary because of technical change. If a new technology requires that workers be given more education, then **b** must change for technological reasons. Or the horses may indeed require more hay to pull heavier ploughs. A strict interpretation of the Marxian concept of subsistence bundle could even attribute most changes in workers' consumption to such technological imperatives; that is, workers' needs (and hence consumption) are determined in large part by their relation to the means of production.

2. The validity of the Marglin–Stone hypothesis – that capitalists consciously consider the real-wage effect before introducing technology – is not discussed here. It should be noted that there is a danger in attributing omniscience to the capitalist class or to individual capitalists in these formulations. Furthermore, the short-run effects of a technical change are solely the effects on cost-efficiency at constant real wages; the balance of class forces does not establish a new real wage for some time.

3. It is assumed here that capitalists have reasonably good foresight. A cost-increasing technical change will not be introduced unless the capitalist expects $\Delta\pi_b > 0$ – and, in fact, $\Delta\pi_b > |\Delta\pi_e|$.

7. The law of value and the transformation problem

1. Assumption A is true if all goods are normal goods, and are gross complements to each other. This follows from examining the Slutsky equation. In fact, the statement of the assumption can be weakened to read:

$$\hat{\mathbf{p}}_{\text{II}} > \mathbf{p}_{\text{II}} \Rightarrow \mathbf{D}_i(\hat{\mathbf{p}}_{\text{II}}) \leqq \mathbf{D}_i(\mathbf{p}_{\text{II}})$$

and a slight alteration of the proof proves the theorem.

9. Simple reproduction, extended reproduction, and crisis

1. H is compact because it is assumed that the technological conditions are such that $\mathbf{\Lambda}_{\text{II}} > 0$. Because $e^* > 0$, $N > \mathbf{\Lambda}_{\text{II}}\mathbf{B}$. Hence each component of $\mathbf{F}$ is bounded. H is clearly closed and convex.

2. To see this: by (9.10) and $\mathbf{p}_{\text{II}}\mathbf{B} = N = \mathbf{Lx}(\mathbf{F}^*)$, the right-hand side of (9.16) can be written as

$$\pi[(\mathbf{p}_{\text{I}}A_{\text{I}} + \mathbf{L}_{\text{I}})\mathbf{x}_{\text{I}}(\mathbf{F}^*) + (\mathbf{p}_{\text{I}}A_{\text{II}} + \mathbf{L}_{\text{II}})\mathbf{x}_{\text{II}}(F^*)]$$

which is simply total profits.

3. Notice that we need not specify budget constraints for individual capitalists because there is only one consumption good. One collective budget constraint suffices.

References

Arrow, K. and F. Hahn. *General Competitive Analysis.* San Francisco: Holden Day, 1971.

Braverman, H. *Labor and Monopoly Capital.* New York: Monthly Review Press, 1974.

Brody, A. *Proportions, Prices and Planning.* New York: American Elsevier, 1970.

Debreu, G. "A social equilibrium existence theorem," *Proceedings of the National Academy of Sciences* 38(1952): 886–93.

Debreu, G. *Theory of Value.* New Haven; Conn.: Yale University Press, 1973.

Dobb, Maurice. *Political Economy and Capitalism.* New York: International Publishers, 1945.

Doeringer, P., and M. Piore. *Internal Labor Markets and Manpower Analysis.* Lexington, Mass.: D. C. Heath, 1971.

Edwards, R. *Contested Terrain.* New York: Basic Books, 1979.

Edwards, R., M. Reich, and D. Gordon. *Labor Market Segmentation.* Lexington, Mass.: D. C. Heath, 1975.

Elster, J. *Logic and Society.* New York: Wiley, 1978.

Fine, B., and L. Harris. "Controversial issues in Marxist economic theory," *Socialist Register,* 1976.

Gale, David. *The Theory of Linear Economic Models.* New York: McGraw-Hill, 1960.

Gintis, H. "The nature of labor exchange and the theory of capitalist production," *Review of Radical Political Economy,* 8(2), Summer 1976.

Gordon, D. "Capitalist efficiency and socialist efficiency," *Monthly Review,* 28(3), July–August 1976.

Himmelweit, S. "The continuing saga of the falling rate of profit – a reply to Mario Cogoy," *Bulletin of the Conference of Socialist Economists* III (9), Autumn 1974.

Immanuel, Arghiri. *Unequal Exchange.* New York: Monthly Review Press, 1972.

Kalecki, M. *Theory of Economic Dynamics.* New York: Rinehart & Co., 1954.

Kemeny, J. G., O. Morgenstern, and G. L. Thompson. "A generalization of the von Neumann model of an expanding economy," *Econometrica* 24(2), 1956.

Lakatos, I. *Proofs and Refutations.* Cambridge: Cambridge University Press, 1976.

Maarek, G. *Introduction au Capital de Karl Marx.* Paris: Calmann-Levy, 1975.

Mandel, E. *Late Capitalism.* Atlantic Highlands, N.J.: Humanities Press, 1975.

Marglin, S. "What do bosses do?" *Review of Radical Political Economics* 6(2), Summer 1974.

Marx, K. *Capital, Volume I.* New York: International Publishers, 1947.

Marx, K. *Capital, Volume III.* Moscow: Progress Publishers, 1966.

Marx, K. *Wages, Price and Profit,* in K. Marx and F. Engels, *Selected Works, Volume II.* Moscow: Progress Publishers, 1973.

Marx, K. *Theories of Surplus-Value, Part II.* Moscow: Progress Publishers, 1968.

Marx, K., and F. Engels. *The German Ideology.* New York: International Publishers, 1963.

Meek, R. "Marx's 'doctrine of increasing misery,'" in R. Meek, *Economics and Ideology and Other Essays.* London: Chapman and Hall, 1967, pp. 113–28.

Morishima, M. *The Theory of Economic Growth.* Oxford: Clarendon Press, 1969.

Morishima, M. *Marx's Economics.* Cambridge: Cambridge University Press, 1973.

Morishima, M. "Marx in the light of modern economic theory," *Econometrica* 42 (1974): 611–32.

Nikaido, H. *Convex Structures and Economic Theory.* New York: Academic Press, 1968.

Nikaido, H. "Refutation of the dynamic equalization of profit rates in Marx's scheme of reproduction." Department of Economics, University of Southern California, 1978.

O'Connor, J. *The Fiscal Crisis of the State,* New York: St. Martin's Press, 1973.

Okishio, N. "Technical changes and the rate of profit," *Kobe University Economic Review* 7 (1961):85–99.

Okishio, N. "Notes on technical progress and capitalist society," *Cambridge Journal of Economics* (1977): 93–100.

Pasinetti, L. *Lectures on the Theory of Production.* New York: Columbia University Press, 1977.

Persky, J., and J. Alberro. "Technical innovation and the dynamics of the profit rate," University of Illinois, Chicago Circle, Department of Economics, 1978.

Robinson, J. *An Essay on Marxian Economics.* New York: St. Martin's Press (1966 edition), 1942.

Roemer, J. "Technical change and the 'tendency of the rate of profit to fall,'" *Journal of Economic Theory* 16(2), December 1977.

Roemer, J. "The effect of technological change on the real wage and Marx's falling rate of profit," *Austrialian Economic Papers,* June 1978a.

Roemer, J. "Neoclassicism, Marxism and collective action," *Journal of Economic Issues,* March 1978b.

Roemer, J. "Marxian models of reproduction and accumulation," *Cambridge Journal of Economics* 2, March 1978c.

Roemer, J. "Mass action is *not* individually rational," *Journal of Economic Issues,* September 1979a.

Roemer, J. "Origins of exploitation and class: value theory of pre-capitalist economy," Department of Economics, *University of California Working Paper No. 125,* 1979b.

Roemer, J. "Divide and conquer: microfoundations of the Marxian theory of wage discrimination," *Bell Journal of Economics,* Fall 1979c.

Roemer, J. "Continuing controversy on the falling rate of profit: fixed capital and other issues," *Cambridge Journal of Economics,* December 1979d.

Roemer, J. "A general equilibrium approach to Marxian economics," *Econometrica,* March 1980a.

Roemer, J. "Innovation, rates of profit, and Uniqueness of von Neumann Prices," *Journal of Economic Theory* 22, June 1980b.

Roemer, J. "Exploitation and class: part II, capitalist economy." *Cowles Foundation Discussion Paper No. 543,* Yale University, 1980c.

Rowthorn, B. "Late capitalism," *New Left Review* 98, July–August 1976.

Samuelson, P. "Understanding the Marxian notion of exploitation: a summary of the so-called transformation problem between Marxian values and competitive prices," *Journal of Economic Literature* 9 (1971):399–431.

Samuelson, P. "The economics of Marx: an ecumenical reply," *Journal of Economic Literature* X(1): 51–7, March 1972.
Samuelson, P. "Insight and detour in the theory of exploitation: a reply to Baumol," *Journal of Economic Literature* XII(1): 62–70, March 1974.
Schefold, B. "Different forms of technical progress," *Economic Journal* 86, December 1976.
Schwartz, J. *Lectures on the Mathematical Method in Analytical Economics.* New York: Gordon and Breach, 1961.
Shaikh, A. "An introduction to the history of crisis theories," in Union for Radical Political Economics, *U.S. Capitalism in Crisis,* 1978a.
Shaikh, A. "Political economy and capitalism: notes on Dobb's theory of crisis," *Cambridge Journal of Economics* 2:233–51, 1978b.
Smolinski, Leon. "Karl Marx and mathematical economics," *Journal of Political Economy* 81 (5):1189–1204, September–October 1973.
Sowell, T. "Marx's *Capital* after one hundred years," *Canadian Journal of Economics* 33 (1967); reprinted in M. C. Howard and J. E. King (eds.), *The Economics of Marx.* New York: Penguin, 1976.
Sraffa, P. *Production of Commodities by Means of Commotidies.* Cambridge: Cambridge University Press, 1960.
Steedman, I. *Marx after Sraffa.* London: New Left Books, 1977.
Steindl, J. *Maturity and Stagnation in American Capitalism.* Oxford: Basil Blackwell, 1952.
Stone, K. "The origins of job structure in the steel industry," *Review of Radical Political Economics,* 6(2), Summer 1974.
Sweezy, P. *The Theory of Capitalist Development.* New York: Monthly Review, 1942.
Sweezy, P. "Some problems in the theory of capital accumulation," in *Sozialismus, Geschicte und Wirschaft: Festschrift fur Eduard Marz.* Vienna: Europaverlag, 1974, pp. 71–85.
von Weizsäcker, C. C. "Modern capital theory and the concept of exploitation," *Kyklos* 26 (1973): 245–81.
von Weizsäcker, C. C., and P. Samuelson, "A new labor theory of value for rational planning through use of the bourgeois profit rate," *Proceedings of the National Academy of Science* 68(1971).
Wolfstetter, E. "Surplus labour, synchronized labour costs and Marx's labour theory of value," *Economic Journal* 83 (1973):787–809.
Wright, E. O. "Alternative perspectives in the Marxist theory of accumulation and crisis," *The Insurgent Sociologist* 6 (1), Fall 1975.

Index

Key words and phrases that appear in chapter titles and section titles are listed in the Table of Contents and are not indexed here. References to Marx are not indexed, except for quotations.

Arrow, K. and Hahn, F., 14
augmented input coefficient matrix, 16

Berge maximum theorem, 63, 165
Braverman, H., 58, 134, 141
Brody, A., 35

Calsamiglia, X., 211
Cambridge equation, 187
class exploitation correspondence principle, 202
class formation, 202
convex production, 36
crisis, 13, 192–5
  fiscal, 193
  profit-squeeze, 133, 193
  realization, underconsumption, 193

Debreu, G., 14, 61–2, 165
degree of monopoly, 23, 25
differential rent, 28
Dobb, M., 132

Edwards, R., 134, 141
Elster, J., 211
equilibrium, 15, 19
  competitive, 29, 76
exploitation
  definition of, 37
  as normative theory, 206
  without profits, 57

factor intensities, 33
Fine, B. and Harris, L., 113, 116
Foley, D., 211
Frobenius-Perron theorem, 16, 110
functionalism, 8, 114
fundamental Marxian theorem, 16, 47, 83, 201
fundamentalists, 132–3

Gale, D., 126
Gintis, H., 134
Gordon, D., 134, 140

Immanuel, A., 175
indecomposability, 45
independence of production, 47, 65
industrial reserve army, 23, 182

Kalecki, M., 23

labor theory of value, 147
  market dependence of, 203
  as value numeraire, 204–7
Lakatos, I., 211
law of value, 155, 201, 203

Maarek, G., 35
Malthusianism, 88
Marglin, S., 58, 134
Marx
  on falling rate of profit, 109
  on labor theory of value, 151–3

Marx and Engels
  on human consciousness, 54
Meek, R., 150
microfoundations, 7
Morishima, 35, 47, 50, 91, 97–8, 111, 125, 202

Nikaido, H., 14, 72

O'Connor, J., 132
Okishio, N., 35, 97, 112, 118

Pasinetti, L., 14
Persky, J. and Alberro, J., 113–14, 123
price expectations, 33, 39
profits without exploitation, 49

reproducible solution
  definition of, 19, 41, 67, 74
  existence of, 20, 44, 67, 80
  quasi-, 42, 80
Robinson, J., 132
Roemer, J., 130, 203
Rowthorn, B., 132

Samuelson, P., 97, 99, 105
Say's Law, 186
Schefold, B., 117
Schwartz, J., 2, 14, 110, 120
Seton, F., 111
Shaikh, A., 113, 116, 119, 122
Smolinski, L., 1, 211
social equilibrium existence theorem, 61–2
socialism, 208–9
Steedman, Ian, 14, 50, 202
Steindl, J., 190, 198
Stone, K., 134, 142
subsistence bundle, 15
  social determination of, 54
Sweezy, P., 89, 132

unequal exchange, 175

von Neumann model, 36, 124
  irreducibility, 126

Weizsäcker, C. C. von, 35, 105
Wolfstetter, E., 35, 105
Wright, E. O., 132